TransLucent

TransLucent

How I put off my natural man

and found a spiritual woman

Katherine

ISBN: 979-8-9876518-0-3 (eBook)
ISBN: 979-8-9876518-1-0 (Softcover)

Edited by Briana Farr
Cover design by Katherine
Cover design © 2023 Katherine Herrmann
Cover Photo licensed from Adobe Stock Image #126783286
Book design by Firewire Publishing
Printed by Book Printers of Utah
Printed in the United States of America

Author's Note: This is a true story. Some names are actual while so many are fictitious. Your guess is as good as mine. If you think it's about someone you know, it probably isn't. Just go with that.

Email: translucent@andhalfatime.com
Facebook: TransLucent

Dedicated for Kindness and Sweetness. Always.

Table of Contents

Foreword

NORMALLY THE FOREWORD WOULD BE WRITTEN BY A CLOSE personal friend—perhaps a friend of notoriety or celebrity, or with great expertise in this field. They would give my story some authority and persuasively explain to you why you should read it. You would feel confident in knowing that you didn't waste your money and that this book would be beneficial to you. Well, sadly, I don't know anyone like that. LOL.

Oh, I did meet Ron Howard once when I was a little kid before he became a famous movie director. His brother was playing on the ward softball team and my father was catcher. I got his autograph, but that's long gone missing. He probably wouldn't remember me, right?

However, I was listening to General Conference on my phone, sitting on the Conference Center plaza, when I heard this part of President Nelson's talk that caught my attention:

Overcoming the world is not an event that happens in a day or two. It happens over a lifetime as we repeatedly embrace the doctrine of Christ. We cultivate faith in Jesus Christ by repenting daily and keeping covenants that endow us with power. We stay on the covenant path and are blessed with spiritual strength, personal revelation, increasing faith, and the ministering of angels. Living the doctrine of Christ can produce the most powerful virtuous cycle, creating spiritual momentum in our lives. [1]

And I thought, "That's my book!" He just said what I didn't know I was saying. So, I was obviously very interested in what he said before that. And I must say it also went well with my book. He's very good at his job.

What does it mean to overcome the world? It means overcoming the temptation to care more about the things of this world than the things of God. It means trusting the doctrine of Christ more than the philosophies of men. It means delighting in truth, denouncing deception, and becoming "humble followers of Christ." It means choosing to refrain from anything that drives the Spirit away. It means being willing to "give away" even our favorite sins.

Now, overcoming the world certainly does not mean becoming perfect in this life, nor does it mean that your problems will magically evaporate—because they won't. And it does not mean that you won't still make mistakes. But overcoming the world does mean that your resistance to sin will increase. Your heart will soften as your faith in Jesus Christ increases. Overcoming the world means growing to love God and His Beloved Son more than you love anyone or anything else.

How, then, do we overcome the world? King Benjamin taught us how. He said that "the natural man is an enemy to God" and remains so forever "unless he yields to the enticings of the Holy Spirit, and putteth off the natural man and becometh a saint through the atonement of Christ the Lord." Each time you seek for and follow the promptings of the Spirit, each time you do any-thing good—things that "the natural man" would not do—you are overcoming the world.

So I decided to make this the foreword.

I won't say I've overcome the world—perhaps maybe a continent or two, and an island. And it certainly wasn't any explicit goal of mine. But it should've been, right? Shouldn't it be all of ours? I just kind of stumbled into this process, as you'll see.

Though we're not friends—yet—I'd say that President Nelson is an unequaled expert in the field of putting off natural men. You should read this book if you want to know how I put off my natural man and found a saintly woman, which was the witty subtitle I'd already chosen for this book.

Introduction

I T IS NOT AT ALL POSSIBLE I ALREADY HAD ANY PRESENTIMENT of my future.

It was late on a Saturday night, September 2018. I sat on my kitchen floor crying. Actually, I was ugly crying. The house was filthy dirty, with garbage everywhere. The dust bunnies were as big as actual rabbits. And there was a lake in the middle of my empty kitchen floor. The hookup for the washing machine had failed and water shot across the room. It had taken me awhile to get the water turned off so everything in the room was wet. I'd installed my "smart" thermostat and all it would do was call for more heat. Stupid thing. It was 75°F outside, but it was over 90°F in my house. I was hungry and didn't have any food. Well, only whatever had come over in the refrigerator, which was on my front lawn. My boxes for the kitchen hadn't arrived. Apparently they were lost in transit. The entryway was filled with a couch from my college days pulled out of storage, and filled with mouse droppings. My living room was full and stacked halfway to the ceiling with boxes of my few personal possessions and garbage bags filled with clothes. There was a tiny path to the stairs. And the only thing that had made it upstairs to my bedroom was my mattress. I wasn't sure where in my living room my sheets and pillows were buried. They'd just dumped everything where there was space.

I'd just moved back into my home after my divorce. We were swapping houses that were next door to each other.

My ex got all the furniture and appliances, computer, artwork, television, my parents, and our kids. She had family that was helping to clean the clean house I had left behind. They were setting up beds, organizing the kitchen, unpacking boxes, and creating a home. Men from the ward set up her washer and dryer, put her refrigerator in the kitchen, and even changed which way the doors opened. My family refused to show up, and the ward wasn't there for me, either. My stuff was just inconveniently in the way. My LGBT friends showed up to help move my stuff over, but they were constantly misgendered by the ward members helping my ex and didn't stay long.

Feeling overwhelmed, I sent a message to my parents with a plea for help. My mom said I could drive to their house if I wanted something to eat. These were the same parents who usually rushed to help people. They only lived a couple of miles away. Still, they didn't answer the call and come.

Sitting there I felt alone, abandoned, and on my own.

So, this is my life now, I thought.

It'd been a hard year. I'd fought to stay married. We went to months of marriage counseling only to have my wife file for divorce when I thought we were making progress. The Church banned me from attending the temple for life. My oldest daughter, Shannon, got married and disinvited me from her wedding and reception. I was forced to leave my home of 24 years and live next door in our rental house. My youngest daughter, Allison, got baptized without me. And my divorce was finalized. A 31-year relationship with my best friend and soulmate was ended. Somewhere in there I went to my homeland of California to say goodbye. I wasn't sure I was returning home alive.

But it was also an amazing year. It was the year that my Heavenly Father really began to reveal His hand in my life. These were the labor pains of a rebirth, of change, of becoming, of learning.

I had no idea what was going to happen, what His plan was. I'm glad He had a plan, because I didn't know what mine was. If I still had one, it was rather short, with a tragic ending of Shakespearean proportions.

A year later, in 2019, I bought a journaled Book of Mormon. One of the best things I ever did. For as much as I use tech, I love being able to underline and write in the margins. One thing I'm good at is seeing patterns, and my first time reading through the pages these words stood out to me: **murmur, remember, and stir-up.** I took those words, printed them out, and taped them to my wall. I will talk about murmur later, and stir-up probably never, but here let me talk about remember.

So many places in the scriptures, the prophets tell their people to remember. Remember how God got them out of Egypt. Remember how God got them through the Red Sea. How He sent them manna, and water from a rock. How they conquered Palestine. How He led Lehi out of Jerusalem and saved his family from the destruction. How Alma and his people were saved from the Lamanites. There are so many times that God acted in doing big things to save His people so they would know that He was God and hopefully their testimonies would grow.

But what if we don't remember? What happens when we forget these remarkable experiences? The Nephites forgot in just a few years that God had made it daylight for three days to signal the birth of our Savior. They forgot doctrine and contended with the church. They lost the Spirit. They forgot the proof—the evidences—that God had been in their lives. They forgot the feelings of the Spirit. They forgot the times they were inspired to act.

And when you forget, you stop keeping the commandments and lose the companionship of the Spirit. We hear this every Sunday as we partake of the Sacrament.

> *...that they are willing to take upon them the name of thy Son, and always remember him, and keep his commandments which he hath given them, that they may always have his Spirit to be with them. (Moroni 4:3)*

You then wonder where God is. Is He real? Why has He forsaken you? Could He really exist?

I had a friend who grew up in the Church and went on a mission, got a degree and a wife at BYU, had a great career and moved to California. When the Church was supporting legislation against gay marriage, he was disaffected. He investigated early Church history and lost his testimony. In just two weeks, he and his family went from monthly temple attendees and tithe payers to atheists. I wonder how he forgot all his spiritual experiences so quickly.

I see LDS mothers and fathers of LGBT kids who come into the LGBT community wanting to help their child, and within a short period of time they end up leaving the Church. How do they forget to remember? What of all the feelings they had in the temple? How do people forget these things?

I've always been blessed with a great memory. Not eidetic, but just down the road from there. It was really great to have in school because I could remember pretty much everything the teacher said and rarely needed to take notes.

I still remember the first time I really felt the Spirit. I was 13 years old, and we took the grand family cross-country trip to see Church and national historical places. Three weeks in the back of a station wagon with my older brother. We were at Carthage Jail in the upstairs room, and the docent was telling the story of the martyrdom. The spirit just filled the room and me. The feeling was so thick you'd think you could cut it, or even see it. I knew then that it was true, and it was a witness of Joseph Smith and his divine mission.

Always remember. Write your experiences down in a journal. Or record them on your phone. Because there are going to be times in your life when you will feel all alone, you will wonder where God is as you are in bondage. It's times like that that you should review your book of remembrances and feel them and know what God has done for you in your distant past and even recent days.

This book is me remembering. It's putting out there the things I remember of God in my life; the miracles and the tender mercies exactly as they happened to me. If someone remembers differently, I'm sorry. These are my scriptures—my small plates, as it were—so that I know how my testimony has grown.

Plus, some crazy stuff about being transgender.

Enjoy!

1.

Prelude

S HE SAT DOWN NEXT TO ME AT DINNER DURING THE JUNE
2022 Utah County Single Adult (UCSA) conference and patiently
waited for my current conversation to end. I turned to her, and she
told me that she heard my testimony[2] at the North Star[3] conference two
weeks earlier. She said, "Don't take this the wrong way, but I didn't think
that people like you could even have a testimony. I don't know why you
were there, but you were there for me. I needed to hear you."

OK, I'll try to not take it the wrong way. LOL

But, people like me?

I thought, *You mean a transgender woman who has medically and socially
transitioned full time, which would not seem to be in accordance with Church
policy and counsel?* I know. I must be a horrible, awful, unholy, unrighteous
sinner, with a soul as dark as fuligin. And perhaps she wouldn't be wrong.
I know many who would agree with her. How could the spirit of light
and truth ever find a home in my heart, right? Well, it does happen on

occasion, believe it or not. Usually on Thursdays. But maybe, just maybe, I'm not the person she thinks I am.

But who am I, as a transgender woman? It's probably easier to say what I am not.

It can be very confusing today, because there are many reasons for the proverbial "man in a dress." It could be Halloween, and he thought it'd be funny. He might be an actor in a Shakespearean play. He might be wearing his traditional costume from his culture. He might be a drag performer (drag queen), usually a gay man who wants to hypersexualize women for entertainment. He might be a cross dresser or transvestite who likes to wear the clothes for sexual pleasure. He might be thinking fashion forward, or trendy, or shocking in order to gain attention. These are just a few reasons. But what differentiates all of them from being me is that at the end of the day, they are male. None of them will say they are a woman.

A trans woman is a person that was assigned male at birth and identifies as female for reasons that may be genetic, biological, or even spiritual.

(Reader, if you want more information on that right now, skip to the *Appendix* for more of my thoughts on how this happens, and come back. If you'd rather get on with the exciting story about my life, which I'm sure you'd rather do, please continue!)

2.

Becoming Katherine

I WAS BORN IN LOS ANGELES IN THE MID-1960S. I'M A PROUD Southern California girl. Raised out in the suburbs, up in the mountains, down on the beach, and at Disneyland.

I come from a large, extended Mormon family, though there were only two of us growing up. I have an older brother named Mark. My parents, George and Launa, came from a long line of Church members. Some were pioneers and early founders of the Church that you hear about in conference talks and Sunday school lessons. The Church ran deep in my family. We are also very conservative Republicans, except for my brother.

My father, also a native Californian, went on a mission to Germany, entered the army and served in Korea, and later learned to program mainframe computers in night school. My mother was from Cedar City, Utah. She programmed computers at Cal State LA before meeting my father. She then worked retail at JC Penney while we were in grade school. My parents didn't let us watch much TV. No Saturday morning cartoons or after school specials. No sugar cereal. My mom cut our hair and made most of our clothes, and my father was raised on "spare the rod, spoil the child." My parents had lousy taste in music for the 1960s. Instead of Elvis or the Beatles, I was raised on Nat King Cole, Harry Belafonte, the Smothers Brothers, Bill Cosby, and the Paint Your Wagon soundtrack. I think I can still sing it from beginning to end.

We went to church every Sunday and had Primary mid-week, making the 5-mile drive each way. My parents went to the Los Angeles Temple monthly and fulfilled canning assignments. They even worked the ward Christmas tree lot. My dad was an elders quorum president and my mom served in the Primary. We were a good, active Mormon family; although Family Home Evening (FHE) was quickly and permanently given up at an early age, because Mark and I didn't get along at all. FHE was the fight that began and ended with prayer, and a song, and maybe a tasty snack. At an early age Mark decided he couldn't stand sharing a room with me and moved into the dining room. It was a small house.

I don't know. Maybe his moving had to do with the fact that I came out to my parents when I was 3 years old. I don't really know much about it; I just know that I told my parents I was a girl. Let me say that again. I told my parents when I was 3 years old that I was a girl. It really does happen. And it does happen that young. Most of my trans friends did the same thing at a similar age. But Mark probably moved out because I was a precocious kid, identified as gifted in kindergarten, highly creative, and I was also tall for my age. In other words, I could excel at being the annoying little sister.

Now would be a good place, or perhaps just a place since there really isn't a good place, to explain a little more about my parents. SPOILER ALERT: I don't have one of those heartwarming stories of acceptance and love like you might find on your LGBT bookshelf from Charlie Bird[4], Tom Christofferson[5], Becky Mackintosh[6], or Ben Schilaty[7]. (And you should read all their books if you haven't.) My book is a train wreck. It's a 200-car pileup that you won't be able to look away from.

My parents have never accepted me as their daughter or supported me in transitioning. They will usually remember to call me Katherine, which is now my legal name. (I'm also legally female.) They might even spell it right. But they make little effort to use my she/her/hers pronouns. More on our current relationship will come later.

They would tell you that everything of my early story is not true; that my stories are either complete fabrications, or at best, may have happened, but just not the way I remember. They have always declined to tell me how they remember these events. Their silence is confusing. I'd love to know their truth and see how it matches up with mine. Are they not telling me to avoid further family contention? Or are they not telling me because there is something to hide? And what might that be? Is it to protect them? Or protect me? They apparently want to take these secrets to the grave and will likely do so given their advanced age and poor health.

I don't blame my parents for how they treated me as child. I'm sure they did what they thought was best or were counseled to do in those times. I'm sure they thought that if they ignored the problem, if they didn't encourage it, that I would naturally desist. I clearly didn't.

I'm sure that my declaration of being a girl at such a young age must have shocked them. This was years before there would be Pride or the word "transgender" was even invented. There was nothing from my parents or TV to influence me at that age. However, my parents did go on the *Let's Make A Deal* game show as twin girls, my father wearing a short wig and white blouse. Hmmmm. LOL.

It was especially difficult back then because no one ever talked about this. And there was no internet or social media. There was no one cheering trans people on. Gays were not out and proud in movies or on television. Sure, some actors and entertainers were a bit flamboyant like Liberace or Barry Manilow, but they didn't publicize their sexual orientation. They feared what would happen to them.

I know, from a very young age, that I wanted long hair and to wear dresses. Cliché? Sure. But back then that was typical of most little girls. I hated boys' clothes and I never wanted to wear a suit and a tie. (And I still never have.) I did not look forward to being a deacon because I knew what would be sartorially required of me. I mostly played with the boys my age in the neighborhood for lack of another choice, but when I was at their houses, I was attracted to what their sisters were doing.

For a time, I had a best friend, Mihoko, who was a girl visiting with her family from Nagoya, Japan. Our families were really close, and I was so sad when she moved back home at the end of third grade. I was never good friends with any of the boys. They were just so different and our interests dissimilar. I was never their first choice to be with. They rarely came to my house. I've never had a best friend. And this has been true all of my life—from grade school, into college, to even now.

My father was into model airplanes and trains, cars, wedding photography, and woodworking. My brother was into science, including chemistry, biology, and zoology. They liked scouting, hiking, and shooting guns. I, however, liked being with my mother, sitting around the campfire with the women—cooking, going to the fabric store, canning food, and helping her make clothes, quilt, and even wash dishes. I've always found washing dishes to be therapeutic. I tried to like trains. I tried to like science. My parents signed me up for Little League, but I was pathetic. I couldn't catch and I never got a base hit, but did manage to get walked a couple of times. And I discovered I liked soccer a lot better. It was probably the shorts.

My brother loved science fiction, but I found my home in fantasy discovering *The Lord of the Rings* in fifth grade. My parents were completely clueless about both. I had no idea what a trilogy was and started with *The Two Towers*. It was a bit confusing, but I still did a book report. I eventually read them in order, and then *The Hobbit* and *The Silmarillion*. Later my brother would introduce me to *Star Wars* and *Doctor Who*.

It was during the time of early grade school, when puberty started, that the dreams and desires to be out as a girl really started to grow. Daily, they colored everything that happened to me. And I knew I couldn't talk about these growing feelings with anyone. I promised myself that I would have to keep them a secret.

I remember in the 1970s, the Church emphasized gardening and food storage as well as journaling, and every Christmas I'd get a shiny new journal from my parents. Well, I'd watched enough Brady Bunch to know that no matter how hard you tried, people always ended up reading your journal. With these feelings, I didn't know how to write about my day without including them. They were a part of everything; hence why I never journaled other than the weather for the first week of January. After that, my journal ended up lost in the bottom of one of my desk drawers.

Sometimes kids get asked, "What do you want to be when you grow up?" And they would say they wanted to be an astronaut, or stewardess, or doctor, or cowgirl, or the president, or a vampire slayer, or whatever. I wanted to be living my life as a woman. I may be one of the few whose childhood dream actually came true. I also thought of being a dentist. Oh well.

Without any sisters, I idolized my girl cousins: Jill, Jan, Cindy, and Cherie. When we'd get together, I wanted to spend all my time with them. Unfortunately, they didn't see me as one of the girls, and I was left with the boys. Being the youngest, my boy cousins found me to be easy prey for their machinations. Worst of all, one of my cousins was a star school wrestler. I hated being with them.

I was a Boy Scout, and even an Eagle Scout at the 11th hour and 57th minute. The scouting and camping part was fine; I just hated the boys. I remember my ward would go on a kayak trip through Flaming Gorge, Utah, each year. And when we'd camp at Hideout, I'd go another 20–30 yards up the trail. Not only was there a beautiful unobstructed view of the reservoir, but I was away from all the crudeness, lewdness, and gross things that they were doing. They could laugh at pull-my-finger for hours. I could never understand their sense of humor. I hated the way they'd talk about girls, watch R-rated videos, and then went to church on Sunday and were seen as worthy priesthood holders. It was not anything I wanted to be a part of. Still, I had to endure them.

That was another hard thing about being transgender back then. You couldn't come out, and if you did, what would have happened? Do you think anyone would have been accepting and affirming? Would my cousins have even talked to me? Would any of the girls in church or school? I think we know the answer to those questions. I would have been relentlessly teased and bullied. It was a good thing I already had found out from my parents that it was not something to be talked about; it was something to be ashamed of. It wasn't right. I wasn't right. I had to hide who I really was.

People are surprised when you finally come out and declare you're a girl, and they think that you just then made some choice. No, you've been living a lie trying to satisfy society's expectations for all those years. You've always been the girl, you just never got to be one completely with all the others. You didn't get to live your full life; you had to live at times a reduced life. But it was still your life, and it wasn't all bad. That's why we say things like, "In my other life…" when we speak about our past selves.

So I wanted to be like the other girls. I wanted to be doing things with them and dressing like them. I wanted to dress like Madonna, and Cindy Lauper, and do *Flashdance* so badly. I wanted the mini skirt and the off the shoulder sweatshirt. It was hell stuck in a world where creativity was mixing your layered polos and pegging the collar. Yeah, I didn't do that either. How do you dress in junior high when you can't wear any of the girl clothes you want, and you absolutely can't stand the guy clothes? Let's just say I wasn't ever going to be on the cover of GQ, or Vogue. It was mostly androgynous jeans, beach t-shirts, and a hoodie. I was from California after all.

I wasn't able to experience girl clothes till after we'd moved to Utah in 1979. It never occurred to me before that to borrow from my mother. I wonder why? We'd moved from a tiny two-bedroom house to a massive five-bedroom home. However, a lot of things just got dumped onto the floor of the family room of the finished basement as my mom dealt with her dying mother. And it was there I saw these three 1950s satin prom dresses falling out of a trash bag with their crinoline petticoats. I just had to, and I finally found the courage and the opportunity. And they fit! They were so beautiful. I loved them. Especially the yellow one, which, I learned recently, was my mom's graduation dress.

I would find time after school before my mother got home from work, or my brother from school, to explore what was there on the basement floor. It was a dream come true, but it also caused a lot of shame. I'd close the gate across the driveway and put the dog out in the yard. I'd hear the gate open when anyone got home and that would give me a few minutes warning to get presentable. Having to sneak around like this just reinforced to me how wrong this was. Because you never needed to hide good things, right? I was a bad girl.

And after stuff got sorted and put away, I'd explore all the closets and under the stairs to find boxes, chests, and suitcases with clothes from my mom's younger days. (My mom denies that she ever had any of her old clothes around the house. She says I must have stolen them from someone or shoplifted. What stores sold homemade clothes from the 1960s? This was from the woman who taught me to never steal, not even a pin. Thanks, Mom!) I'd carefully memorize how they were folded and organized so that I could return them exactly so no one would ever know. But then I got bold, and I started keeping clothes in my bedroom to save time. That is what we call in this business a stash.

I wonder how my life might have been different if I'd had an older sister. I asked my friend Samantha if she ever had a stash of clothes when she was young. She said she had three older sisters. Anytime she wanted anything, she'd grab it off their floor and when she was done, she'd throw it back on their floor. Her sisters were slobs. They never knew. Lucky girl.

And with puberty progressing, my body was going through the usual changes you'd expect of a boy. Puberty was an endless losing war against a body that was changing in ways I didn't like. OK, I didn't take much notice of my voice changing to a lower pitch or my shoulders broadening. So that wasn't alarming. But there was hair growing in places I didn't want. I hated shaving my face. I shouldn't have to do that, right? It was a constant battle of which I hated more: shaving or having facial hair. But at least I could socially do that. My legs were another issue, and I had hobbit feet. And I plucked my brows constantly so I would have two instead of one. I was getting taller, and that was fine. Or I thought it was fine to be the tallest in the family. I didn't see that as a problem then. And then there were no breasts, nor a waist, hips, or a butt happening for me. Sigh. But the absolute worst was the genitals seemingly having a mind of their own. This boy body really sucked.

I knew boys in grade school, from talk on the playground, who were all excited about puberty and becoming sexually active. I had no idea what they were talking about. To me it was a mystery and an annoyance. I didn't understand having a penis. It was foreign to me. I didn't even like looking at it. I didn't want it and wished it was gone. But I had no idea what was supposed to be in its place. And I certainly didn't want it becoming aroused. I didn't find anything of the experience enjoyable. It caused me great distress.

So during the rare occasions I had opportunity in my house to explore my girlhood by trying on clothes, I didn't need my body reminding me in embarrassing and uncomfortable ways of my misfortune of birth. The clothes just weren't tailored to accommodate this situation. And I intentionally didn't want this association. When this happened I'd have to stop and change my clothes. I wouldn't allow the icky boy world to intrude. I wasn't ever wearing girl clothes for sexual gratification. I was wearing them because that's what girls wear. The sexual element destroyed what joy I was having.

So I tried to do something about this. I would use string or rubber bands to constrict the blood flow to my genitals so they wouldn't grow. It helped, and I hoped that they would just die and go away, but then it hurt. I'd worry about what the consequences of that result might be. Could there be complications? Might I die? How would I even know at this age? It was a worry. This was something I certainly couldn't talk to my parents about and was unlikely to be covered in the World Book Encyclopedias in the family room.

When I was older I'd stand naked in the kitchen with a knife in hand aware of how far away was the nearest hospital. By then I was less worried about loss of blood than I was of severing the important nerves necessary for satisfactory confirmation surgery. Also the knife wasn't that sharp.

So it's never been for me about dressing for sexual arousal or imagining myself having sex as a woman for pleasure either. I'm not a cross dresser, transvestite, or autogynephile (AGP). I don't fantasize about having sex with women or men. And I've never done porn of any kind.

One of the symptoms of gender dysphoria is having a strong desire of wanting to be rid of your primary sexual characteristics. I've illustrated how deep and strong the discomfort had been for me. Now that I'm on cross hormones (HRT), I no longer have these strong desires. (HRT can be helpful for some transgender people in controlling gender dysphoria. The church does allow HRT for this purpose.) I'm now at peace with my body, or maybe it's simply a cease fire. Because if I had the money and opportunity to have bottom surgery tomorrow, to have my body corrected, I would be there bright and shiny in the morning waiting for the doors to open.

But I did feel guilt and shame for having these desires every day. This wasn't normal, right? Wasn't I supposed to be a boy? But I wasn't, and I didn't want to be that way at all. But wasn't I? The boys I knew weren't feeling this way, right? Why did I? Why did this feel so much more normal? I was broken, and bad, for feeling this way. It must be wrong for me to be wearing girl clothes even though it gave me peace and happiness and completeness.

I would pray that God would fix me. No, not to get rid of the girl feelings. Being a boy wasn't who I was or ever wanted to be. So I prayed that the boy part of me would go away, both body and brain. That I'd wake up some morning and my body would be right. I'd have all my girl parts and just my girl thoughts. None of that icky guy stuff would remain. If God could perform all those miracles in the Bible, why couldn't He do this one for me, too? But He never has.

Then one afternoon after school in 1979, my parents invited me to go with them in the car. "Where are we going?" I asked.

"To see a therapist."

"Why?"

"We need to work on some family communication issues." Huh. At that age what did I know about therapists? I had no idea what communication issues we could be having. And why was my brother not coming?

The therapist made small talk, and then explained about ways we could better communicate with one another. I had no idea what this was about. I didn't pay much attention. But finally, he excused my parents so he could talk to me alone. He asked about school and my hobbies. And then he abruptly said, "Do you think you're a girl?"

Woah! Why is he asking me this? How could he know? Oh, crap.

I remembered a few months earlier that I'd broken my prime directive—don't write about this. So why did I? The answer was because I found it therapeutic, like talking to someone, to make my thoughts and feelings concrete. Putting them on paper made them real, gave them form and substance. Stupid girl. But what did I do with those papers? I never found them when I looked later. No matter, I had to deal with this now. Apparently, my parents knew. What do I say? What could happen? And in a split second my brain came up with a very cunning plan—flat out denial. Ok, not very original; but I figured it had the greatest probability of success for my continued happiness.

"No."

"You don't want to live as a woman?"

"No."

"So, you don't want to be a girl?"

Again? "No." Thank you for all the rephrasing. Had this guy gone to law school, too?

After having beat that horse, he changed the subject and moved on and made some more meaningless small talk in hope to disguise what had just happened. I learned about pretense that day. Did he believe me? He quickly excused me and called in my parents. He talked to them for a while and we left. I assume he told them I denied everything. But they still had the papers as proof. I've been told lately that if I hadn't denied it, I probably would have been put into some sort of conversion therapy. It's not like my parents would affirm me in those days, right?

My parents deny this meeting ever happened; that if they did take me to a therapist it wasn't about being a girl. When I ask them why a therapist would ask me these questions out of the blue their only answer is that he was really good at his job. I'm sorry, how does a therapist in 1979 look at a 13-year-old boy and deduce that he thinks she's a girl? Really? He'd have to be a mind reader like Carnac or Kreskin.

But I now knew why I was there without my brother, and it wasn't about our communication. But it should have been. I thought I was going to be in big trouble when I got home. My father was legendary with a belt or razor strap. Yes, we owned an actual razor strap. But nothing was said. My parents went on like this hadn't happened; it was never talked about. Yes, apparently, we did have communication issues. And we still do. They could have easily confronted me with what I wrote and shown that I'd lied to the therapist. And where would that have gone?

It was now 10 years since I first told them at age 3, and perhaps till then they'd thought they were successful in me desisting. Nope. Not in the least.

My relationship with my parents was damaged from this event. Up until then I think we had been a fairly normal family, but now my parents really knew. And I never had the same relationship with them. We weren't close. There was this distance and distrust. There was this perpetual elephant in the room. I had to double down on being secretive and protecting myself.

All through junior high and high school, I played cat and mouse with my parents. I would stash my mom's girl clothes in my room, and then sometime later, after days or months, I'd get home from school and the clothes would be gone. They were nowhere to be found. I looked everywhere—from where I got them to everywhere they might have gone. I finally got really good at hiding my stash, so it never was found again. But I eventually ran out of all of my mom's old clothes.

My parents made sure I didn't do anything to out myself. Dressing up as a girl for Halloween I found out was a huge "No!" My junior year I got my cousin to offer to help me do just that. She started warming up the curling iron and looking for a dress when my mother called and demanded that I be home in 5 minutes or else. When I got home, she told me that I couldn't dress as a girl to the Halloween party because my friends would surely know it wasn't a costume. Something my wife would repeat a couple decades later.

But my senior year, I guess I finally caught that infamous teenage rebelliousness bug and I started to transition. I refused to get my hair cut. I didn't trim my fingernails. And I began to change how I was dressing as much as I could with what I had. If only I'd thought to have gotten my ears pierced during this rebellion.

It should have been obvious that my earlier denial was a lie. I was doing what I wrote about, what they'd been told. They knew. It still wasn't talked about. Did they still feel like if it wasn't talked about it would go away? Were they told it was somehow natural and I'd still probably desist? Or were they just in denial too? Did they not know what to do, or were they actually hiding a secret from me?

Sometime after I graduated from high school, my mother put my hair up in those hard, pink curlers for the night. Ouch! Not a good night's sleep. Beauty is literally pain. In the morning she took them out and she'd brought a tray of her Estée Lauder makeup. She did my face and angrily said, "You want to be a girl. Fine! You're a girl." I can still hear her saying this and the tone. I don't recall having told her anything. And I don't remember how I got her to curl my hair, but she obviously knew. But this wasn't a mom and daughter bonding moment of affirmation. It was done to further shame and humiliate me. I floated the rest of the day on a pink fluffy cloud, but I had nowhere to go. I couldn't go out with friends like this, even if I'd had any. So I just walked around the backyard and the house. She never did this again. I guess her plan to shame me into desisting didn't work.

When my brother moved back from Santa Monica in 2015, we finally had a chance to have a real talk for the first time in over 30 years, since before his mission. And over a couple curries he told me that he was bipolar, and I told him I was transgender. That brought several memories back to his mind. He told me that soon after he'd gotten married in January 1985, he had a talk with our father. "What is going on with my little brother?" My brother had gotten back from his mission in August 1984 and was soon engaged and busy with school and getting married. He'd missed much of my high school years and growing my hair out.

My father told Mark that I was "third sex." OK, I wasn't sure what that meant and had to Google it when I got home. Basically, it means that I'm intersex, neither male nor female. It was an interesting choice of words for my father to use back then. Not the sort of thing you learn on the news or in Sunday School. My father claims no memory of this conversation, or why he would have said that. But I wonder why he would say that.

My father also told Mark that my mother had found stuff in my room and burned it in the fireplace. Huh. My father couldn't tell my brother what she found, but I can guess now why I never found the clothes from my stash, though that seemed a bit extreme. I figured they'd gone to Deseret Industries. But maybe it shows how much my mom was traumatized about this. My father says my mother never told him what she burned, and my mom claims to never have found or burned anything from my room. Why would my brother make this up? And why would my father not want to know what was burned?

It seems that as my parents clearly knew I was stashing women's clothes and looking more female, that the more obvious answer would have been to tell my brother that I was a transvestite. How did they arrive at third sex? Was there something from my birth I don't know about? Had they recently talked with a therapist? But it explains why when I stayed overnight at my brother's place that Mariam, his wife, offered to French braid my hair. I LOVED that. Apparently, she knew something.

I was politically active at an early age. I loved watching the nightly news with Walter Cronkite, and I would read newspapers from front to back. I also would watch *The Phil Donahue Show.* At that time, men in dresses were played purely for comedy in TV and movies. I remember Klinger in *M*A*S*H,* Dustin Hoffman in *Tootsie,* and even *Bosom Buddies* with Tom Hanks. They weren't transgender, but I was kind of jealous of them publicly being able to do what I wanted privately, even though it was fictional and for laughs.

I had no idea what sweeps week was at the time, but Donahue would have his annual transsexual/transvestite show. OK, these were finally real people, but they were laughed at and ridiculed. People in the audience would shout nasty condemnations at them. Nobody was standing up for them. They weren't normal. They were freaks. They weren't loved. They weren't me, right? How could I be like them? I'm not a freak. I'm not a freak! I saw myself as different from them. How could I come out and be treated like that? It just reinforced the need to hide who I was.

But the gender dysphoria was raging and getting worse as puberty progressed. The more testosterone there was in my body, the more the discomfort in my head.

Is gender dysphoria just a feeling? What is it like to feel like a woman in a man's body? I'm reminded of the lesson in Seminary about how to describe what it feels like to have the Holy Ghost by trying to describe what salt tastes like. Elder Packer shared an experience he had:

> *"Then," I said, "assuming that I have never tasted salt, explain to me just what it tastes like."*
>
> *After some thought, he said, "Well, I suppose you could say that it is not sweet and it is not sour."*
>
> *"You've told me what it isn't, not what it is." After several attempts, of course, he could not do it. He could not explain, in words alone, so ordinary an experience as tasting salt.* [8]

How do I explain my "ordinary experience" of feeling gender dysphoria so that you understand? It's hard to describe these things to another person who has never experienced them.

If it is a feeling, maybe it's similar to depression in that it is constant and persistent with you. I've heard it said it's like car sickness, which doesn't ever go away. Maybe it's like that feeling like you know you're coming down with the flu. It's not a passing feeling like happy; it's that growing feeling in your body and joints for hours that something is not right, telling you that you're going to be really sick the next day.

Or maybe gender dysphoria is a feeling like your conscience—the Light of Christ—nagging you that you did something wrong, or like a constant worry. But instead of thinking of whether you turned the oven off this is telling you your body is wrong. It's not right. You're a girl. That message is with you every moment of every day. Sometimes it's just humming quietly in the background like the air conditioner, and then at times it's yelling and nagging you. It's not, "Oh, I feel like a girl." It's telling you that you are a girl. Demanding your attention and action. So maybe gender dysphoria is not just a feeling, but a force or compulsion? Like that feeling when you've spilled tomato sauce on your white blouse and you can't change and you feel self-conscience and everyone is looking at you and all you want to do is put on some clean clothes so you can stop thinking about it.

You want this continual feeling to go away. You want the calm. You want to be comfortable. Sure, you can try to fight it or ignore it. You might be able to distract yourself from it for a while, but then it is back. And then you want that peace again. You desire and crave that sense of normalness. You want to see yourself and be yourself. And that happens when you're being a girl. Transitioning helps alleviate the dysphoria.

My friend Karen Penman says that gender dysphoria is like having a balloon that is constantly filling with air. You can occasionally let the air out and relieve the pressure through transitions, or you can wait for it to explode. Exploding is never good. It's not pretty. No seriously. The clothes you're wearing are not pretty.

Often when trans women begin to transition, they usually go through what we call the "pink phase." They try to live some missed girlhood by wearing clothes that are far too young for them and haven't been in style for a generation or two. They look ridiculous. Also modesty may be an issue. We didn't attend young women classes where this was drilled into us. This is where it helps to have a girl friend to guide you. The phase hopefully passes fairly quickly without too much embarrassment or cost.

Gender dysphoria only went away for me when I was being that feminine girl. That meant putting on a dress and makeup and looking in the mirror. Or painting my nails. Is this playing to a stereotype? Maybe. But I essentially had been playing the tomboy every single day of my life. Maybe that's fine if you're a tomboy, but that wasn't who I was. Putting on a t-shirt and jeans like every boy and girl can didn't tap into my feminine self that wanted to also be expressed.

After being on HRT and having normal female hormone levels, I can now look at myself in a mirror and see myself regardless of what I'm wearing. No makeup in a t-shirt and I'm right there looking back. The dysphoria for me is completely gone. (This doesn't happen for everyone who starts HRT. For some it is only lessened, if anything.) There's no longer the compulsion to be more female or feminine. I am now female 100% of the time.

It's an unnerving feeling. I had gender dysphoria for decades informing and validating me that I was transgender. How did I know I'm transgender? Because of the gender dysphoria I felt. And now it's gone. I'm feeling normal for once. And at times I'm thinking maybe I'm not really transgender. Maybe I never was. And then I see myself, and I'm like, right, there's a reason I'm feeling normal; it's because I now have the right hormones and I'm being me. I'm living my truth, as the youngsters say. Ok, sure, I have body-conscious issues. I look in the mirror and see a body that's not quite what I'd like, but then so does every other woman. But it's at least me now.

And it's at this point where you have to decide if you want or need more medical transition. Frankly, some girls are never going to pass no matter how many surgeries they get. And if that's what you think will bring you happiness, then it is a pointless and expensive challenge. Some cis women let their body-conscious issues drive them from one plastic surgeon to another till it's one surgery too many. You have to be happy with yourself for who you are. One more surgery won't make you happy.

I'm fine with who I am. My other life was still a good life even with gender dysphoria. And I still had a good life detransitioned in the closet. I had a wife and family, a good job and home. Sure, I wish I was cuter, and I probably never will be. I still might go under the knife, but it's not out of any compulsion. If I die with my natural face and body, I'll be fine. It's not consuming me. But I wouldn't pass on an opportunity.

There are other things in my life that are more important. Being transgender isn't more important than your salvation. If being transgender is more important than the Church, or keeping temple covenants, or following the prophet, then you really need to take a break and think about what you're doing. That probably makes me a bit hypocritical; but it wouldn't be the first time. You'll see. Keep reading.

My bishop met with me to call me on a mission when I was about nineteen. That had been drilled into me since I was little. My father had gone on a mission to Germany, and he was proud of that and tried to teach us German. Didn't happen. My brother went on a mission to Nagoya, Japan. So, it became my turn. I took the papers home and read through them.

The first part was easy, and then came, "How often do you think about suicide? Never? Rarely? Sometimes? Often?" Where was daily? Or even hourly? "And if so, why?" How do I answer that? Next question. "Do you have any mental issues that we should know about? If so, explain." Um, sure, I guess they should probably know about my gender dysphoria, and I'm a girl, but how do I begin to explain that? And when I do, then what happens? With no easy answers, or even any answers at all, the application went in my desk drawer and got lost to time. The bishop didn't follow up. He probably knew it was a long shot. I thought about it, and I've had regrets, but I just didn't know how to do it. I was only surviving because of my long hair and how could I cut that and go on a mission without killing myself? There was simply no way I could imagine where I could pretend to be male for two years and live.

I was doing what I could at the time. Most people thought I was just being a rocker, or a hippie, or a druggie. Mostly the latter. I got asked for drugs or a smoke often when I was riding the bus to the university. My mother got asked if she would speak in Relief Society about her "special" child. On clarification, they made it clear that it wasn't for my giftedness, but it was my obvious illegal drug use. My mom almost tore them a new one because she knew that wasn't true. And it wasn't. What I was doing was medicating my gender dysphoria by transitioning a little. When I finally saw myself with long hair, I began to see myself.

I eventually saw a therapist at LDS Family Services. The only thing I could figure was happening to me was multiple personalities. It was in all the made-for-television movies then. Today it's called dissociative identity disorder (DID). I mean, why else did this "boy" have girl thoughts and think of themselves as a girl and want to live as a girl? Made sense, right? Yeah, it only took the therapist a couple questions to determine that wasn't the diagnosis. I also saw a respected psychiatrist at the University of Utah—same thing. Strangely, none of them thought transgender.

My parents weren't very helpful, either. There was the constant, daily nagging about how I needed to cut my hair and fingernails, and how I looked so much better before. They were still trying to get me to desist and be their son, but I was trying to deal with my girl brain. Let's just say she wasn't on the same page. She wasn't all that interested in doing homework. As a result, I took a 3.6 GPA to a 0.4 in four quarters, and then the University gave me more free time to spend someplace else. I didn't have a real job; I was working part time for a fireworks company. I had no money. I had no ability to fully handle the gender dysphoria and truly live as myself. My life was in shambles; I was in a deep depression, so I began to consider ending my life.

It was a very dark time for me, and it was a scary time for my parents, too. Music became my escape. I listened to a lot of Depeche Mode and other new wave and alternative music, KCGL/KROQ-type stuff. One afternoon I crashed onto my bed, lights out, door closed. I just wanted to sleep the day away and be numb; but suddenly I felt a presence in my room near the closet. It was dark and menacing. I'd been attacked spiritually before, but this was different. I cowered under my blankets, facing the wall, eyes closed, and fought and prayed for them to go away. Then something *changed* and I realized that it was now an angel there, and I didn't want to see an angel either. I was ashamed, broken, and bad. A horrible, awful person. I wasn't good enough. I wanted them to both leave me alone and go away. I was then no longer being attacked, but I waited, and waited, and after a while they were finally gone, too. I don't know what I would have seen if I'd had the courage, or faith, to look, but I'm pretty sure looking back I would have seen God. I have regrets.

In June 1986, my father took me on a trip to Las Vegas for the National

Computer Conference. My cousin was in from Berkeley and was going to be showing his product. He had a pretty girl along who was to be the proverbial "booth babe." I liked hanging out with her. The conference was huge, and it was interesting seeing all the latest technology. My father took me fake sky diving, and to "An Evening At La Cage" with Frank Marino as Joan Rivers. I know, right? It was classier than your usual drag show. Here were these men getting to impersonate beautiful, glamorous women. I was so jealous. What was my dad thinking?

On the way home we stayed at my grandparent's home in Hurricane, UT. I let the adults hang out and I went upstairs to my room, and I did what I always do: I explored all the upstairs bedrooms with their closets, dressers, and trunks full of old clothes; and found dresses and things and worked up the courage to try something on without getting caught. I guess they heard me prowling around, and my grandfather asked what I was doing. I didn't know how to answer that. How could I tell him? So my father helped me out by also asking what I was doing. I still couldn't say.

Suddenly, they all took a jump to the Island of Conclusions and decided that I was upstairs doing drugs. My reticence to admit what I was doing, the long hair, and the look on my face all confirmed their suspicion. There was a lot of yelling, and my grandparents kicked me out of their house. They called the police, who could tell I wasn't on drugs, and they gave me a ride into St. George where my father paid for my Greyhound bus ticket back home. My friends Greg and Gloria let me stay with them a few days till my parents cooled down, and I wanted to go home. That burned the bridges with my grandparents and my father.

Later that hot summer, after fasting for 24 hours, I drove my truck up the hill and hiked with no water or food up to the back of a canyon, above my house, to end my life. I didn't leave a note. I told no one where I was going. That's how I roll with suicide ideation. I won't reach out. I'm not going to make a phone call. In hindsight, I realized it probably would have been days or longer before I was found, or if I was ever found. And it was there at the back of the canyon, amongst the pines sitting on a log by the stream, that God intervened in my life.

Five years earlier when I was a sophomore in high school, I had a seminary teacher who challenged us over Christmas break to gain a testimony that God lived. We were given a handout with suggestions of things to do that would bring the Spirit and help us to achieve this goal. Things like fasting and praying, reading scriptures, listening to church hymns, etc., etc. I did all those things, even religiously. But Christmas passed and it was soon to be New Year's Eve and I was worrying that I was going to return to school a failure. It became a struggle. And then one night it happened. No, the heavens didn't open with hosts of angels, nor even a single angel. I was walking my dog through the necropolis at night (it's a quiet place at night, usually), and I just got this feeling in my breast that grew. It wasn't huge, it wasn't burning, but it was just there that God was present and had been listening.

As I now sat at the back of this canyon, I was thinking through all that I was dealing with and how I was just through with it all and no one cared or loved me. I was arguing my justification for what I was about to do, and that feeling came back, and I felt, "**I love you.**" Ok, so maybe no one mortal loves me, but my Heavenly Father still did. He was still here with me. That got me thinking: if my Heavenly Father loved me, then maybe I could get through this, but I was going to need help. I told Him that I was going to need a girlfriend.

A girlfriend? Yeah, maybe that was self-serving and a bit of a reach, like I was a catch in my current state, but it was really what I needed. Someone here in mortality that would love me and was uniquely qualified to help me with being a trans girl. I prayed every day for this girl to be in my life; "Send me an Angel" by Real Life was my song. And I worked on my depression and my attitude toward life by myself. I'd realized in my few experiences that there wasn't a therapist who could help me. Basically, I faked being happy. When people asked how I was doing, I said cheerfully, "I'm great!" I'm still pretty good at it, but now I say, "I'm fabulous!" Same thing. Shhhhhhhh. Don't tell anyone. It's our secret.

I still couldn't take college classes, but I could attend the Institute of Religion. How I never graduated from the Institute I'll never know. I must have taken every class. I got active with the LDS Student Association (LDSSA). I went to dances. Danced in the fountain, and met people from the church's fraternity and sorority, ΣΓΧ and ΛΔΣ. Mike Mollinet introduced me to the guys in the ΔΧ chapter, and I suddenly had all these brothers who spent much of our time hanging out with sorority sisters, mostly ΔΛΧ chapter.

The following fall quarter in 1987, I was rematriculated on probation. And then one day as I was crossing Marriott Plaza, I saw a girl with my friend Nancy, and I knew she was the one I'd been praying for to come. This was the woman I'd marry. Yes, it doesn't just happen at BYU. But I didn't tell her that.

Her name was Valeria and she lived about a mile from my house. We started talking, meeting at The Bay for dancing, and eventually dating. After 6 months we were kind of into each other and I wanted to go steady. The plan was to marry this girl after all. But I'll admit that I was not an easy person to date. I had never really dated before.

Being a transgender lesbian, was hard in high school. You're a girl who is attracted to the girls. So, your thinking goes something like this walking down the hallway. *Hey, there's a beautiful girl. I love what she's done with her hair, and makeup, and that outfit is fabulous! I wonder where she got it. I wonder how I'd look in it. And what a cute body. I wish my body looked like that. Why can't I have boobs? I wonder if she'd go out with me? Why would she when I'm a girl who looks like a boy?* Yeah, there's the question. Do you want to be the girl, or date the girl? I think a lot of the straight guys just jumped to the end with the going out part. As a result, I didn't date at all till now.

I was 21 and had no idea what I was doing. I'd never had a real friendship, let alone a relationship before. I couldn't even talk to my brother, or parents. How do I communicate with this girl? I was scrambling and making a whole bunch of mistakes and it was undeniably very hard on her. I was a horrible, awful person at times, not understanding the games I didn't know I was playing. I was overthinking everything. I was also harboring this huge secret that was probably causing a bunch of these problems because I needed to tell her, but I didn't know how or when to tell her.

Eventually came the time that I couldn't put it off any longer, and I decided I had to come out to her. I wrote a six-page letter explaining that I was transsexual (I didn't know the word transgender yet), that I'd been wearing women's clothes, that I had girl brain and thoughts, and I wanted to live my life this way. I gave it to Nancy for the two of them to read.

The next day I found out that I was dumped. She had been thinking of leaving me anyway and this just made it easier. She then realized that she'd known the whole time from things I'd said and did, and what her father had told her about me. Her father already thought I must be gay. OK, I was dating his daughter, but he didn't mean it that way. When she told her parents about the letter her Father told her, "Sometimes girl spirits end up in boy bodies and you don't want to date, let alone marry anyone like that." He took an immediate dislike to me, and I never saw him again till his funeral. I was never allowed to be in the same place as him.

But Valeria and I managed to stay friends and saw each other at institute and other activities. She dated many of my fraternity brothers, even inviting me into the girl's restroom to help her get ready for her Spring Formal date. We would get back together and break up all summer long. Sometimes twice in a day. Having this secret now out in the open didn't necessarily make things easier between us. It was now a struggle of what to do about it and understand it together. And I don't know that she came to understand it the same way I did. She didn't think of me as a woman.

But despite all that, I don't know what it was, maybe my quick wit and sarcasm, irresistible good looks, amazing taste in alternative music, or love of British television, but by fall 1988 we were going steady and in love.

Soon after, she moved out of her parent's house and into an apartment. And there I asked her if I could borrow her clothes. At that time, I didn't have any girl clothes. She cautiously agreed. She wasn't exactly an enthusiastic ally. But for my next birthday, she bought me a complete outfit: shoes, tights, skirt, belt, and top. And she gave me her bra from high school which I stuffed with cotton balls. My first clothes that were all mine. I got changed and we went out walking around her Salt Lake neighborhood in the daylight. I was on top of the world. I was finally living my dream. I was finally free.

She later taught me how to do makeup and paint my nails. The first time I saw myself with makeup in the mirror, I was like, *There you are.* I finally saw myself fully staring back for the first time of my life. That was life changing. A confirmation of who I was.

It was then I decided I needed a girl name.

In college I'd gotten tired of my birth name. Everyone was only interested in the long-haired hippie camping on couches in the Institute until they found out I was already a member and not going to be a conversion success story. They didn't really care about me. No one did. So, I looked for a new name that I could use to hide who I was.

I loved the Shakespearean play Twelfth Night with all the gender bending comedy. You had a girl who was pretending to be a guy who had a girl falling in love with her, right? Her name was Viola, and she went by Cesario. Yeah, I couldn't realistically use either of those names in modern-day Utah. But as Cesario, Viola was getting mistaken for her twin brother Sebastian. That could work. I liked that name. It was also the name of a character from my favorite science fiction book, *Nova* by Samuel R. Delaney. Although he went by Damned Sebastian, and wasn't I for what I was doing? So, everyone at the Institute, including Valeria, for many years, and some still even today, only knew me simply as Sebastian. No last name. Like Madonna or Prince. I was Viola, pretending to be Cesario, but people could mistake me for Sebastian. It worked.

So here would be a good time to mention, NEVER ask a trans woman what was their birth name. We call that our dead name for a reason. That person is dead. They never were us. It's from that other life. You're curious; I get that. Maybe it's interesting for you, but it can look like you only see us still as that male person. You simply don't need to know.

Why is my name Katherine you ask? I really hated my male birth name my whole life. Ugh. I never, ever, ever liked it, not even in grade school. Sorry 'rents. And going with the feminized version was an even worse option. I'd been called that before. So I'd chosen a clever new boy sobriquet of Sebastian a few years earlier, but how do you choose your own girl name? Something that you'd use for the rest of your life, maybe even legally? I wanted something that my parents would have named me as their daughter. But it's not like I could ask them.

I might have gone with Jennifer if we didn't already have 15 billion friends named Jennifer. So I found a book with the top 100 popular girl names for when I was born. I immediately tossed out the top 20 or 30 since I wasn't that popular, and started reading through the list. Somewhere around 60th was Katherine. I decided to go with what I thought was a boring, traditional, perhaps even Germanic, spelling. Just like my parents would have chosen. Sorry, it's not really all that exciting of a story in comparison to Sebastian. I'm not named after anyone at all.

And I still usually just go by Katherine, with no last name. That's how I introduce myself today. And I've never had any friends, or family, long enough to have a shortened nickname like Kathy or Kate. But I've tried to go by Kath since I heard it in the TV show *Broadchurch*. That hasn't stuck either. So I'm just Katherine.

For the next many years Valeria and I continued to go shopping till I'd gotten rid of all my male clothes. I'd go to work in androgynous girl clothes and then meet her for dinner at her place, and I'd change into something more comfortable like a skirt, or dress, or oversized sweater and leggings. Nobody seemed to think it weird at work that my tops had shoulder pads and said "EXP" across the front. When her roommates retired to their bedrooms, we'd sneak out and walk around the Salt Lake City Avenues. Other nights we'd sneak out and go to a restaurant like Olive Garden or rent a movie at Blockbuster. On Sundays after church, I'd change into a Sunday dress like her, and we'd go to a park to walk and read scriptures.

We'd go places that we were pretty sure that we, or I, wouldn't get recognized. And as far as we knew I didn't. I found out a couple years ago that I was seen by someone who worked with my cousin Jan. She told her sister Jill and my Uncle Don and Aunt Maradene. They didn't understand, but they kept it to themselves. They also were thinking I was gay but were confused that I was dating a girl. From what I've been told by my mother,

I think it was the only secret Maradene ever kept. LOL. When I finally was able to come out to my cousins, they were all very accepting, and we had some girl's-night-out dinners, but we were missing that bond that hadn't developed over many decades.

And Valeria hated Halloween. You have to realize that Halloween was like the only time a trans girl could be in public with friends as herself without being out. So I made the most of it. We'd go shopping for weeks so I had a new outfit for every party. I always won the company Halloween costume contest. They all thought I had borrowed my girlfriend's clothes. Nope. Not at all, but I probably changed my clothes three to five times before leaving the house.

And for Valentine's Day we'd buy matching bra and panty sets with all the hearts and things. But we were good young women and never got a peek at each other. It was just fun!

By 1994, I'd gotten my life together and things were going great. Being essentially socially transitioned the past 5 years, I had my gender dysphoria under control. I'd gotten tossed from the University a final time and told never to come back. But I'd managed to make a career from my self-taught programming skills using the home computer, and I had a good job as a software engineer. I'd bought a car and a house and a dog, Ardath. But there was just one problem.

I didn't know how to marry Valeria.

3.

There and Back Again

OK, I DID KNOW THE MECHANICS OF HOW TO GET MARRIED, but there was just one problem. Can you guess?

We'd tried to get married on Leap Day 1992 at the Los Angeles Temple, but when I'd gone to get my temple recommend, I'd brought up with the bishop being transgender and living as a woman. I thought I needed to confess that, right? I didn't know what the policy was. And I just had all this built-up guilt or shame or embarrassment from doing something not normal. He needed to know, right?

He said he'd have to get advice. When the advice came back a week or so later, he said that the First Presidency didn't think that what I was doing was a great idea. He obviously was not directly quoting them. But he said I needed to cut my hair and change back to boys' clothes if I wanted a recommend. Well, I really wanted to get married to Valeria in the temple. We'd talked many times over the years and had agreed it would be the temple the first time and only time. I'd also done some studying at the

University medical library, and I'd decided that I wouldn't do any medical transition till I had all my kids. Being married and having a family was really important to me, and worth some sacrifice. So, with her support, I whacked my hair and detransitioned, digging out what male clothes I still had and putting away my girl clothes. That was a miserable experience. It wasn't me. But I endured for the reward at the end.

Six months later for September we made tentative wedding plans again and I met with the bishop. He told me that I didn't cut my hair short enough and that he didn't think that I'd really had a change of heart. That after I got the recommend that I'd go back to being a girl. Well, he was right about the last thing. I didn't intend to stay detransitioned. He said come back in another six months. Uh, no. I wasn't doing that. I moved my records to where Valeria lived and broke out my girl clothes. My parents told me many, many years later that that bishop told them that how he handled my situation was his biggest regret as a bishop. I've wondered how he thought he might have handled it differently.

So nothing had changed. It'd been over 6 years since we met, and 2 years since I last tried to get a recommend. That was a long time to be emotionally vested and I still had no idea how to get a temple recommend. And without one, we wouldn't get married. I figured it was soon going to be time, if not way past time, for Valeria to cut her losses. We couldn't keep going this way, and she needed to find a guy she could marry, even if he didn't have luxurious long hair and a wardrobe to die for.

But when I came home from a business trip in May, she picked me up at the airport. She said, "Me and your mom have been talking."

"Oh? What about?"

"We think that me and you should get married."

"Oh. Did you pick a date?"

"June 10th."

I figured in my head that was exactly 3 weeks away. Not a lot of time. I pretended to think through my schedule and teased, "I think I'm free that day."

"Good, because we already booked the Salt Lake Temple." Nice.

She set about making her white wedding dress. I wouldn't get to wear one. Sucks to be me. We learned from the last engagement and planned on a very small, family-only guest list, thus limiting the damage if this went sideways. My father would naturally be the photographer. The reception would happen a month later at our home. And we bought matching negligees from Nordstrom for the honeymoon. (IKR? We returned them unused. She wore it better anyway.) But I still had no idea how to get a recommend. Why would now be any different than two years ago? What was she thinking?

With a week before our endowments and sealing, push came to shove. I scheduled a visit with the bishop. WARNING! OK, I'm not proud of this. This is not a shining moment of my life. Don't try this at home. But I was between a rock and hard place. There was a wedding all planned, again for a third time. What was I to do? I'm a very honest person. My integrity is a key character attribute of mine. I can't lie. So what I came up with in desperation was this: I heard that bishop's had the gift of discernment. To copy policy from President Clinton, it would be all "don't ask, don't tell." I'd answer the temple questions honestly, but I wasn't going to volunteer any information about how I dressed and lived unless the bishop directly asked. And if God wanted the bishop to know, then God could inspire the bishop to ask. I've since been told by my friends who have been bishops that it doesn't at all work like that. Oops. I didn't know.

So, as you might guess, he didn't ask, and I didn't tell. I walked out with a shiny temple recommend and saw the stake president with the same results. The stake president was the son of President Hinckley, so he should have known if he needed to, right? Again, not my proudest moment. And I felt a bit of guilt about this for many years; it took all of my will not to walk out of my endowment session.

I take some solace in the fact that at the time, and I didn't know this, but the only policy in the Church's *Handbook 1: Stake Presidents and Bishops* then was that those that had had an elective transsexual operation couldn't go to the temple, or those who were planning on it. I hadn't and I wasn't. So, by any published policy, being transgender and, sort of, kind of, transitioned shouldn't have prohibited me. I wonder what the First Presidency really said two years earlier.

Well, while I didn't get to wear a wedding dress (next time for sure), I put together some of my best men's wear and we got endowed Thursday night and married Friday morning. We waited for a while that morning, but Valeria's father ended up not coming. I was disappointed. She told me recently that she didn't even invite him. She didn't want him there. The poor men in the temple had no idea what to do with me. Apparently, I didn't fit the mold with my long hair and without a tuxedo, I received no attention.

We didn't wait to start having a family. We would end up eventually having seven kids, six of them daughters. I know. You'd think that would be lots of drama, but it wasn't. However, the house had only one bathroom. I'm so glad I have my kids.

But each pregnancy was a hard thing for me. I couldn't be pregnant. As my wife progressed through all the changes of having this life grow within her, I was useless. Every day was a reminder of how my body was broken. It was wrong and beyond modern medicine to fix. It was hopeless. I wanted to have children. I wanted that connection. I wanted that experience. I wanted to be a mother. And it was never going to happen for me. I was born sterile.

Mother's Day and Father's Day are hard days. I'm female, but I'm not the mother. I'm my kids' father, but I'm not male. I want the jewelry and chocolate, not the ties and cookies. My kids still refer to me as their father. It's weird. But I figure it would be wrong to be called their mother. My wife went through the rigors of pregnancy, labor, and delivery of eight children. I figure with that she's earned the right to hold the title all on her own. I wouldn't dare take that honor from her.

Sure, if I was a teenager today, I'd probably decide to go on blockers, hormones, and have surgery, and I wouldn't have a family. So, I'm glad I was born when I was. But I'm really torn sometimes. I'd have loved to be able to be myself from my youth. So I'm not going to fault anyone who does transition, because I understand. They don't have to go through the misery just because I did.

But sometime after the birth of our second child, Valeria says to me, "We need to have a talk." Sure, why not. What could happen? "The girls are at an age that they can tell that you're not dressing like the other dads. I don't want the kids to think they have two moms. You can't dress like that around the family anymore. Maybe when the kids are adults you can retransition."

I was not expecting this conversation. I was gobsmacked, but it made some sense, right? I could make no argument. What families had two mothers? Gay couples? Were we in a same-sex marriage? I hadn't thought of us like that, I guess, because we weren't looked at like that. I wasn't recognized legally or religiously as female. And what should our kids think?

There was also a hidden threat, but I didn't know then what it was. I did the math. Coming back out in my mid-forties wasn't too old, right? So I reluctantly agreed. And we began packing up all my clothes, makeup, shoes, etc., and storing them in the back of the shed all properly moth balled. Soon after that I wasn't allowed to be me for Halloween. For the first time in forever, I had to come up with male Halloween costumes. Ick. And then I couldn't be me even in the privacy of our bedroom. I'd spent the past 10 years being me, living my truth. Maybe I wasn't out publicly, but I was out as much as society would have accepted at that time. I had been happy, and now I wasn't.

It was hard in the closet. I did keep my long hair, so I was able to still deal with the gender dysphoria. Because of that Katherine was always still present. But I had to relinquish all the femme to my wife, and I felt like I'd lost a connection with my daughters. I had to stand back and give my wife space. I was supposed to be the man now, and I didn't do that very well. I'm so glad I had all my daughters. Having the reverse with six sons would have killed me. I'm not sure how I could have ever been a role model to them. Boys and men weren't anything I wanted to deal with.

And it was during this time that I could feel the Spirit working on me for many, many months. It wasn't much other than, "something is coming" and "you need to be ready." I had an idea what it was about. It could only be one thing. I'd have to cut my hair shorter. And then the phone call finally came inviting me to visit with the stake president. *That* I wasn't expecting. I was called to be the ward executive secretary. And I was told that being the secretary meant I was in the bishopric and had to abide by church grooming rules. Yes, I probably again didn't cut it as short as they wanted, but it was still a large sacrifice.

My first day in the bishop's office he invited me to become familiar with everything. So after our bishopric meeting was over, I went through all the drawers and filing cabinets. It was a dusty graveyard of ancient forms, reports, and handbooks. I found the Church's *Handbook 1*. Not knowing I wasn't supposed to read it, I started flipping through it stopping at things that caught my eye. One of those was when I saw the word transsexual. Surprise! The Church has policies for members like me! It's not exactly something that gets talked about across the pulpit or in elders quorum because, really, how many people does it affect? Using the index, I read through all the policies about "elective transsexual operations." I wasn't worried about it too much since I wasn't planning on having surgery; wouldn't even know where to begin even if I had the inclination or resources to do so. We were still having kids after all. But when I next renewed my temple recommend, I brought up to my bishop about my girl past and how I wasn't currently doing anything. Since it had been in the past for many years, he decided it wasn't anything to be concerned about. And the guilt of "don't ask, don't tell" passed away.

By October 2012, after about 15 years of misery, I had put on over 100 pounds. I reached a point I couldn't be in the closet anymore. And I'd had another *me* experience. I'd looked down in the shower and saw that I finally had my boobs. Ok, they weren't going to win any awards or get me that centerfold magazine spread, but they were mine. It was time. I wanted my body. So in November 2012 I told my wife, "We need to talk," and I returned the favor. But at least I took her on a weekend getaway to a hotel with dinner before I told her that I couldn't stay in the closet any longer and I'd needed to begin retransitioning.

Yes, I was miserable. And I'd sit in the chapel and look at the men on the stand and think, "I have absolutely nothing in common with them." Going to elders quorum was like being on Mars, when I was from Venus. I didn't want to be like them. I was tired of being something I wasn't. I was in my mid-forties. Sure, maybe I was having the infamous mid-life crisis. But I wasn't buying a sports car or getting a younger wife. I was buying heels. I saw a life that I wasn't enjoying, my life, and I didn't see it changing, and I didn't want another 15 years of it. But I figured that in retransitioning I was consigning myself to hell. I was a horrible, awful person.

Valeria told me later in marriage therapy that she knew I was miserable, she just thought I'd continue to hunker down and endure it to the end. Oh, nice. Was I really supposed to sacrifice my happiness for everyone else? It created an interesting paradox. As long as I endured in my misery, then everyone in my life was happy. And if I was happy, then everyone in my life was miserable. Why can't we find that place where we can all be happy?

I was carrying decades of imposed shame and societal condemnation. I couldn't point to anything in particular that I was doing that was bad, but it had to be with the way everyone reacted, right? I'd be ending a very long self-imposed detransition. I'd be going back to what I'd confessed to my bishop years earlier. What would happen now? Again, I was between a rock and a hard place. And I had to decide what was best for me.

I consoled myself that the terrestrial kingdom wasn't that bad from everything I'd heard. I was that miserable. And I didn't know what else to do. At least I could be happy for a few years before the judgement of eternity. Maybe my family would come visit me. And where would I go if I took my life? Maybe I might luck out and sneak into the lowest level of the celestial kingdom. Who knew?

In fairness, when I told Valeria what I'd decided, I wasn't planning on coming out publicly. I was just turning the clock back to when we first got married. I figured we'd have a weekend getaway every so often so that I could be out in public, but otherwise my transition would be private, even still secret from the kids. But as she pulled back from me emotionally, I felt more alone and was left to make decisions unilaterally, and I felt less of a need to moderate the transition. That probably caused her to pull back even more in a regrettable cycle.

Dr. Laura Schlesinger would talk on her radio show with married couples where one decided they didn't want children. Well, that is kind of one of the main purposes of marriage and a large expectation. So for the husband or wife to decide they now didn't want children was a change in the marriage contract. Divorce was reasonable so that the one could find someone they could have children with.

There are things that you have an expectation won't change like values and goals, and that wedding vows and covenants will be kept. But you also can't marry expecting that some things will change. Like you can't marry the non-member thinking that they will join the church, or your spouse will give up porn, or live the word of wisdom, or stop carousing, or become a financially responsible individual. Because they may never do any of those things. Your marriage and love can't be conditional on what someone will become.

I think I'd made it pretty clear who I was at the beginning with my coming out letter. I was transsexual. This is how I wanted to live my life. As a woman. And she'd helped me do that. She'd dated me for 6 years essentially as a woman. I was wearing women's clothes every day; some that she'd made. Sometimes there was makeup and jewelry. And we did buy lingerie for the honeymoon. I may not have come out publicly, and not because I didn't want to, but I think we both knew that would have been a bad thing at that time. Did she marry me thinking I would naturally desist on my own, or did she plan on changing me? I don't know, but I don't think so. Did Valeria change the contract 15 years earlier putting me in the closet? Was I changing it now? Was I just as bad?

I had been woefully ill-prepared getting into our relationship at the beginning and that made it a torturous experience falling in love. And now I wasn't any more prepared for our relationship falling apart over the next 6 years. I again had no idea what I was doing. I had no experience with divorce, and I had no intention of getting divorced. That didn't stop me from making a lot of mistakes trying to keep our marriage together and navigate my retransition without her. I tried to do good things, but quite often I was wrong.

Here is an important safety tip for trans couples thinking about getting married: it's actually necessary to talk about these things before you get engaged. We obviously didn't. Oops. I didn't have any expectation that I would detransition. I never thought about it. I didn't think how it would work with the kids. It's not like there were books or movies on this at the time. And I don't know what she was thinking. But the other thing is this: it's good to get these crucial conversations on paper so that 15 years later you both know what you understood.

So many times, I hear of couples getting married and the husband is trans, and they come out right before they get married. The wife thinks, "Oh, once we get married that won't be a problem." Like having sex with her will cure anything. Well sure, sex, as fun as it is, doesn't cure all problems. It doesn't cure infidelity, abuse, mental illness, or porn addictions. And it certainly doesn't cure gender dysphoria. I know a couple where the trans husband was never able to consummate the marriage and after a couple years they got divorced. If you read about Caitlyn Jenner, she talks about how Kris Kardashian knew before they got married, but Kris claims she didn't know. Caitlyn was on hormones, had breasts, and was transitioning when they were dating. And coming out after marriage usually ends up in divorce. Wives who are straight and haven't signed up to be married to a woman do not stay very long.

I'm always amazed at the ability of moms who will fight like dragons for their LGBT kids but will cut and run if their own husband is LGBT. If you're transgender and thinking of getting married, document what your spouse knows and what the expectations are for social and medical transition and gender roles in the home.

When a spouse begins to transition, it is often the case that the other spouse will make ultimatums. Like, "I don't want to ever see you as a woman." Or, "You can't pierce your ears." Or, "The kids can't know." Or, "You can't transition at all." Be careful with these. You might find they aren't so bad as you think.

Remember, this person is still your spouse. The one you fell in love with many years earlier, and maybe for many of the qualities that came from their female life that you weren't fully aware of. Don't assume that things are going to go badly or you won't be able to handle it. As long as they are keeping their covenants, you may find that you can be now even closer in your marriage without this huge secret. Love, attraction, and even sex, will find a way.

They also say, "When one woman comes out of the closet, another one goes in." It can be a hard situation for your cis spouse in going from the only woman in the relationship to sharing those perks and that uniqueness.

Well, as you might expect, Valeria wasn't thrilled by the news of my desire to retransition. I thought we were just going back to how we were before. It was supposed to be no big deal. I'd envisioned that we still loved each other and were sealed together as a couple, and as parents we'd figure out how to make this work as a family. What I didn't understand was how much she would feel she would need to protect the kids from me. I would be seen as a threat and danger.

She saw her perfect Mormon home being destroyed. BOOM! In a giant mushroom cloud. She saw her husband giving up eternity. She was now horrified to think of her husband in a dress, even though she'd made a few for me. She tried to understand why she was accepting when we started dating, but was now intolerant. She decided it was because she was now more righteous. Possibly.

She would spend the next couple years trying to fix me. I was broken and obviously what I needed in my life was more religion. My fall from grace had reignited her diligence to be even more spiritual. The usual movies and TV we watched, while not horrible, were no longer good enough. The bar was raised in our house. She would accompany me on my morning runs riding her bike beside me. It was great to be able to spend the time with her and I would have liked to talk about us, but she only ever wanted to talk about the gospel. Every conversation began with how she was preparing to teach her Sunday school lesson, or some conference talk she'd recently read. Our weekly FHE became a periodic veiled lesson in how I needed to change.

But I hadn't left the church. I still had a testimony. I still believed the

Church was true and led by a prophet. I went to church every Sunday. I was still going to the temple, wearing my garments, and keeping our covenants. I knew the doctrine as well or better than her in these morning discussions. And my father would do the same thing when he would join me for runs. But none of it was what I needed. I'd had the gospel my whole life and I'd been transgender my whole life. Being transgender wasn't a function of low spiritual strength. I was still here because of my spiritual strength. I needed love and acceptance for who I was. Not judgement and rejection.

But as I said, it felt like to me that she'd emotionally pulled out of the marriage. We were now just two people living together. She told me that if the kids ever found out she would divorce me. I'm proud to say that my two oldest kids didn't find out till they were legal adults. So I feel like I kept the original bargain. I just didn't know there were going to be five more kids.

The five more kids would have pushed my retransitioning from 2015 to 2028. I wouldn't have made it another 16 years till I was in my early 60s. Valeria told me later if I hadn't gone in the closet, we would have stopped having kids. So I have to say that as hard as it was, and has been, it was totally worth making the sacrifice. I can't imagine not having my last five kids. Isn't that what mother's do? No regrets.

I made a plan now that I had all my children to begin medical transition. But everything I read said that taking estrogen puts on weight. I was already some 280-plus pounds. I didn't want to start from there. So I started exercising and eating less. I found testosterone was actually good for one thing—weight loss. I was losing about five pounds a week. (Yeah, men suck. I've never been able to do that again.) Within 9 months I was down to 190 pounds. My fighting weight from high school was 170 pounds, so I felt pretty good about that at my age. I was running 4.5 miles every morning and about 25–30 miles a week. I was in the best shape of my life in a long time. (My wife wasn't happy about this.) I kept the weight off for a year and I began seeing a therapist for a WPATH[9] letter to begin hormone treatment.

Another important safety tip: only take your wife to marriage counseling and not to your personal transgender therapy. Valeria found out I was having these sessions and I thought it could be good to have a moderated discussion. Instead, my therapist thought it was a good time to drop a rock in my pond by telling my wife, "She needs to get divorced, leave the church, have surgery so she can live her true life as the woman she is." That was shocking for me since I didn't want to do any of those things. I didn't want to get divorced, and I didn't want to leave the church, and having surgery would definitely cause me to leave the church. This just widened the divide between us.

After about a dozen sessions, I got my letter and made one of the weirdest phone calls to an OB/GYN for an appointment. Sure, I'd been with my wife to dozens of visits, but this time it was for me. The doctor took one look at me and said, "Girl, let's get you started." She had me read and sign self-consent papers and never asked to see my letter. WPATH was now allowing self-consent in some cases. I didn't need to have gone to the therapist, but it was good to have been through the process and have the letter as proof of my diagnosis.

After two days of a low dose of estrogen and an anti-androgen, my testosterone had gone to zero and my estrogen was high. I was at female normal levels. And that's when an amazing thing happened. My gender dysphoria went completely away. I literally felt this fog in my brain lift and sunshine shone in for the first time. The constant background noise of the dysphoria ended like someone turning off the air conditioning. My brain was quiet. I could think thoughts. This sudden and permanent ending of the dysphoria was evidence to me that what I had been dealing with my whole life was somehow biological, and not psychological. My brain was no longer fighting with my body. It finally had the hormones it always wanted. It was like getting half my brain back. And also, with the thoughts about sex every 15 seconds ending, it was like getting the other half of my brain back. And what thoughts do you think when you finally for the first time in your life have a fully armed and operational girl brain? I thought of shoes. LOL. Just kidding. Maybe.

Other things happen with hormones. Your pheromones change. I lost that manly musky smell, and now have the sweeter girl smell. (My wife hated that, too.) Your skin changes. It's smoother and the collagen in my face adjusted, giving my face a more female shape. I don't have the usual wrinkles around my eyes and face like other women my age, which makes me look a about 20 years younger. People have thought I'm Shannon's older sister.

I think it was the last time my wife and I went to the temple, she took the elevator, and I took the stairs and got to the front desk ahead of her. My recommend was scanned and the man said, "Sister Herrmann, welcome to the Bountiful temple." I was so glad Valeria didn't hear that. But it warmed my heart. We were doing sealings that night. The sealer asked for our last name and then he said, "Brother Herrmann, is this with you your wife or your mother?" I think he came near to passing through the veil right then.

When women find out my real age they ask, "What are you doing to have such great skin?" Well, actually nothing. I don't buy anything weird or expensive. I just use a normal moisturizer before putting on makeup. I'm just doing estrogen. The same thing they've been doing. However, I've been only doing it for 8 years. Sorry, but don't hate me quite yet. There's more.

Your fat will redistribute somewhat, and your boobs will grow. OMG, I had no idea how much that hurt! Something I never was told in school. But the worst is when they stop hurting meaning they're done growing. Trans women will usually grow to a cup less than their sisters, or mother, but I wasn't asking. And it helps to start earlier in life when you have more growth hormones. But I came out alright. I hadn't lost what I had before I lost weight and only added more.

And I'd been on an anti-androgen for many years that had an uncommon side effect. It caused all the hair below my shoulders to stop growing. Valeria had one rule when she started helping me transition—I wasn't allowed to shave my chest. But I did shave my legs and pits every week. I had a fairly hairy chest and legs, but my back was smooth. This had made it hard to buy clothes in the past. Not that many necklines that will hide the chest hair. I luckily wasn't like my father who still had genes proving us ape descendants. So I only had to shave my chest and legs once more. I haven't shaved my chest in ten years, and I only shave my legs every couple years to get rid of the peach fuzz. Ladies, now you can hate me, right?

Another change was that my ability to feel emotions was expanded. I had been emotionally constipated my whole life. My mother's mom told me I had a tender heart, and I did, but I couldn't feel those things. I couldn't cry. It's like guys have the emotional equivalent of the restaurant box of crayons for kids. They have four. And what they don't realize is that girls have the Crayola box of 96. It's like going from black and white to color TV. I love how I can now feel things and cry at the end of a Nicholas Sparks movie. I can feel the Spirit during sacrament meeting. It's so nice to be human.

Being on estrogen will not raise the pitch of your voice. You can learn to pitch it up a bit through speech therapy, and there are surgeries that can restore what your girl voice might have been. Estrogen also doesn't make you shorter or narrow your shoulders or widen your hips. It will make the hair on your body and face finer and grow slower, but it won't remove it. And if you've lost hair on the top of your head, it's not coming back that much, but having less testosterone might help save what you've got left.

Not having testosterone makes it a lot harder, even impossible, to lose weight. Before, I could lose five pounds by walking upstairs, but now if I nearly kill myself exercising and starving, I can lose maybe five pounds in a year. As they say, "Welcome to womanhood!" But with that also came losing my libido which was such a blessing. It's so nice to not be thinking about sex all the time. Haven't really missed it. I've always seen women differently, but now the sexual aspect is gone. Sure, I still notice their bodies and compare, as women do, but it's now a lot easier to be friends and see them completely. And yes, I can still get warm and passionate and everything. But I'm in control of it. Physical intimacy is something I can want on my own terms.

Living as female full time has taught me lots of things. I didn't get to bear any of my children or experience a lifetime of misogyny and sexism and marginalization. (Maybe I have some, since being the long-haired man in Utah and in our church was not an easy path.) But I see things in a new perspective being in a world that I wasn't before. I hear your stories and I see your lives, and I experience much of it firsthand now. I feel the struggles that men just don't get or take for granted. My respect for women has only increased, pushing that pedestal higher to a tower.

Anyway, all this is to say that going to start hormones had crossed a line with my wife. She went to the stake president, and eventually the bishop. They began helping her with an expected divorce.

She hoped that I'd run off back to my homeland of California, to San Francisco specifically, where I could live the lifestyle, and be far away from the kids. What is that transgender lifestyle? I don't know. I'm from Los Angeles. The implication from San Francisco was undoubtedly that it would be filled with immorality and wanton sex, I guess. However, I was a Latter-day Saint woman. Since when did I ever want to do that? Why would I want to break my temple covenants? And then there were the times she simply wished I was dead, and my kids wouldn't have to see me.

I was no longer part of the marriage, or perhaps better said—at some point the kids became a higher priority than me. Her mama bear instincts had kicked in, and she needed to protect the kids and keep them safe from their crazy father. (Safe meaning not seeing their father in a dress.) She'd forgotten who I was and replaced me with an image from the internet or from people she'd talked to about how trans women behaved.

I didn't know how bad things had gotten and that she was having these conversations. That's when I learned more about another way God spoke to me. I call it the Cloister Bell. Yes, it's a *Doctor Who* reference. When the universe is about to end or something else similarly bad then the Cloister Bell of the TARDIS would start to toll to warn the Doctor.

And the Cloister Bell was tolling for a second time in my life. What it really was ended up being the most awful, horrible feeling in your entire life. The Spirit is screaming at you that something is wrong. Doom is coming. It will keep you up at nights, not able to sleep, for days and weeks on end. Several years later I read in the *Ensign* magazine what this feeling was. It is the Spirit offended. It is Hell. And it must be a shadow of what eternal Hell is like. You do not want this feeling! Do not offend the Spirit by not following its promptings.

My first and previous experience with it was in February 2000 when I'd changed jobs. The company I was working for was going under and I had three written job offers in hand for much more money. I had a lifeboat, but my company was making me offers to stay—really good offers. But wasn't it a sign that I should leave since I had these offers? That's how I'd seen this situation in the past. Why would I stay at a company going out of business?

We prayed about this decision. We fasted. We went to the temple many, many times. And every time Valeria would tell me, "You should quit. That's what God wants you to do."

And I'd be like, "Sure."

And I guess I felt what she did, temporarily, but then that feeling would soon leave and I'd feel like I should stay. Really, I was feeling like I should stay, but every time we talked as a couple, she would have me feeling like I should leave. And ringing in my ears was how my bishop and church leaders would always say, "Husbands, listen to your wives because they are naturally more in tune with the spirit." And I doubted myself. Maybe I was wrong, and she was right. I'm supposed to listen to her. And she was so certain.

So, I told them I was leaving, and it felt wrong, and I signed an agreement with the other company, and it felt more wrong, and I was desperately looking for a way out of this. How could I stop this quitting? I wanted some miracle to happen that I could point to as evidence to show my wife that I shouldn't leave. But it didn't come, and I'd signed a contract, and I was listening to my wife. And the Cloister Bell was ringing. I didn't know what to do.

I couldn't sleep. It was loud. Deafening. There was no way I could fall asleep in bed, so I would sit on the living room couch and just stare into space, and I would pray. Eventually, I would fall asleep praying on my knees. (I used pillows.) After a couple hours sleep, I'd go to work with the bell still ringing. Nothing helped. This huge, overwhelming sense of wrongness wouldn't go away. It made the gender dysphoria look like grade school amateurs. There was nothing else but this doom. I'd majorly screwed up, and the Spirit was telling me. But I didn't understand or know how to fix it. I couldn't quit and go back, right?

Valeria didn't understand what I was going through. I tried to explain, several times. But she would just ask me to come to bed like that would fix it. But that wasn't helpful. I'd just lay there unable to sleep while she was peacefully dreaming. It was something that only I was experiencing.

It was many weeks before I could sleep in my bed. And it was months before it had quieted enough to something of a dull roar. My old company did implode a couple months later. They laid off everyone but three people to keep the lights on while they searched for a buyer. And I felt somewhat vindicated. Hadn't I done the right thing in still having a job? The right thing for my wife and family? But I also found that where I was working was awful. It wasn't like I thought it would be. I hated working there, and I prayed to get out.

During all this time, I would go to lunch with Mark, an old work colleague. The one rule was we didn't talk about work. But one day I was out shopping for roofing shingles with my wife, and I told her I needed to meet him for lunch.

She said, "What for?"

"He's going to offer me a job." I don't know why I said that, but sometimes I just know things. (Like when I told my friend Greg who was doing IVF that he was going to have triplets. That all the eggs they had planted were going to take. Called it.) And when we had lunch, that's almost exactly what Mark did. He told me that they were soon to be acquired and they wanted me back. It was a miracle. The bell finally stopped. I found out that if I'd stayed, I wouldn't have actually lost my job and I'd have made a ton more money and been better off. Oops. It's like someone knew what was going to happen.

But now the bell was ringing again out of the blue on a Sunday night. Why? I hadn't quit my job. I hadn't done anything wrong or made any life-changing decisions. OK, maybe not lately. You know what I mean.

So, what was going on? I felt impressed that I needed to look. Eventually I logged into my wife's computer account and found her text messages and emails with the stake president, and the accountants and therapists he had directed her to that would help with a divorce. And the bell stopped. I'd had no idea that this was taking place; that things had gotten that far.

The third and, so far, last time I felt the bell was during the divorce process when I'd thrown in the towel. I'd given up. And the bell started to toll. And I immediately started to think, "What has my wife done now???" And I checked her email and messages, and there was nothing. I couldn't find anything. So, what was it? I eventually figured out it was me. I needed to make choices and not let her drive this process. I needed to fight. And with that the bell stopped.

I learned from the Cloister Bell that I needed to stand on my own. It was always about me. That I needed to heed what the Spirit was telling me. I couldn't just lean on my wife. I'd never really done that before. My wife wore the pants in the family. Things were always done her way. I needed to develop my own relationship with the Spirit and learn to do what it directed. This was something I was not terribly good at doing. It was easier to let her make these decisions.

I realized that I needed to get help if this marriage was to be saved. I'd heard from my therapist that there were actual LDS couples who stayed married with a trans spouse. A miracle! I asked her if I could talk to one. She couldn't reach any. But there must be some help out there, right? So, I began searching the internet. I finally found two groups: TransActive and North Star. Both were for active LDS members who were LGBT.

So I took my wife to the TransActive/Wasatch Front Transgender FHEs and the North Star conference. Let's just say that my wife meeting all these other couples and transgender members didn't help. She thought we were all crazy and should get locked up in the asylum. She thought North Star was inconsistent in encouraging gays to not have relationships while not discouraging transgender members to transition, and never went back. She learned from the other spouses how awful their marriages are and told me every month or so of one of them getting divorced. They were echo chambers of pain amplifying the hurt and tragedy they were living through with their husbands. This was not the support I was looking for. Almost all of these wives had found out their husbands were trans long after they were married, or right before they got married. We were unique in that my wife knew and helped me for 6 years beforehand. Everyone thought I was so lucky to have had a wife that helped me transition for all those years. But nobody in these groups understood why she felt so different now.

It was soon after starting HRT, and not long after going to these trans activities, that we separated. We still had a small house with seven kids and all the upstairs rooms were full, so I took the downstairs living room couch. I tried to hide this from the kids by getting up earlier and sneaking up to the master bedroom before family prayers.

Another thing the Spirit told me was how to read my wife's personal journal on the computer without knowing the password. I've never told her till now. There was a security hole. I read about my wife's hurt and the things she felt but didn't say out loud. It was deeply painful, hard, and hurtful for me to read. It broke my heart. I was shattered. I didn't understand what she was going through. And instead of using this information as a weapon, I wanted to help her. I loved her. What might I do so she could love me, or at least not see me as a horrible person? How could I make her life better?

As long as I was living downstairs, I gave up running in the morning, and spent that time cleaning the living room, kitchen, and entryway. I decluttered and put things away, swept and mopped the floors, washed the dishes by hand, cleaned the counters, vacuumed the couches and chair cushions, dusted and varnished the wood. And every night when I came home it was a disaster again from seven kids doing homework, playing, and eating snacks. "I just cleaned up this mess!"

And I made a waffle breakfast for the family every late-start Tuesday before school for family prayers. There was hot chocolate with whip cream and sprinkles, bacon, sausage, scrambled eggs, and fruit. And I cleaned it all up afterwards. I noticed how my wife didn't have time for breakfast before church because of all the kids that needed to get ready. So I got up earlier and made her a special breakfast in bed each Sunday. And I found massage creams and I'd work over her feet and back. When I'd go shopping, I would make sure to get something for her. I knew her size and what styles she liked. I worked really hard to make things better.

But I noticed that there was never any appreciation given for my efforts in her journal. The only journal-worthy things were the many times when I still screwed up. I think one of our many marriage therapists, Blaine Hickman, said it best, "It doesn't matter how good of a wife you are, you're not a husband." True. But she always said she wanted to have a wife like I did.

A year later in August 2016, my oldest daughters, Shannon and Cathryn, would be told by Valeria about me being transgender. She beat me by a month. I don't know what her reasoning was, but I figured when I had my orchiectomy in September things would blow up. Since they now knew my secret, I didn't feel a need to hide from them. They got to meet their real father in all her glory. They would move out in December to an apartment, not wanting to have anything to do with her, leaving me their bedroom. I bought a bed and left the couch after over a year of residence.

A couple months later in January 2017 all my kids would know after my stake president told me about a forthcoming church policy—more on that later—and my wife would file for divorce that summer. The next day I went and finally got my ears pierced. A year later the divorce would be finalized and our 31-year relationship, 24-years of marriage, would end with me doing exactly what I told her in my 6-page coming out letter at the beginning that I wanted to do.

I honestly never thought our marriage would end. I thought we were soulmates. She was the divine answer to a year of prayers. I thought to the very end that my wife would realize and remember that I was a good person, that I was keeping my temple covenants, and that this wasn't much different from how we'd spent our first 10 years together. There was no reason for us to break up. She could still love me.

I guess I was wrong about that, too.

She told me that she needed to set an example for our daughters of the kind of man you marry and to whom you stay married. She couldn't do much about the first, except not tell people she knew before we got married. And by this time, I probably wasn't at my best. Our marriage wasn't at its best. It'd been years since that night in the hotel. Years of rejection, separation, disagreement, misunderstanding, hurt, and suffering for both of us. My announcement had set so many gears into motion that by now the least of our problems was that I was transgender and wearing a dress. I still thought we could clean up the mess it created with counseling.

She then told me that God wanted her to divorce me. I knew then that it was over. You can't argue against revelation. But I couldn't wrap my head around why God would want this, especially during the times that I thought we were making progress in therapy. I've learned that He had His reasons, as you'll read about. I couldn't have done all these things, learned all these things, and been in my marriage. In a way, my first therapist was right. I did need to get divorced in order be the woman my Heavenly Father wanted me to be. No regrets.

When I was notified on July 23, 2018, that the judge had finalized our divorce, I immediately felt relief. I'd done everything I knew to keep the marriage. But I also did my best to make sure our divorce set her up as well as I could for success. She was still the mother of our children, and I wanted her to thrive. I had a clear conscience. I was ready to move on.

I still love my wife. Not in a romantic way, or like we'd ever get back together again. But I've never hated her. I still think of her as a best friend. But while we kept in constant communication, texting and such, it took me years to be able to be in the same room as her because of the hole in my heart.

———

With my marriage story ended, let's wrap things up with my parents. They will only admit that they found out I was transgender in 2013 when my wife told them I was coming out of the closet. My mother yelled at me, "You don't walk or think or even act like a girl. All you care about are your boobs!" My parents met with their stake president who counseled with them to just love me. While perhaps my parents loved me, they didn't love me as their daughter.

In 2015 as I became active in LGBT groups, I met many parents of transgender kids. I heard of their journeys to understand, accept, and love their kids for who they are. I regularly invited my parents to attend, but they largely refused. They said this was all too sudden and they needed more time. I gave them the phone number of some local parents who had a trans daughter. My mother didn't call them for a year, and then 6 months after that they had a brief lunch. My mom came home and told me that I was nothing like their daughter. I didn't understand why she would say that. Of course I'm not like *their* daughter. My mother explained that their daughter was transgender and I had Asperger's syndrome. I'd never been told that before. This was a characterization based upon anecdotal evidence and not any professional diagnosis. But even if so, how does that invalidate my lifelong experience? My mother was looking for alternative explanations.

They always needed more time, and they always had another excuse. Now years and years have passed.

My mother would confront me about why I wanted them to attend these groups and meet these parents. She told me that it was obvious that I wanted her to change, but she didn't want to change. She loved me, her son, and that was it. She didn't need to do anything different.

And it was true, I wanted my parents to change. I wanted to feel loved for me, their daughter. I thought they could be like my friends Brooke and Steven and have that awakening as they did when their son came out gay. I thought if they could see how other parents of LGBT children loved and accepted their kids, they might do the same. They chose not to. That's not how they wanted to be.

One day as I was going through divorce, I was feeling depressed and alone, and I just really needed to feel loved by my mother. My parents weren't very sympathetic. They were team Valeria during the divorce. They told me that they were sorry that I was suffering the consequences of my choices. I told them it wasn't a choice.

It was Sunday morning, and I really didn't want to attend my home ward, so I texted my mother to tell her I was going to come to church with her. I'd recently read a Church blog post *Navigating Family Differences with Love and Trust* [10]. The author had a wonderful experience having her gay son and pregnant daughter with her in church. Couldn't I have that too? My mother texted back panicked and told me in no way was I allowed to go to church with her. I guess not.

My friend Samantha had a loving and accepting family. Her mother was sick and was spending a lot of time in the hospital and in recovery homes. She would write often about how she and her mom were bonding and having wonderful experiences together.

My mother had recently started having heart problems that had resulted in periodic minor strokes. One morning I ran into my mother at the post office. We briefly spoke, and she told me that she was headed to the hospital to have her heart checked. She was having arrhythmia. She left and I got my mail, and I thought maybe it would be good if she had someone with her. But I didn't know where she was headed, and I left for my next errand. Our paths happened to cross a couple miles away and I saw it as providence.

I found a parking space at the medical clinic before her and waited at the front doors. I saw her coming through the parking lot. And when she saw me waiting, she stopped and turned around and retreated back to her car. I followed her and found her sitting in the car with the door open. She told me that I was not allowed to go in the clinic with her. She said she would rather die there in her car in the parking lot of a hospital from heart failure than have me with her in the clinic. I stood there and thought about all the possibilities, but I didn't see I had much choice and I left. My mother would rather die than be with me. How could I be responsible for that? I found my car and cried for a good long while.

My mother spent the summer of 2021 working on a photo album for their coffee table. My father was a photographer and they had pictures of the family and of their many, many trips to exotic locales around the world, and from their several foreign church missions. When it was completed, my mother asked me to look through it. I thumbed through the pages. In the front were the earliest pictures of family with my mom and dad as kids, as they dated and got married, and a few pictures of their two children. Then there was the overwhelming bulk of the album with their trip photos, and finally in the back were photos of their grandkids.

It seemed obvious to me what my parents were really proud of. It struck me how few pictures there were of their family, and that there were not many pictures of me, and none of me from the past 10 years, since my transition. I told my mother, "There are no pictures of me."

"Of course there are."

"No. There are no pictures of ME."

"Oh."

A couple months later my mother invited me to look through the photo album again. I noticed that there were many more pictures of the grandkids put in the front. And as I was going through the vacation photos, buried between Thailand and China, were three pictures of me. They were head shots, closely cropped so you couldn't see my clothes, and two were in black & white so you couldn't see my makeup. I had to think hard where these photos even came from. But it was clear that my mother didn't want me as part of the family or seen as her daughter.

I love my parents. And I would love to have a mother-daughter relationship, but that's just not going to happen. I would try to do things with my mother. "Let's go get dinner? Or lunch?"

"No, eating out is too expensive"

"Let's go to a movie?"

"No, I'd just fall asleep"

"Let's go get a pedicure?"

"No, I've never had one and don't want one."

"Let's go shopping?"

"No, I have everything I need."

No matter what I suggested, she always had an excuse. Even things I knew she'd done recently with friends and family. She only had one suggestion for me. "Why don't you come over to the house?"

I came to call them my prodigal parents. You know, from the parable of the prodigal son. My parents were dutifully waiting for their prodigal daughter to finish her life of riotous living and squandering her inheritance. (Except I wasn't getting one. They don't want me spending it on bottom surgery.) They were waiting for me to hit rock bottom, learn that I wasn't really transgender, and they could welcome their son home.

I think as parents, it's easy to jump to prodigal parenting. "Hark! Our children are straying from the divine path and doing things we don't condone. So, what do we do? We will wait in the house till they come back." But Jesus gave two parables before that about recovering lost items. I love how Roy Bean has tied these three parables together in his *Ensign* article, *Rescuing the Lost: Counsel for Parents and Leaders*[11].

The first parable told us we needed to go find our lost sheep. We need to find them where they are. We need to *want* them in our fold. And the second was that we need to clean our houses. We need to make a place where we can find a lost coin; a place where a coin would find a home.

Those first two parables require work by the parents to learn and to understand, and perhaps even to change. Love is an action. You can't just say you love someone. Words are cheap. Even our Heavenly Parents require of us to show our love through action.

If ye love me, keep my commandments. (John 14:15)

We're not allowed to draw near to Him just with our lips. Sitting at home and saying, "We love you," is meaningless.

My relationship with my parents has waxed and waned over the years. Currently we don't have a close relationship, and I may only see them once or twice a year at most. They don't invite me for family dinners at Thanksgiving or Christmas. They prefer to spend the time with their daughter-in-law and grandkids. They want their son.

I just want to be loved by my parents.

4.

Embracing the Future

I N SPRING OF 1979, MY FAMILY MOVED TO UTAH. (YEAH, I
still hate the cold and snow.) My father had the idea to attend the
General Priesthood Session of Conference in person. So we stood on
the lawn between the North Visitors Center and the Tabernacle for hours
till they let us in to sit on hard wood benches with no leg room. My father
decided to make this semi-annual discomfort a tradition.

We came every April and October and waited. But I got to see great
moments with President Kimball and Elder LeGrand Richards, President
Benson and Hunter, and watch President Hinckley make his way up from
being the third counselor in the First Presidency. There is always something magical in how the building comes to a dead silence as soon as the
prophet enters the room. I have a lot of great memories from those times.

And when the Conference Center was built, we stood in that overflow
line, too. And when my parents would go on vacation or when we were

fighting, often I would still come by myself. In my other life, I've been to a lot of priesthood sessions; at least one or two every year for 40 years.

There came a time a few years ago after I'd started HRT when I'd go stand in the overflow line and I'd start hearing security say things as they walked along the line like, "Only priesthood holders are allowed in the priesthood session." While there were women sharing snacks with their family standing in line, they were talking to me. I wasn't wearing makeup or jewelry, and I was wearing menswear. Women's slacks and dress shirt with an open sweater or blazer, a tie or scarf. I'll admit that I was making a minimal, half-hearted effort to present male.

Eventually the time came when I got to the front of the line to receive a ticket for the session that I had to show my driver's license and temple recommend to prove I was a priesthood holder. They did give me a ticket. And when I crossed the street to the Conference Center I got carded again outside the doors, and after I got through the metal detector, and when I got up to the balcony. The lawyer and seminary teacher from Boise I had met in line had watched with a certain amount of curiosity as I had to jump through all these hoops that he didn't. He wondered what was going on. I explained it to him. He thought it was good to know in case he ever had a trans student.

I was sitting at the back of the balcony waiting for the meeting to begin when a man with an earpiece stopped next to me. He told me that women weren't allowed in the priesthood session and asked if I was a woman. Not answering his question directly, I told him I was a priesthood holder. He asked for my ID. He looked at it and handed it back. I told him I was transgender. After he left, I realized that my days of attending the priesthood sessions were coming to an end. Soon I would not have an ID showing me as male.

A year later, I was in line with my brother, nephew, and father. The security guy stopped and said, "I think I know the answer to this, but they're yelling in my ear that a woman is trying to get into the priesthood session. Can I see your ID?"

"Sure. Yes, I'm transgender. Could you radio them across the street, so I don't get stopped there too?"

"Sure."

I still got carded. But what really brought it to an end was my father telling the security guy, "This is my son. This is my son." Over and over. That hurt. That really hurt. I'd have rather had my father call me his daughter and not have gotten in.

My brother scolded me for even coming. "Why do you come to priesthood session when you're a woman?" Well, I'm a creature of habit. I love traditions. I've been coming for like 40 years. In a weird way I enjoy the priesthood session. Would I rather go to the women's session? Sure. But I didn't have anyone to go with and I was hesitant to try alone. And if I got carded there, they would throw me out for sure. But it's not like there's any super-secret stuff going on just for men.

You have to understand, there's no single way of being transgender. My other life of being male is still part of my life, as weird as that is. But women can't hold the priesthood! Mormon women don't want the priesthood! Well, this Mormon girl does. And I don't know that anything can be done about that short of excommunication, which I certainly don't want.

In the summer of 2020 a woman named Karen told me, "I'm sure it's just like what it says in your patriarchal blessing."

"What do you know about my patriarchal blessing?" She didn't know anything, she just assumed it was like any other girls' with talk of finding a worthy husband and having children, but I've learned that there are no coincidences. I got out my blessing and read it again.

At every visit as a young woman with my bishop, he would ask me if I'd gotten my patriarchal blessing. I'd tell him I hadn't. He'd tell me how wonderful they were, and I was sure that was true. He'd fill out a fresh recommend and tell me who was the stake patriarch, and I'd file the paper in my desk drawer with the others. I didn't know that I wanted to receive one. OK, I really did want one. I'd read my parents. But what would the patriarch say about someone like me? Would he be inspired that I was female? Then what would happen? How to explain that? But what if he didn't? What if I got some male-oriented blessing? What would that mean? Would that confirm that I was just some mentally ill young man? This was a blessing from God, and which gender would God bless me as? It was just safer to not take the risk and find out. When I was 36, married with kids, and firmly back in the closet, I figured it was maybe time to find out.

I'd never thought of my patriarchal blessing as anything special. There were no great revelations from the last time I read it, but I saw some patterns I never noticed before. So I took the text and broke it apart and rearranged the clauses. I put all the statements of blessings I'd already received in one pile and all the promises of future blessings in another pile, and I found one blessing that didn't go in either. It said, "At this time you have been blessed to receive the Holy Melchizedek priesthood."

I was blessed with the priesthood right then, but wouldn't be in the future? My priesthood was temporary? Sure some people might say that it was just an unfortunate turn of a phrase and I shouldn't read too much into it. Maybe. But don't we always find new significance in our patriarchal blessing as time goes on? Was this another confirmation of who I am?

Many years ago a trans woman was telling me how she wanted to be excommunicated and re-baptized back into the Church so she didn't have the priesthood, because women aren't supposed to have it. I told her that she'd probably have the priesthood again when they restored her blessings. I had thought we'd just be those women in the Church who held the priesthood.

However, I believe I can say now that this part of my patriarchal blessing has been fulfilled. I don't think I have the blessing of the priesthood anymore. Not too long ago I was asked to help give a healing blessing for a lesbian having surgery the next day. No one has ever spelled it out to me what exactly I'm restricted in doing, so I performed the anointing. During the blessing, it didn't feel wrong or bad, but I didn't feel anything like I normally have giving blessings in the past. I imagine that was the last blessing I'll ever perform.

Being able to give my wife and children blessings was something special that only I could do for my family. I couldn't get pregnant or be the nurturer, but this was something as their father and husband I could do. The three Ps of a father are: Preside, Protect, and Priesthood. And now with the divorce, I'm worthless in that regard. So I'm trying to find my new role in my family.

Being dependent upon men for performance of religious ordinances is a different feeling. It's interesting to watch them go about their duties now from the other side, knowing that was something I once was able to do. But then I never felt like I was one of them before. Not having the priesthood doesn't feel so much like a loss. I think now I have a different connection to God. And I wonder what other parts of my blessing might be fulfilled in ways that I could never have imagined even a few years ago.

And something else interesting about that interaction was that Karen was wrong. There was no mention at all of marriage or even of having a spouse in my patriarchal blessing, but there were many mentions of my children and how I needed to bear my testimony to them.

The last years I went with my family to priesthood conference was when I first heard of Peter Mooseman and his "Hug A Gay Mormon" activities. I saw him on Main Street when he created a living room on the sidewalk, and I dragged my father to go find him and give him a hug at General Conference.

"Here's a hug from a trans Mormon," I told him. Eventually we met at some LGBT activities, and I kept telling myself that I was going to join him, but I would forget. There should be an app for that.

October 2018, I remembered. I used all my scant Illustrator skills to create a sign and had Office Depot print it. It read:

**Embrace A
Transgender
Latter-day Saint**

There wasn't any particular added meaning to "embrace" other than to hug. I was just trying to graphically balance out the other longer lines. But some members were clearly put off by the thought. While they might give a hug, they didn't want to endorse or condone transgenderism.

Saturday morning I walked up to the corner of the Conference Center and was filled with anxiety. Was I really going to do this? Was I really going to publicly out myself to all these people? Peter wasn't there yet. My courage was fading. But he came. And we had our signs and we hugged people. Media people freely took our pictures. We occasionally got asked to comment for newspapers. I always declined.

I should say that all of us that stood on the corner with our signs, the queers, the bisexuals, the gays, and the transgender, all had different experiences with the church. (Sorry, there were no lesbians but me.) We all perhaps had different reasons for being there and hopes for outcomes. But the great thing was that while we were there, it was all about being present and showing that there were LGBT Latter-day Saints who supported the Church. We had nothing bad to say. We weren't protesting. We weren't advocating for change. We were there to just smile, give hugs, and be the unofficial greeters.

It was a lot of fun. "Welcome to Conference!" we'd yell.

"Good Morning!"

"Enjoy your session!"

"Drive safe!"

"Have a happy conference weekend!"

"See you next year!"

I liked to improvise a bit with, "This session has 10% more doctrine."

"I saw the dress rehearsal. This one's really good."

"Not a rerun; all new talks this session."

"Get a good nap. You won't want to sleep through the next session! Wives, keep your husbands awake."

"Don't forget to fill out those Yelp reviews."

And "Girl, you're rockin' it!" Surprisingly, some women don't appreciate compliments on style from a trans woman. But I guess that year of theater in high school paid off and all those times I worked trade shows in my career. I tried all sorts of lines. Some worked, some bombed, but maybe it gave someone a smile.

We stand on the corner where church employees who can't take the tunnels will cross the street from their underground, reserved parking spaces. So you never knew who you would see. Quite often we'd see the general presidencies of the Relief Society and Young Women, and their board members. It was like a semi-annual fashion runway for me. You can't go wrong copying their classic style. I'd get up each morning and think to myself, "What would Sharon Eubank wear?" They all ignored us. But we'd get glances from other people, and we'd get scowls from a few. Some mothers would put their hands over their children's eyes. That hurt. But we also got smiles, some double-takes, and quite a few hugs.

People would walk by and look at us and walk another 20 feet and turn and run back to give us a hug. One young woman from Idaho ran back and gave us all hugs and had her picture taken. As she got her hugs the tears just started to flow harder and harder. As she started to walk off, we called her back. "Are you alright?"

Her answer was, "I just feel my Savior's love." I was told later that a man wrote on his religious blog how he was very transphobic, but he saw my sign and got a hug. He wrote how it had changed him.

I've been hugged by actors, international super models, general authorities, mission presidents, and brothers of an apostle. But the special ones are from the moms who tell us they have an LGBT child, and they want a picture of us so they can show their child and give them hope. That is inspiring to me. I'm flattered and humbled. I never thought of it that way. But if some child who is LGBT can see us out and at Conference and loving the Church and it helps them to stay? Then sure, I'll try to be that hope. The other special ones are from the youth who will leave their friends with quizzical expressions as they come over and hug us and whisper in our ear, "I'm gay" or "I'm queer," or "I'm trans." And we whisper back excitedly, "Congratulations!"

I've been interviewed by two local television stations and made the evening news. My picture made front page of *Apple News* when the Church reversed the policy of exclusion, and it made the front page of the *Provo Daily Herald*, just above the fold. And it's still regularly on news sites and broadcasts, in memes, in FAIR presentations, and wherever someone is talking about the intersection of LDS and LGBT people. You can even buy a high-quality image of me from Getty. I make no money off that. I literally became the poster child for the Church for being transgender.

Church security never gave us any problems. We were harmless. And right there with us were also a half dozen local police officers. The religious protestors with their signs declaring Joseph Smith to be a liar and a fraud were not fond of us, especially me. I found that they held me in more contempt than regular Mormons, or even gay Mormons. I was an abomination. I know because one of them followed me halfway down the block yelling "Abomination! Abomination! Tranny walking!" at me over and over. But I always welcomed them with a cheery "Good Morning!" and a smile.

In April 2022, the Church began having in-person General Conference after two years of the Covid-19 pandemic. And I was now by myself. All the others had moved on with their lives in different ways, but I thought that there was still a need for transgender representation. The gay moment had passed. Could I do this by myself? I reminded myself that Peter did it alone for many years. And I wondered what miracles would happen now.

On Saturday, a tall man on his way out of the morning session hurriedly gave me a hug in passing and shouted back, "Here's a hug from a newly called General Authority."

"Who?"

And then a woman was hugging me. "Here's a hug from a newly called General Authority's wife."

"Who?"

And then there were kids hugging me. The wife yelled back. "And here's hugs from the kids of a newly called General Authority."

To my knowledge I'd never been hugged by an actual General Authority before. I thought they were the ones who routinely avoided and ignored us because it would be bad optics. "Who? Who is this General Authority?"

She stopped and told me. I figured he'd go down in history as the General Authority with the shortest calling of just 2 hours. LOL.

Between the Sunday sessions, a woman touched my arm in passing and said, "Thank you for being so cheerful and positive." as she walked by.

I turned and said, "There's another option? I'm a Latter-day Saint woman." She paused and looked back, and a playful grin formed on her face. She might have thought it was amusing I thought myself a woman. Or maybe she liked the idea that LDS women are naturally cheerful people. I don't know, but I could tell from her clothes that she was in one of the presidencies, which made this a particularly special encounter.

In October 2022, I was again alone. But that Saturday I was once again hugged by a fairly recently called General Authority, his wife, and family. He'd made it 6 months. I teased the church leaders as always with, "Have a great lunch!" as they headed over to the office buildings. And as they came back this time, there was a man standing in front of me with a box. He said, "We were talking about you and thought that you probably didn't have time to get lunch. So we brought you one." I was gobsmacked. This had never happened before. *They were talking about me? And thinking about me? They brought ME lunch?* I was so close to crying. I thanked him and gave him a hug, and he went with his date into the session. As the church leaders were filing back for the 6pm General Session, once again this young man was standing there. "We figured you also didn't have time for dinner." And now I did cry.

"Who? Who are you?" He told me that the young woman with him was the daughter of a General Authority and told me his name. It was someone with whom I wasn't very familiar. I was overwhelmed by the charity.

On Sunday, I had several church leaders stop and ask a bit about me and my life, I couldn't say much in 5–10 minutes, but this was new. I also had mission presidents and missionaries that wanted pictures with me. These weren't the LGBT friendly people of previous years.

As I told each of them things like, "Goodbye! Thanks for coming! Drive safe! See you next year!" that afternoon, I had so many quietly respond as they departed:

"Thank you for being here."

"Thank you for being so cheerful and happy."

"See you next year."

Those responses were even from many who we see sit on the stand. I can't wait for April 2023.

But that first Saturday evening in 2018 I had tickets to my first ever General Women's Session with my friend Liv, I ditched my sign and we walked on to the plaza and waited in line. I got through the doors, through the metal detector, up to the balcony, and in my seat without getting carded once. That felt so good. I was finally home in the right session with my sisters, the women of the Church.

Then during the opening prayer, I opened my eyes and saw a man with an earpiece down the aisle looking right at me. Sigh. Never open your eyes during a prayer. When the prayer was over, he was gone. And then over my shoulder I heard "Ma'am, would you please join me at the top of the balcony?" I grabbed my purse and headed up the stairs. At the top were a half-dozen men that surrounded me. He asked for my ID. I handed him my driver's license. I was just a couple weeks from getting my corrected birth certificate and a new driver's license showing my corrected name and birth gender. I guess all good things come to an end.

He looked at the license and at me and asked, "Is this yours?"

"Yes." Like I carry other IDs? Fake IDs?

"You're not who we thought you were. There's a woman who looks like you that causes problems." He handed me my license back and they all walked away leaving me standing there.

My first thought was wondering what poor unfortunate woman looked like me? I'm so sorry for her. And what was she doing to have Church security looking for her? I guess the Church doesn't care if a "man" is in the women's session after all. I went back and took my seat.

All my government IDs are now corrected. After the divorce was finalized, I went to court and had my name legally changed. I then sent all the paperwork to the great state of California to have my birth certificate corrected. It now shows that I was born Katherine, a girl. I gave a copy to my mom for our family history. My parents weren't happy. My father especially since he had blessed me with my birth name. I then spent months and years removing my dead name and correcting my gender in all the places in my life. It's a process similar to when women have a name change when they get married or divorced, except I wasn't changing my last name. This is another of those things that makes trans different from being gay. I couldn't get into the priesthood session now even if I wanted to. And I don't.

But arriving Sunday morning, I learned that Peter never paid attention to the closing remarks of the priesthood session. People have to be in their seats early for *Music and the Spoken Word.* By the time he arrived at 9am, most people were already in the Conference Center. But there are some people who apparently like to sleep in.

We were joined that morning by two friends named Jordan. At 10am the sidewalks were empty, and we gathered our belongings. Peter was going to watch from his condo a couple blocks away. We weren't invited because he claimed it was too messy. So the rest of us were headed to Temple Square to listen from the loudspeakers. And at that moment a woman walked up to us and said, "The Spirit told me I'm supposed to talk to you guys."

And this is the time and place when I first learned of my Heavenly Father's plan for me. It had just been a month after I'd been crying on my kitchen floor after the move. When I thought I was alone and my life ahead was unplanned and unimportant. And then this happens.

What? Peter and I looked at each other. We clearly had no idea what she was talking about. We were on the corner of the Conference Center outside of General Conference, where at that very moment a prophet, seer, and revelator was conducting the meeting. Why would the Spirit want her to talk to us? We looked back at her.

She said, "Well, maybe I can tell you a bit about myself. My name is Symphony. I'm an endowed member of the Church and I live my life according to the Spirit. Every day I ask the Spirit what I should do. I don't even set an alarm for the morning. I get up when the Spirit tells me to." Wow.

"The Spirit told me to come to conference yesterday. I came and managed to get a ticket to the afternoon session. This morning the Spirit told me to go back to the conference center." She seemed surprised by that. "When I got to the conference center I looked around and didn't see anyone." She must have been down by the flagpole and fountain. "The Spirit told me to go to the other corner. When I got halfway up the block, I could see you standing there with your signs, and the Spirit said to go see you. So here I am."

Huh. Well, while she was talking, I was silently praying for guidance. I was thinking of that scripture that was something like, "I'll tell you what you need to say in the moment you need to say it." D&C something or other[12]. But as she finished, I had nothing. I looked at Peter and he clearly also had nothing. Now what?

She said, "Well, I told you a little about myself, maybe you could tell me your story?" Those were the magic words. That is something every LGBT person knows how to do.

Peter went first. We invited her to walk with us as we traveled down the Main Street Plaza. Peter explained how he as a teen found he was attracted to boys while in scouting, and he hoped to find a nice LDS man to marry, and hopefully the Church wouldn't excommunicate him, and he was done. He said goodbye and went home. Well, that took five minutes. Jordan and Jordan both took their turns, but their stories were fairly similar and took even less time. She then looked at me.

"My story is a bit different." LOL.

I then shared my story with her, much of which you read in the prior chapters. I told her about my childhood, meeting my wife, getting married, having kids, and eventually getting divorced. There was laughter, and there were tears falling on each other's shoulders as we held each other. After a while we could hear that the morning session was ending and we needed to get back to the corner. I'd spent almost two hours sharing with her.

We invited her to come give hugs with us, but she said she needed to be getting back home. "Oh, where do you live?"

"Los Angeles."

WHAT??? No wonder she was surprised this morning. She'd expected to leave early that morning to make the 10-hour drive back home, but instead she'd spent many hours here with us at the direction of the Spirit.

Symphony did come back to the corner for a short time. There we were met by some friends Kris and Blair. Symphony gave hugs and was first to offer to take pictures for people. But the time came, and we said our goodbyes and she left. We haven't heard from her again. But God wasn't finished.

Soon it was 2pm and the afternoon session started. The Jordans left, Kris caught a train, and Blaire went home, too, leaving just me and Peter. He went to his condo, and I walked down the Plaza and sat inside the East Gate by the temple to listen to conference.

While I sat there, an elderly couple came in the East Gate holding open a large map of Temple Square. They saw me and came over and asked, "Could you tell us where the Tabernacle is?"

"Sure, it's the large silver domed building right there," I said. (The Church should really do something to make it more visible and identifiable. It just blends in.)

"Are you from here?"

"No, I'm from Los Angeles, but I live here now."

"Oh, how long have you lived here?"

"Long enough to go to school, get married, and have seven children."

"Can I ask you a personal question?"

I thought I knew where this was going. "Sure."

She leaned in and whispered, "How many wives does your husband have?" Don't laugh, reader.

I decided to keep my explanation simple. "He has only the one." I then shared the last 100 years of Church history with polygamy.

"Well, we're from Michigan and we're so glad to finally make it to Salt Lake City. We bought a motor home and we've spent the last 4 months touring all over the Western United States. We came here to see one thing." Can you think what that might be? I'll wait.

"A wagon."

What? Not the temple, not the tabernacle, not the choir, not genealogy? The Church has obviously missed something in their marketing.

"We want to see a wagon that the pioneers pulled across the plains." I had been thinking they meant a Conestoga wagon that was pulled by oxen. "We heard the story of a little girl who pulled a wagon across the plains in the snow, and when she got here, they had to amputate her frozen legs." I knew exactly what she was talking about then.

"That girl's name is Nellie Pucell. And I'm her great, great, grand-daughter," I replied.

That always brings tears to my eyes. I told them her story of how her family came from England and crossed the plains with the Martin and Willie Handcart Companies. I shared how her parents died, and how she had her legs amputated below the knees without any anesthetic. She ended up in Cedar City as a third wife and raised six kids in a log cabin with a dirt floor. She made her living doing laundry. In 1991, I was present when President Hinckley dedicated a statue to her on the university campus where her cabin had stood, and he spoke of her story in the following Conference[13].

The Spirit was so strong, and we both had tears in our eyes. They apologized that they needed to get going, with so much to see. I informed them that they could find a handcart in the Church museum on Monday. And they were gone. But God wasn't finished.

I settled in and tried to figure out who was now speaking and on what topic. After a while I saw a man approaching from the direction of the temple. When he got close enough, I easily recognized him. It was my friend Greg, a fraternity brother.

We'd sat next to each other in seniority order for many years. (Yes, it's weird.) He was also my straight crush in college. Please don't tell him. It could be awkward. But we had a connection. There have been numerous times when either he or I would call when the other was thinking about them. He was my first and only call when Valeria and I found out our third child, a boy, was a miscarriage at 20 weeks. He dropped everything and came and got Shannon and Cathryn. My fraternity brothers and their wives took care of them for the next several days as we recovered.

We hugged and shook hands. I said, "What are you doing here?"

"Looking for you," he said.

"How did you know I was here?" I knew he wasn't on social media, so he hadn't seen my posts.

"I didn't."

He explained that a couple hours earlier during the afternoon break while he was taking a shower, the Spirit told him to go to Conference. He got dressed and asked his triplets if they wanted to go to Conference downtown with him. They all looked at him as if he was crazy. He drove the short five miles from North Salt Lake and had been watching conference from the Tabernacle balcony. A few minutes earlier the Spirit had told him to leave. He came outside and the Spirit told him to go east along the temple and then he saw me.

We hadn't seen each other in a couple years. We talked for a few minutes, catching up, and then I could hear that conference was ending. I'd missed both sessions today. I invited him to come to the corner and give hugs. He said he needed to be getting home. We hugged and he left.

I walked back to the corner. Peter showed up and we hugged people till they were all gone. I then left for home. A man stopped me on the sidewalk and said, "Are you transgender?"

"Yes."

"I've never met a transgender person before."

I said, "You never forget your first." He said they were headed back to Arizona.

I kind of floated all night in a daze.

The next day during lunch at work I was thinking about what had happened. Sometimes I'm slow. A woman had been inspired to drive from Los Angeles to Salt Lake City to talk to me and hear my story. OK, maybe she came for other reasons, too. The world doesn't have to revolve around me; but she could have listened to conference at home. I'm amazed and inspired by her obedience and her ability to know what the Spirit wants her to do every day. That's commitment to drive 10 hours—700 miles—by a prompting. But why would God do that?

And then there was the couple from Michigan. What are the odds of them hearing the story of my great-great-grandmother and showing up after four months of driving right when I, her descendent, was sitting there? Has to be astronomical, right? Why would God do that?

And then for the hat trick, why would God have my brother come on short notice to just show up and see me? Why would He do all three of these things?

I didn't have any easy answers other than, "Because He can." But as the weight of the experiences began to settle on me, I found I couldn't work anymore, and I left.

Why? Why would He do this?

As I've thought about these three witnesses, as I call them, I've come to understand that:

(1) He wanted me to know that He was real. He knew who I was. He loved me. And He knew where I was and what I was doing. You maybe could explain away one of these witnesses as coincidence, but all three? Not a chance. This is how much my Heavenly Father loves me; that He'd do something so mind-blowingly impossible that I can never deny. Maybe it wasn't two figures in a grove, but it's good enough.

(2) I realized that this was a blessing for all the hard times I'd been through. This was the prize, the reward, for being faithful. But I also realized that it was a blessing for what would come. This was something I needed to hold onto for the hard times that would soon follow. How exciting is that going to be?

I'm sure Abraham started at the bottom learning to receive revelation and act upon it. He endured all kinds of hardships that strengthened his testimony. And as he showed faith and obedience, his trials grew, but so did his blessings. They grew together till he reached a point where God could make the big ask for him to sacrifice his son so that he could receive the greatest blessing.

Our experiences build on each other. We go through trials, and if we are faithful then when it is over, we will be rewarded with strength and preparedness for the next trial. We're a better person, and our testimony increases and strengthens. It's a cycle.

(3) I believe the reason for my three witnesses was for three distinct messages to me. The first was that I needed to share my story. I've done so whenever anyone has asked. They just don't realize that it's going to be a three-to-four-hour commitment. And now with this book, which I'm finally doing, many people will be able to know it at their leisure.

The second was that I was a pioneer. I get told that all the time—I'm clearing a way for those behind me. Maybe. The fun thing about pioneers is that they quite often die. Anyone play Oregon Trail lately? It's hard. But is this harder than what Nellie went through? Is what I'm doing harder than having my legs amputated? Is it harder than watching my parents give up in a snowstorm? Is it harder than raising six kids in a log cabin doing laundry? I don't think so. She's an inspiration to me, and I think of this witness whenever things seem tough.

The third message was that I still had friends and I would find friends. I didn't have to be alone even though I'd lost my family and ward. There still would be people that would come into my life and help me when I needed them.

I don't know for how much longer I will go and hold my sign. Peter has decided that he's done. Blaire moved to Florida, so she's out. And Kris tragically died earlier this year, not by suicide. I'm the last. I guess I'll keep going as long as it seems the right thing to do. Maybe there will be a new generation to hand it off to, or maybe it'll no longer be necessary. But I'll miss it when it ends. I'll miss meeting all the wonderful people. It's been such an amazing experience each time.

5.

TransMission

I'T'S BEEN 10 YEARS SINCE I HAD A CHURCH CALLING. IT BOTH-
ers me. I was raised in the Church and my parents always had a calling. I remember President Hinckley speaking in Priesthood Session
on how every convert should have three things:

> *Every one of them needs three things: a friend, a responsibility,*
> *and nurturing with "the good word of God" (Moro. 6:4). It is our*
> *duty and opportunity to provide these things.* [14]

And isn't what is good for the convert also good for the member? I
remember interpreting this list at the time as every member should have a
friend, a calling, and a quorum/class. Having a responsibility, the opportunity to serve, is what we do in the Church. We are a lay ministry. It's
what my family always did.

I always had a calling from the time I was twelve. I served as the deacons quorum secretary, teachers quorum secretary, priests quorum secretary, Sunday School teacher, elders quorum teacher, elders quorum secretary (twice), ward executive secretary, newsletter editor, and assistant ward clerk—historian. I also served on the ΣΓΧ Interchapter twice as a publicity officer and historian.

They tried to call me to be ward executive secretary again, but I was beginning to retransition and, frankly, the men in the bishopric weren't people I wanted to be with at some unholy time on a Sunday morning. And why? I was never a good secretary. I never took meeting notes, and I hated calling people for appointments. What I was good at was collecting and crunching data and making beautiful reports.

Plus, it was getting redundant; you can't go home again, and I couldn't do what I'd done before. I learned that from my second time as elders quorum secretary. The new president worked differently and had other expectations. I felt the new bishopric just wanted to keep their eye on me. "Enemies closer" and all that. I didn't say no. Our family never believed in saying no to a calling. It wasn't how I was raised. Callings were inspired. How do you say no to inspiration? I just never got back to the stake president. I guess it was a pocket veto.

But looking through that list, I can't help but see a pattern that I was always a secretary or a teacher. Not once was I a president or counselor. I've never been called to be someone who made decisions or contributed to them. And never was I in the Young Men, Primary, or scouting. As an adult, I was kept away from all the impressionable young minds full of mush. I wasn't exactly seen as a role model for the young men. I hadn't gone on a mission. And you can't have a man with long hair around the youth. What lesson would that teach them?

When my priesthood leaders became aware of my retransition, I still would ask my bishop for a calling. He said I could have a calling and he would look into it, and then he would never get back to me. After a couple years, my stake president and bishop met with me while I was living in my rental house. The bishop told me that they'd looked through all the callings and they first eliminated all the callings that were gendered. That meant all the bishopric and clerks, elders quorum and Relief Society, Young Women and Young Men, and maybe even Primary. They then looked through what was left and decided that there wasn't a single calling that someone in the ward wouldn't oppose. I wouldn't have a calling. This was surprising.

I was always taught that callings came from God. It was His church. I don't think I've ever seen in a ward someone object to a calling during Sacrament Meeting. And I've heard when there are objections that unless the reason has merit, they are then asked to pray about it till they can sustain the calling. So, what I was being told by my bishop was that there were people in my ward who were "uncomfortable" with me, and that their feelings mattered more than the desires of God. The bishopric wasn't even willing to determine what God might have in store for me. They weren't willing to stand up for me and teach the ward about love and understanding. The haters won. At a time when I was alone, vulnerable, and struggling; finding few friends in the ward; and not being allowed to go to a gendered third hour class or quorum, I was now being told I couldn't serve. My ward passed on every opportunity to provide any of the three things I needed. This was a blow.

Now, when I lament that I don't have a ward calling, many people tell me they don't either, and how wonderful it is. I don't understand them. Is there just not as much of a need for service? Does it seem like there are fewer callings in a ward these days? And why wouldn't members want to serve? A few years later, I was talking to my brother about this. Mark told me he also hadn't had a calling in years, so he went and found one elsewhere. He volunteers at another denomination's local food pantry. Huh. Ok, I'd still rather serve my church, but I can't. So what would I do? Where would I find a calling?

As you might suspect, I did eventually stop attending my home ward. More details will come later. I stayed with them for over a year giving them time to adjust to the new me after I came out publicly in February 2017. But still missing a friend and being denied a way to serve or feel sisterhood, I left to find these things someplace else. I hoped that I might find a ward that was accepting that I could make my new home ward. I had LGBT friends who thought their bishops and wards were really great, and they were, until stake presidents became aware of me. Sigh. So the Summer of 2019 I was out of wards to attend. Well, I certainly wasn't going to go back to my home ward, and I'd run out of friends to attend with. I was out of options, or so I thought.

Without any ideas, I did the only thing I could. I took it to God and asked, "Father, where am I supposed to go to church now?" And He actually told me! He gave me an image of a ward building in West Bountiful. I knew the place, since I ran by it practically every day. "Are you sure?" Some part of me was worried that I was projecting my thoughts and desires. Was this really from God? I wasn't sure. I'd never been to this ward and didn't know anything about them; I had no reason to choose this ward. But I still worried that I was making something up. Sister Marjorie Kimball once said:

> *Never suppress a generous thought.* [15]

And Moroni said,

> *For behold, the Spirit of Christ is given to every man, that he may know good from evil; wherefore, I show unto you the way to judge;* **for every thing which inviteth to do good, and to persuade to believe in Christ, is sent forth by the power and gift of Christ;** *wherefore ye may know with a perfect knowledge it is of God.* (Moroni 7:16)

So, as they say, if the inspiration is for something good, then you should probably follow it.

I decided to show some faith and find out. I got up that next Sunday and showed up at 9am for sacrament meeting. That's the nice thing about our Church here in Utah—you can't swing a dead cat without hitting a ward building, and there's always a service at 9am.

Almost always. Sometimes earlier.

I attended sacrament meeting. It was fine. I went to Sunday School, where in the lesson the teacher referenced Tom Christofferson's book *That We May Be One*. I raised my hand and added to her thoughts. People came up after and thanked me for my contribution. They asked if I had moved into the ward, and I told them I was just visiting. They asked where I was from. I told them I was from Los Angeles. (Sorry, I am not from Utah. I've just lived here temporarily for the past 40 years.) They hoped I'd come again.

I went home and thought, *Mission accomplished!* Then I asked, "Where do I go next week?"

The answer was, "Go back." Oh.

The next week I went back to the same ward. Sacrament meeting was fine. In Relief Society we had a lesson about hard trials in our lives. A woman named Brandi began to share her story and all the ladies began crying. They obviously knew her story, but I didn't. The tissue box was taken off the piano and passed liberally around the room. She eventually mentioned her divorce. I knew that hurt and pain. And then she mentioned she had a trans teenage son who had left the Church and was doing things she never taught him. Now I had tears flowing and they passed me the tissues.

After the lesson I introduced myself to Brandi and came out to her. We became Facebook friends and got together later to talk about her son. Now we see each other occasionally at singles events.

After that week I was saying again, "Mission accomplished! Where do I go next week?"

Again the answer was, "Go back." Oh.

The next week I went back. But this time as soon as I entered the doors to the building I was immediately filled with the Spirit throughout my whole body. That had never happened before just going to church. *Oh. So, we're really doing this.* It was Fast Sunday. I was going to be bearing my testimony.

This was something that I'd been pondering from earlier that year.

When I'd been attending my friend Kelsey's ward she told me that a trans teen girl had killed herself. The bishop had spoken with Kelsey privately to get more insight since she was gay. She told me the family was devastated. They found out in the suicide note. I wanted to rush to their side and comfort them, but I was told they really wouldn't want to see me. They were as upset their daughter was trans as she was dead. As the saying goes, "Better to have a dead son, than a live daughter." No wonder she took her life. More than half, 57% actually, of trans kids will attempt suicide in an unaccepting home[16]. Another saying is, "Be careful who you hate. It might be someone you love."

I'd been wondering what might have been different if I hadn't been attending that ward in stealth, just being one of the many women. Just being myself. What if I'd been out? What if this young woman had known and could have maybe talked with me, or just realized she wasn't alone? What despair she must have felt hiding in the closet and hearing what was unknowingly being said about her by the people she loved most.

I went to a *Listen, Learn, and Love* meeting at Bountiful High School with Richard Ostler. In this meeting Alyson Deussen wished that more adult LGBT members would be out to give our kids hope. Her gay son had taken his life in high school. This was also something I'd heard often in my times at the Conference Center giving hugs. People wanted my picture to give their kids hope. How can I give hope? Or be hope?

I also attended a fireside with Dennis Schleicher a couple months earlier where he talked about a time he was visiting a ward in Virginia. It had been Fast Sunday and he was inspired to bear his testimony. In closing, he was inspired to say, "And I'm gay." Afterwards many members came up and talked to him because of this, and he was able to give them advice and help heal a ward in trauma.

These three events had been bouncing around my head all Summer, but I wasn't sure what to do about them. Bearing my testimony was something I only did once a decade. And here I was at this ward being told I was to bear my testimony. After the sacrament the bishop bore his testimony. He said about everything I was thinking of saying and sat down. No one got up…and no one got up. The minutes passed and the Spirit got stronger and stronger. Finally, I was like, *Fine! I'm going!* And the Spirit pulled me out of my chair and dragged me up to the pulpit.

I bore my testimony. I don't remember everything I said, but it was pretty typical. I think I talked about my pioneer heritage. But as I closed, I said, "My name is Katherine. I'm a Daughter of God. And I was born transgender." After the meeting just a couple people came up and talked to me. I looked around for Brandi and her son, but they weren't there. Her family was sick and had stayed home. Huh. It was kind of anti-climactic. Nothing special happened, and I went home. (I also went to Kelsey's ward later that day and bore my testimony.) It was September 29th and this was to be the start of a most amazing day that would end with Harmony, but I didn't know it yet. And I'll get to that.

Was my mission accomplished now? "God, where I do I go next week?"

The Lord gave me another image. It was an a-frame church, the Bountiful 31st Ward. Huh. I attended there for a couple weeks and then on Fast Sunday when I passed through the doors of the chapel the Spirit came over me. I knew I was bearing my testimony again. After finishing and sitting down, a woman jumped up and came back to sit next to me. And I was passed a note thanking me for my testimony. They welcomed me into Relief Society, but it was time to move on.

"Heavenly Father, where I do I go next week?" I was simply given an area of Bountiful. I opened up the meetinghouse locator and looked for wards in that area. There was one that felt right. The Bountiful Hills Ward. I attended for the month and showed up for Fast Sunday.

I was running late and arrived right at 9am. I sat in the back, as is my preference, and waited for the meeting to begin. It didn't. So, I got out my phone. I soon realized that there was a man standing in front of me. He introduced himself as the bishop. I told him I was Katherine and was just visiting. He sat down next to me. Huh. Not what I expected. He explained to me how he'd talked to all these many people by name about me. I'd never heard of them, but apparently, they were all the people I'd sat next to in Relief Society and Sunday School in the previous month. Wow, a bishop that does his homework, impressive. Maybe even scary. But where is this conversation headed? Isn't the meeting supposed to be starting?

He then explained to me that when I came the first Sunday that friends of his from the Bountiful 31st Ward had been there and recognized me. They told him what had happened in their ward. He told me that he didn't want any social justice malarky going on and left me a warning. He said I could still bear my testimony if I felt inspired, but I needed to keep it focused on the Savior. And he left, walked up to the pulpit, and introduced the stake president presiding on the stand. Oh dear.

I initially wasn't sure what he was talking about. Then I remembered— it was right after General Conference and I'd referred to President Oaks talk about how some members, and I didn't say which members,

> *feel marginalized and rejected by some members and leaders in our families, wards, and stakes. We must all strive to be kinder and more civil.*[17]

I wasn't pushing any agenda. Is it a social justice agenda if the First Presidency says it? Don't we talk about the talks from General Conference that had meaning to us? I didn't even mention LGBT. I felt like I was just giving a normal testimony, but maybe people might construe it that way by my saying I was born transgender. Did they? It wasn't my intent. I just wanted that girl sitting in the congregation, hiding in her closet, feeling despair, to know that I was transgender too, and I had a testimony, and she could have hope. What do I do?

I was feeling so much anxiety and adrenaline, that I didn't know what I was feeling. I couldn't hear the Spirit if it was yelling in my ear. Eventually the bishop opened the meeting up for testimonies. With 20 minutes available, three people rushed up to the stand. The first woman took 10 minutes with a long and rambling thank-timony. I'm thinking, *This isn't happening. What does it mean if I don't get to bear my testimony today? Wasn't this God's plan? Should I just move on to another ward?* But the next two finished in two minutes, and no one else got up.

I still didn't know if I was feeling the Spirit, but I decided to keep to the plan. I started walking up. And when I made the steps to the stand, four heads turned and looked my way and dared me. I gave them my best smile and took the pulpit and bore my testimony. I remember talking about Nephi and his brothers and not murmuring against God and the Church and the great and spacious building. After I finished, I went to go back to my seat, but I couldn't move because someone was holding on to my arm.

I turned and found myself looking up at the stake president. He put his hands on my shoulders and said, "Thank you for bearing your testimony. You're welcome here anytime." And then he gave me a huge hug. I've never seen that happen before or since. After the meeting I was swamped with people coming and talking to me. I talked to the stake president's wife, who informed me he was actually just a counselor. Good luck with that. But last was the bishop. He told me that he hoped he hadn't offended me and that I was welcome any time in his ward.

When I got home, I had a text message from my friend and "monster" Emily Swensen. "Did you bear your testimony today in the Bountiful Hills Ward?"

"Yes, how did you know?"

"We're with friends in St. George and they got a text message that they'd missed the most amazing testimony given by a trans woman named Katherine. I figured it must be you." Ha, lucky guess.

That night I gave a fireside with The Utah Hearth in Holiday, UT. When the fireside was over two women came up to me and said, "Did you bear your testimony in a ward on the west side of Bountiful a few months ago?"

"Oh, West Bountiful? Yes, I did."

"Well, a trans teenage boy heard your testimony."

"Oh, I thought Brandi said they were sick and missed it."

"Who's Brandi?" This story wasn't going where I thought it was. "Ok, let's start over."

"There was a trans teenage boy who had dropped out of the church years ago who woke up that morning and felt inspired that they needed to go to church. He looked around and found a ward to attend and heard your testimony."

I looked heavenward and thought, *Oh, this is real.* This isn't some delusion of grandeur of mine. That was real inspiration and I followed it. I'm really on the Lord's errand. I was really at that ward for a reason. His mission was accomplished.

It's kind of like the stories you hear from missionaries who tell how they had what they thought was a golden contact that didn't pan out, but years later they joined the Church. You don't always know who you might affect. You don't always know why God wants you to do what you do. But sometimes you do find out later, and it's magic.

I came to call this my TransMission. Some mission calls don't come under the signature of the First Presidency. Every month I go to another ward. I start attending a ward on the second Sunday, and I attend through the first Sunday for testimony meeting, bear my testimony with my trade-mark ending, and move on.

Every month I make it a matter of prayer to know where I need to go. Sometimes it's a flash of an image. Sometimes it's shown in a dream. Sometimes it's just an area. Sometimes it's just wherever seems next by looking at the map. Sometimes I'm not sure it matters because there are LGBT people in every ward, and they all are hurting. God and I are still figuring out how to communicate with each other. It must be like me trying to talk to my dog.

I've never had to do this before. I didn't go on a mission. Maybe missionaries learn to do this, but I hadn't. So this has very much been a learning experience. I won't say I'm perfect at it; I'm nowhere as good as some women I've met. I may have forced some destinations; or I may have gone with my own thoughts at times. But I think I've learned Heavenly Father can work with my imperfections, because every ward will certainly have someone who is LGBT. And there are so many LGBT members who could use some hope. He will make it worthwhile even with my weaknesses.

I went to a ward in North Salt Lake, and after bearing my testimony a woman jumped up and came back 15 rows to sit next to me. She thanked me for my testimony and for listening to the Spirit and saying exactly what she needed to hear. She invited me to her house for dinner. She explained over dinner that she had a gay son who was telling her that if she loved him that she should leave the Church. She asked how can she choose between her love for her son and her love for her Savior? She can't. But it is a fallacious choice that LGBT people force on others.

I went to a ward in Farmington and afterwards a girl came up with her friends. She told me she was queer. I'd already guessed that weeks earlier when I first saw her. LOL. Her friend was bisexual and not out. She explained that she had been thinking she couldn't stay in the Church and would have to leave. She asked me, "Can I stay in the church if I'm queer?"

"Of course, you can! Look at me and I'm in the church." I told her she might not be able to be as queer as she'd like, but that the Church was true, and she should work to go to the temple.

I went to another ward in North Salt Lake and the stake president was on the stand. I wasn't sure what would happen. I knew he was the stake president because the previous week had been Ward Conference and he'd talked to the Relief Society. How was this going to go this time? After I sat down, he closed the meeting. He said, "This morning I was going to go to my ward; we meet at the same time. And the Spirit told me to go to another ward. So I came here. I've been sitting here on the stand for the past 40 minutes wondering why I was here. And now I know that God wanted me to know that He loves all His children."

Why didn't God just have me go to his ward? Wouldn't it have been easier and just as good? Nope. He needed the miracle through both of us being obedient.

I went to a ward in north Bountiful. I don't know how the bishop got from the stand to where I was sitting in the back so quickly. He must have flown over the congregation. But he said to me, "We can't possibly understand what you are dealing with, but just tell us how we can help you." I felt bad that I was leaving. He so much wanted to help. I've found a lot of wards where there are bishops who really want to help, with Relief Societies that have an abundance of charity.

Sometimes when I first go to a ward I'll find out it's their Fast Sunday because of General or Stake Conference was the previous week, or it's the next week. So it's just a one and done sort of thing. One of those times it was Mother's Day. I hadn't planned on bearing my testimony. It was Mother's Day. I'd only planned on getting chocolate. I usually wear flats for Fast Sundays where I'll bear my testimony because the podiums don't rise high enough, and it's uncomfortable to lean down. But now I'm here and wearing heels when there comes a time when no one got up and the Spirit said, "It's your turn." I met some grandparents afterwards who were raising their two trans grandchildren. They seemed like a really great ward, and I was tempted to stay the rest of the month, but I already knew which ward was next and I moved on.

One time I was headed to a ward, and I was running late. I thought, *I'll just go to this ward here on the way.* But the Spirit said, "No. Keep to the plan."

"But I'm going to be late, and this ward is right here."

"No, keep to the plan."

"I'm going to this ward."

"No." I turned into the ward anyway and went into the chapel only to find out it was a YSA ward building. I didn't even know there were such things. Oops. Ok, I guess the Spirit knew what they were saying. Sorry.

I pretended to be a parent of one of the speakers and then left and went to the other ward. There I found the Relief Society room. A woman came up to me and asked who I was. I introduced myself as Katherine from Los Angeles. She asked me my last name. I'm always hesitant to do so because I like a single name, and because I didn't want bishops tracking me down. (I think it's fair to say that the memo has gone out to all the wards in the area. They all know now who I am when I arrive.) But she was really insistent. So I told her. "Are you related to George and Launa?"

Ummmmmm. That's a really great guess. How does she know this? "Yes. They are my parents."

"I'm your cousin Adam's wife."

"Oh! Hi. I guess it's been a while." Awkward.

I was headed to a ward by Eaglewood golf course. I'd memorized the way there with all its twists and turns. Brigham Young did not lay out this city. But I also put it into my maps for my phone to guide me just in case. As I was getting close to where the ward was, I found myself unexpectedly passing another ward building and the Spirit said, "Here." So trying to be quicker to obey I pulled into the parking lot and walked up to the doors. And I'm thinking, *Why am I here? This isn't the plan.*

What do I do? Do I stick to the plan or go here? I decided to stick to the plan this time. I got back in my car and left following the directions of my phone. It soon became obvious that I was not headed anywhere where I should be headed. I was going in circles. I stopped and looked at the map. I'd somehow gotten the wrong street address into my phone. I'd been at the right building, and I drove back. An elderly couple there invited me to have dinner at their house with another ward family or two. I didn't come out to them, and maybe I should have, but we were having such a nice talk. They didn't seem so happy about my testimony the next week.

Another time I was praying about which ward to go to next, and I had a dream of a ward with a chocolate brown brick. I knew of several. "Which one?" I asked. The dream pulled back and I saw the street corner. It was a building I knew. I'd been thinking of going there, but I'd been reluctant to go because I knew it was my friend Samantha's ward building, and it just never seemed like the right time.

So I started attending there. It was a good ward. In Relief Society a woman talked about how her husband had come out as queer a year ago, and he's also left the Church. She's had some trials. I didn't say anything, but she brought this trial up in every single meeting. So after church one week I talked to her briefly, but still didn't come out to her.

I was a bit surprised then, when I came for testimony meeting and they read in her records. What? How long has she been coming? I thought that she'd been attending the ward when her husband left last year. I thought this was old news to everyone. Well, the two of us bore our testimonies that Sunday. After church I asked her, "When did you move in?" She told me July 9th. Huh, that was the day before I came. If I'd come any sooner, she wouldn't have been here.

There was a ward in North Salt Lake that I'd thought about attending for a long time but it just never seemed right, until the month that it was. I was surprised to hear that there were two seventies presiding over sacrament meeting. I Googled their names and found out who they were. I looked up to heaven and chuckled. Sometimes God makes it really obvious. One of the seventies was a fairly recently called General Authority who gave hugs with his family. Right?

When the meeting ended I asked a woman about this curiosity. Were they just visiting? It wasn't stake or ward conference. She said they both lived there. Oh. That means that they'd be there for Fast Sunday. I'd never born my testimony in front of a General Authority before. This could be interesting. Maybe my last day? But seriously, I wasn't worried at all. I knew that God had a plan for me being here at this time. The Seventy and his family hugged me again—no sign required—and his wife invited me to Relief Society. They had moved into the ward just the week before. And, yes, I bore my testimony as usual. I also had a wonderful experience of getting to meet with the bishop and Seventy afterwards and found out the reason we needed to meet. It was an answer to so many of my prayers and a blessing after so many trials.

There are no coincidences. I'm always amazed by God's planning.

I've been welcomed and invited back by bishops and Relief Society presidents, and members all over the county, but unfortunately they haven't all been good experiences.

In one ward I sat down after bearing my testimony and waited for the meeting to end. I saw that a man in a suit had gotten up, and I assumed he would be announcing the closing song and prayer. After a while I realized that's not what was happening. I tuned in and heard him talking about the Family Proclamation. Something about you couldn't choose your gender. Uh-oh. This was a first. However, this is what bishops are supposed to do. It is literally their job to correct false doctrine in a meeting when it happens. I don't think what I said was wrong and needed correcting, but I'm not going to fault him.

After the meeting I had a few people come up to me. One woman told me how there was a girl crying. "Why?"

"Because of the bishop's closing remarks."

"I can't have a girl crying. Where is she?"

She led me out to the foyer to meet this girl, and she asked if she could have a hug. Of course! We talked a little. She was this woman's daughter. They told me how their bishop was not very accepting of LGBT people, and they wished I'd keep attending. Yeah, I'm not sure how well that would work out for me. I'm sure he'd be thrilled.

Another ward started out fabulous. The first Sunday I showed up they were having Fast Sunday, but they seemed like such a nice ward that I decided to push to the next month. They were very welcoming and friendly even though there wasn't a second hour. And after I'd born my testimony, I was swamped by people wanting to thank me. One man told me how grateful he was his kids were there to hear my testimony, because it was the best he'd ever heard. Wow. I thought maybe this was a ward I could make my home.

The next week was Ward Conference, so I decided to come back knowing the stake president would be in attendance. Well, I met with the stake president and bishop the next week. The stake president was very accommodating and was anxious to see about moving my records. That had never happened before. But the bishop started making comments about how he didn't want any social justice stuff happening. I was confused. I asked him if I had done anything or said anything wrong in my testimony. He said he didn't want any of the social justice in his ward. That it was his responsibility to protect the youth of his ward. He had to protect them from me? I told him I'd changed my mind about attending his ward. I didn't need a bishop who saw me as a troublemaker and somebody to protect against before he had even gotten to know me.

At another ward no one talked to me. I sat in Relief Society both weeks and no one even said hello or asked my name. They completely ignored me. But at another ward nearby, they were so friendly. The Relief Society president sat with me and Harmony during Sunday School. I didn't bear my testimony in that ward because it was July 4th, and this ward was very patriotic. It was just a continuous line of people bearing their testimonies, and I didn't want to infringe on their time.

I had an opportunity a year later to go back. While I was bearing my testimony a woman in the front rows just had this huge smile and was just beaming at me. Afterwards she invited me to their home for dinner. She had a son who had recently come out as bisexual after his mission and whose church attendance was failing. She wanted me to talk to him. A year earlier wouldn't have been good.

Once when I was looking for a ward, I thought I'd identified which ward to go to, but then I clicked on another ward building in the stake and the Spirit just filled me. Aww. Right stake, wrong ward building. I went to the ward, and they were the nicest people. Amy in Relief Society invited me to her house for dinner. It turned out that I'd once lived in a ward with her husband, and my father had taken their wedding pictures. Huh. We had a wonderful conversation.

The women sat next to me in meetings and made me feel so welcome. The next week I was invited to attend their Relief Society birthday dinner. I'd never celebrated the birthday of the Relief Society, and I was invited to an Inklings[18] meeting at a woman named Jessica's house. I didn't know what that was. It was something that best-selling author and popular inspirational speaker, Emily Bell Freeman, started.

Well, I showed up to the Inklings meeting to find that Emily Belle Freeman herself was sitting across the circle from me. That was amazing. She kept looking at me the whole meeting. When it was over, she came over to me and said, "Do I know you from somewhere?"

"Oh, I've been a volunteer at Time Out For Women, but I'm too starstruck to ever talk to you there."

She laughed. "No, someplace else."

"Like a conference that speaks about difficult LDS subjects that most people don't understand?"

"Yes."

"Oh, right." I'd totally forgotten that she'd been a keynote speaker at North Star a year earlier. Amazing how people remember me.

The next night at the birthday party the women treated me as one of their own. Amy even made me a special, unique gift in anticipation of my coming. Ahhhh. The Relief Society president sat next to me for dinner, and we ended up having a very long conversation. I explained my situation. She invited me to keep coming even with all the troubles I'd had with priesthood leadership in the past. I told her I would think about that. Maybe I'd found a ward that could be my new home ward. Maybe that was why the Spirit had been so unusually strong.

Well, I came the next Sunday for testimony meeting. Amy and her family sat with me as we anticipated the bearing of my testimony, but it wasn't meant to be. The bishop got up and bore his testimony and then he announced that he had been given some counsel and he thought it inspired. He invited six members of the congregation to bear their testimony, and if there was any time left, he'd see about opening it up to the rest of the congregation. And then he sat down next to the stake president. Well, my heart fell into my stomach. What was this? I'd never seen this happen before. Was this just because of me? Or did it have anything to do with me at all? Maybe this was just coincidence? There are none, though, not in my life. Why would they not want me to bear my testimony?

What do I do? Amy encouraged me to keep coming. Well, I decided to see. The Spirit was *so* strong. What was going on? And the women were *so* nice. The Relief Society president was so insistent that I decided to come back and not go to a new ward as was my usual. I went back the next week, and Amy wasn't there, and no one sat next to me or talked to me in Relief Society. Maybe it really *was* a coincidence? So I tried again and went back the next week. Amy still wasn't there. And again, no one talked to me or sat next to me in Sunday School. Not even the Relief Society president. Huh. Something was definitely different. This once warm and friendly ward was now ice cold. Something had happened.

As I was leaving the building, I was greeted by two men. They introduced themselves as the stake president and his secretary. They invited me into a classroom. He informed me that even though the women of the ward were wanting me to come that I was not welcome to continue attending this ward or any ward of his stake and that I was to attend my home ward. Did I understand?

"Sure, it's your stake. You get to make the rules." And I left.

I'm disappointed that I didn't get to bear my testimony. And I'm somewhat disappointed I couldn't stay. But I feel like I did what I needed to do. I met those women I needed to meet. I wrote out my testimony and I shared it with them, and I believe they shared with others. Heavenly Father will always find a way.

In another ward I had a bishop ask me to leave in the middle of the Relief Society meeting. Outside I found a stake counselor waiting. They informed me that they'd received policy from the First Presidency that I wasn't allowed to attend their Relief Society. I felt special. They then told me it was a general policy that attendance was based upon gender assigned at birth. Perhaps I didn't know about the policy. Oh, I was very familiar with the actual policies, but I decided not to be contentious. They invited me to attend elders quorum. Awkward. I passed on the opportunity to hang with the guys.

For Fast Sunday, the stake president asked me out of sacrament meeting as it began. His counselors closed the doors to the chapel and stood in front of them to prevent my entry. He informed me that I would not be allowed to participate in sacrament meeting. I was not welcome. So I went home. But not before talking to a woman outside on the steps who had witnessed the spectacle. She had had a trans niece take her life 18 months earlier. I found who I needed to find.

There is still so much misunderstanding and rejection. I'm disappointed in priesthood leaders who give in to their fears. Who decided to break policies by changing how testimony meetings are held and by telling people they aren't welcome. Isn't that what it says on all our buildings? "Visitors welcome." This is not the doctrine of Christ. At a time that many LGBT youth are leaving the Church while the Church is working to promote an image that they care, leaders are actually throwing out a trans woman who might make a difference, confirming the youth's fears.

But one ward I went to I had a particularly cool experience. I'd heard about this ward in Bountiful; it'd been suggested in a Facebook group. I didn't know why they thought I should go, but I kind of put it on my list. I didn't even know who suggested it. After several months of going to the wards I'd prayed about, this ward was finally top of my list. There didn't seem to be any objection by the Spirit, so I started attending. The ward was fine and welcoming.

After I bore my testimony, a woman got up and bore her testimony that she never asked Heavenly Father for anything because He was going to give her whatever He was going to give her. And while that is true, you can't make Him give or not give anything. He still has commanded us to ask.

When the meeting was over, there were several people who came up to me. One in particular was a young boy about 12–13 years old. By his appearance, I guessed he was somewhere in the LGBTQ+ soup. So I gave him my full attention. He just was so happy and engaged, you'd think he was meeting a celebrity. When we finished the woman next to him informed me that she was his mother, and he was transgender. Oh! She continued to tell me how he'd been having a hard time in this ward. There were people intentionally misgendering him and telling him he couldn't go to girl's camp. But especially concerning was that next week he was to get his patriarchal blessing and that was causing a lot of anxiety.

"Yes, I know how that goes. That's why I didn't get my blessing till I was in my 40s."

She went on to say, "I've been fasting and praying for the past two days that someone would say something in testimony meeting today that would give my son hope. And you came."

And that's when my jaw dropped and I looked to heaven. I'm always amazed at how real this is; how it's apparently still real after a couple years. Heavenly Father still has a mission for me. I still can be where He needs me to be when He needs me there.

Here we had the faith of two very different women. One who never asks the Lord for anything, and one who fasted and prayed for two days for a miracle. Two days! Who received the blessing? Though I don't know how the other woman's day went, I'm prone to say it was the faith of a mother for her child. Who was she expecting to say something? Would one of the many ward members who had yet to say something to them just have an epiphany, be struck by the Spirit, and say something new? I don't know. Maybe. But she had faith, and she asked. She months later told me that my testimony had saved her child's life.

How many times has our Savior commanded us to ask?

> *7 Ask, and it shall be given you; seek, and ye shall find; knock, and it shall be opened unto you:*
>
> *8 For every one that asketh receiveth; and he that seeketh findeth; and to him that knocketh it shall be opened. (Matthew 7:7-8)*

And Moroni said:

> *Behold, I say unto you that whoso believeth in Christ, doubting nothing, whatsoever he shall ask the Father in the name of Christ it shall be granted him; and this promise is unto all, even unto the ends of the earth. (Moroni 9:21)*

How many blessings do we miss out on because we don't ask? We miss things that our Heavenly Father is ready and willing to give us, if we'd only ask. Never be afraid to ask. Sure, He might say no, but what if He says yes?

I also began this journey by asking with the simple question of, "Where am I supposed to go to church?" It sounds a lot like the simple question that Joseph Smith asked in a grove of trees. I didn't get a witness of the Father and Son appearing and telling me about the restoration, but I have received many witnesses of where I should go, with some events happening that confirmed their divine source that I cannot deny.

At the recent Utah County Single Adult conference, a speaker talked about how we needed to find our purpose in this life. We needed to ask God what He wanted us to do. Have you asked God? Have you found out what He would like you to do? You might be surprised by the answer.

At this writing after 40 months, I've attended meetings in 42 wards and born my testimony in 40 of them. There are 84 ward buildings in the South Davis County area of Utah between North Salt Lake, Bountiful, Woods Cross, Centerville, West Bountiful, and Farmington. I hope to make it to all of them, but that will take about another 3 years.

Am I really going to be doing this for 3 more years? I don't know. I'll keep doing it as long as Heavenly Father wants me to, or maybe He will find something else for me to do, or maybe some church leader will bring the madness to an end. But right now, I've found a calling.

I can't say that I understand this calling; I didn't look for it, and I never would have expected this. I don't know what the end game is, or how many lives I'm affecting, or really how much good it is doing. I don't get to see the results. But I rather enjoy it. I look forward each week to meeting new people; I look forward to the lessons on how to follow the Spirit. And I have faith in Him whose plan this is, and I hope that I remain up to the task.

I'd like to thank all those who friended me while I was in your wards. Sometimes I can't imagine being stuck in the same ward, seeing the same people Sunday after Sunday. But then I've met sisters in every ward who I would dearly love to keep seeing every week. Maybe I can somehow mash you all up together into a new ward? Those who made sure I wasn't sitting alone, talked with me, welcomed me to Relief Society, and invited me to dinner. I can't remember everyone's names, but you have a special place in my heart. Perhaps we'll meet again.

I love bringing hope to LGBT people all over this LDS community. I don't know how many are in the closet afraid to say something. But I hope that in hearing my testimony that God lives, that He loves us, and that the Church is true, it will help them to keep coming another week, to keep living another day. I hope they see that I'm still here. I'm staying.

6.

The Cathedral and the Bazaar

O NE DAY THESE THREE YOUNG MEN CAME WALKING BY ME. They could have been models. They had that hair and face and body that you could easily see in a magazine or on a runway. Grecian gods might have been a better description, as they had their shirts off, and their pants, and frankly weren't leaving much else to the imagination.

It was a Saturday night, June 2018, in downtown Salt Lake City, and I was at the Pride Festival. I'd volunteered with a Mormon group to give hugs. I was wearing a subtle outfit of pink, blue, and white clothes that I didn't mind getting dirty or even having to throw away. I wasn't sure what was going to happen and was prepared for anything. I was giving hugs with the Oertle family.

The first time I went to Salt Lake Pride was 2016. I wanted to see what it was all about for myself—and it was about as bad as you'd imagine. There were a lot of rainbows, flags, and clever signs. There were a few guys and girls who thought clothing was actually optional. There were drag queens and kings, and fetishes I don't even have a name for—and I don't want to know. I just wanted to forget I ever saw them. And I was amazed at all the corporate sponsors, local and national. Walking around the festival I ran into a few friends and stopped by the Mama Dragon booth to see my moms and get hugs. But when I left, I vowed I'd never go back. Why would I want to visit Sodom and Gomorrah again? And I didn't the next year.

This year, I yelled out to these guys, "Would you like a hug?" They looked at me and wandered over.

"You don't want to hug us."

"Why wouldn't I?" They turned around and I could see that their backs were covered in glitter. And by that I don't mean that some fairy flew by and sprinkled them. No, this looked like it'd been applied with a trowel.

I sucked it up and said, "Of course I'll hug you!" And in turn I gave each of these young men a hug. And then I said, "And you get a sticker!" I had sheets of stickers that said "Hugged By A Mormon." But after I said that I realized I wasn't sure where to put them. Awkward. So, I just handed a sticker to each of them.

They looked at the sticker and one of them said, "You're a Mormon?"

And I cheerfully replied, "Yes, I'm a Mormon."

There must have been something different in how I said it. Maybe I let my voice down a few pitches, or something, but he looked at me and said, "Wait. YOU are a Mormon?" He put emphasis now on the beginning as he realized what I was.

"Yes, I'm a Mormon."

"We used to be Mormon."

"Well, you could be again." They didn't seem inclined, but it had them thinking as they wandered off.

The surprise in his voice of finding out that I was a trans woman and still considered myself LDS said a lot. I've learned that doesn't happen that often. But it's a familiar scenario to me. I consider myself LDS, but they don't see me that way, and I'm LGBT, but I don't see myself that way. I'm in both the LDS and LGBT communities, but my membership in both is awkward. Not really one, and not really the other. Sound familiar?

Getting into the LGBT community is really rather easy. Just declare which combination of sexual orientation and gender identity you subscribe to and you're in, as long as it isn't cishet (cisgender heteronormative). They will accept you, and affirm you, and love you. They welcome you with arms and homes wide open. It's really amazing how that happens. They aren't judgmental about who you love, or who you are, or how you dress, or what you do. They accept you, affirm your identity, and support you. There aren't conditions on their love. It's like being transported to a completely different world of perpetual sunshine and puppies, a Big Rock Candy Mountain.

Often when we are facing struggles in life we can find support and comfort within our families and our faith communities: the people with whom we've had long relationships, have similar values, and who know us the best; people we have relied upon in the past that we trust. But what do you do when it is exactly these people that are the source of your struggles? Where do we go then?

I was given a quote to read in Relief Society, that I barely made it through without crying, and I kept it. It was from a talk by Elder Gerrit W. Gong entitled *Room in the Inn*:

> Second, He entreats us to make His Inn a place of grace and space, where each can gather, with room for all. As disciples of Jesus Christ, all are equal, with no second-class groups.
>
> All are welcome to attend sacrament meetings, other Sunday meetings, and social events. We reverently worship our Savior, thoughtful and considerate of each other. We see and acknowledge each person. We smile, sit with those sitting alone, learn names, including of new converts, returning brothers and sisters, young women and young men, each dear Primary child.
>
> Imagining ourselves in their place, we welcome friends, visitors, new move-ins, busy individuals pulled in too many directions. We mourn, rejoice, and are there for each other. When we fall short of

*our ideals and are rushed, unaware, judgmental, or prejudiced,
we seek each other's forgiveness and do better.* [19]

Where is this magical, mythical place called The Inn? Is it near Shangri-La? If you think about your own ward, is it anything like this? Has anyone in the Church ever imagined themself in my place? Because this inn is not a place I've found in the walls of a ward as an LGBT member, but it is like a place I've found in the Pride community.

In 2015 I looked for support groups for LDS transgender members. I did it initially as a place to find married couples who could serve as a role model or give advice to how my wife and I could better navigate this situation and save our marriage. That failed in a big way, but it became a place where I was welcomed, and people mourned and rejoiced with me, and I could get the support I needed that I wasn't getting in my home or from the Church.

I spent most of my life trying to deal with being transgender by myself, and dealing with it with a girlfriend and spouse, but now I knew real people who knew what I was feeling and going through.

Once I announced I was transgender, there were all sorts of activities I could attend and Facebook groups to belong to. You have gayme nights, dinners, FHEs, and Transgiving. And I could show up as Katherine in a cute outfit and no one was bothered. I wasn't shunned or glared at. And people talked to me. We shared about how things were going in our lives. You know you're at a trans event when the men are in the kitchen discussing hysterectomies and the women are in the living room discussing their prostates.

It was through these groups that I met my first trans woman. Maybe I'd seen other trans women before in passing, but trans women are a lot like pregnant women. You don't want to walk up to a pregnant woman and congratulate her and ask her how far along she is only to find out she's just plus sized. Well, you don't want to walk up to who you think is a trans woman and find out she's not transgender. Plus, if she is transgender, she'd probably just rather not be outed. Pretend she's completely passing and move on.

So after nearly 50 years, I got to talk with someone who had and was going through similar things in their life; someone who knew what gender dysphoria was. And as we say, "When you hear one trans story, you've heard one trans story." And it's true that everyone's story is unique, but it's also true that if you hear enough stories you hear many commonalities. It was good to not be alone.

One group I particularly enjoyed was the Wasatch Front Transgender Family Home Evening. It is sadly no more. It was started by a woman who had a transgender son and felt inspired that she needed to do something. We met monthly on a Sunday at various homes from Ogden to Orem. There were prayers, hymns, a spiritual message, and snacks. Just like any normal Mormon FHE. There were couples and kids. It was a family thing at times.

I usually attended alone since my wife was convinced we should all be committed. But after I'd come out to my whole family in January 2017, I had an opportunity to take my kids with me and show them that there were others like me, and they had kids too. They weren't alone either. My wife and daughter Meaghan were in New York City the same weekend as FHE. It wasn't a problem till my oldest two daughters, Shannon and Cathryn, who had moved out, found out about my plan.

They confronted me and explained to me how I couldn't take my children to the FHE. They said I wasn't allowed to force them to go this activity. The shrillness of their argument and the terror in their voices communicated that they expected this FHE to be mistaken for a satanic ritual including child sacrifices, or something. Not sure where they would get that idea. I explained it's just a bunch of harmless Mormons having an FHE with prayers, hymns, and snacks. It was nothing out of the ordinary, except perhaps who was attending. And that I wasn't forcing my kids to go, we were just going as a family activity. If it came down to it, yes, I could force them to go because they were minor children, and I was still their father. But I invited these daughters to attend. I told them if they thought that this FHE was so dangerous to their siblings, maybe they should come and be there as a protection. They were horrified and declined and ran off to call their mother.

The FHE went as expected. I saw my friends. I introduced my kids to their kids. My kids mostly zoned out and spent the time playing games on my phone. Again, much like the usual FHE in our own house. Afterwards they got snacks and met more of my friends, and we went home. Apparently, the high priestess wasn't available for sacrifices that month.

My kids and I had a great time over that week. We went bowling, out to dinner, and we went to a movie. My kids were not at all hesitant or bothered as far as I could tell from me presenting female. It was no big deal.

However, for Shannon and Cathryn, this was apparently my Rubicon. Cathryn hasn't spoken to me since. She wrote me a message once. She wouldn't tell me why she was mad at me, but that maybe when we were dead we could again be friends. I have something to look forward to now in the next life. Shannon would still talk to me on rare occasions, but it was definitely colder. Our relationship has never recovered, and she too now won't talk to me. I guess what I still don't understand is where this fear exhibited by my children came from. They only found out I was trans a few months earlier.

I have been involved in many LGBT organizations focused on LDS members. They are not all the same. Some focus on the kids, and others the parents. None focus on adults like me and their relationship with their families. And their commitment to LDS values can vary. Some are very pro-church, and some aren't very religious, and some are more for those who are leaving or have left the Church.

What I have seen time and time again is LDS people creating yet another LGBT support group. They may even be inspired—I believe that many of them have been—to create these badly needed groups to fill a void that families and wards aren't providing. But what happens is they become their life, and they lose focus and their foundation. What starts as a Church-positive group for struggling LDS kids, and even adults, drifts as their wants and desires collide with the orthodoxy of the Church; and as they adopt the language and beliefs from the secular LGBT community. They exchange their identity as a Latter-day Saint for being an LGBT ally.

You start to hear how Church and priesthood leaders are imperfect; them making mistakes turns into leaders being bigots, homophobes, and transphobic. Church leaders are no longer inspired, and your own personal revelation is more authoritative. You can have a personal relationship with Christ and his perfect gospel of love, and you don't need a fallible church getting in-between you and God. The Church is unnecessary.

I've come to call this Mormon Protestantism. Like modern-day Martin Luther's, they are protesting the role of the Church and the ordained priesthood leaders as unnecessary, hammering their list of objections metaphorically to the temple doors. I've never quite understood that. Obviously, the Church is necessary to perform the saving ordinances of baptism and endowments—at a minimum. Even Jesus couldn't be saved as a sinless, perfect person without being baptized by those with proper authority. And it is Christ's church; He leads and guides it through His prophets, seers, and revelators. You can't remove the Church and still in any way claim to be Mormon, which seems to be the antithesis for why the organization was created in the first place.

I also encountered more than a few members who with excitement were looking forward to the day when several of the more "troubling" apostles would be dead. Yeah, you know who they're referring to, or could guess. They seem to think if these apostles were out of the way and we got in younger more progressive apostles then the Church could be LGBT-friendly, maybe even allowing gay marriage.

I found this view rather distasteful. How could you actively advocate for the death of God's apostles? These are men *called* of God. It's His church. I'd imagine if He, as their boss, was unhappy with their performance at their annual review, then His HR department has ways of expediting their dismissal and finding a replacement. But He obviously hasn't. So I can only assume that Heavenly Father is satisfied with how they do their jobs. Why would someone think that their replacement would be any more progressive?

In his talk "Two Commandments" in the October 2019 General Conference, President Oaks said:

> *Meanwhile, we must try to keep both of the great commandments. To do so, we walk a fine line between law and love—keeping the commandments and walking the covenant path, while loving our neighbors along the way. **This walk requires us to seek divine inspiration on what to support and what to oppose and how to love and listen respectfully and teach in the process.** Our walk demands that we not compromise on commandments but show forth a full measure of understanding and love. .... **Our walk opposes recruitment away from the covenant path, and it denies support to any who lead people away from the Lord.** [20]*

I've found this to be wise counsel. You can't stay with groups that will recruit you away from the covenant path, and I have left many groups because of these opinions of Church leaders. I've tried to linger and be a positive influence, but in time I'm inevitably drowned out, and my voice isn't welcome, so I move on. I see these people later and they've left the Church, and they look miserable and seem to have lost that light.

In a fireside I gave for The Utah Hearth in November 2019, I spoke to this. One of the other words I picked up on in the Book of Mormon was "murmuring." Laman and Lemuel were always murmuring and finding fault with Lehi, and especially Nephi, but also God and His angels. They were never happy. No one ever said the right thing. They never got what they wanted. And they especially hated how their younger brother Nephi was chosen by God.

Heber C. Kimball said:

> *I will give you a key which Brother Joseph Smith used to give in Nauvoo. He said that **the very step of apostasy commenced with losing confidence in the leaders of this church and kingdom,** and that whenever you discerned that spirit you might know that it would lead the possessor of it on the road to apostasy.[21]*

I read a story about Brigham Young once, which I can no longer find, maybe I'm making it all up, that went something like this: A man came to Brigham Young and told him about all the concerning stories he'd heard about Joseph Smith. Brigham Young replied, "I could think about all these things that Joseph Smith has done, or might have done, and I could lose my testimony and leave the church. Or, I could remember he's a prophet of God."

All this murmuring about Church leaders by the community was an echo chamber of apostasy. They would question the words of the leaders, call them imperfect. But that really is just a manifestation of the famed great and spacious building. I've come to realize that the overall Pride movement, with the various organizations and their supporters, are nothing less than a wing, or perhaps several floors, of this building. Nephi talked about how the inhabitants of this building were at war with the apostles. How they ridiculed and shamed those on the covenant path into letting go and coming and joining them. This was literally what I was seeing come true week-in and week-out. People were losing their testimonies by listening to the collective wisdom of the world and feeling shamed and condemned, letting go of the rod and leaving the path, becoming one with the chorus, and repeating the process.

Be certain that you are affiliating with groups that have your values and that your walk isn't with those that would take you off the covenant path.

Am I saying these people are evil? My heavens, no! Well, not all of them. LOL. Just kidding. I have a lot of friends in the LGBT community. (Or I did.) Many of them are friends who have left the covenant path, or never started. I have a lot of friends who are in that building. Some of them today still believe that they are doing Christ's work. That they are more enlightened. They believe they are doing good and will be on the right side of history. They are good, loving, moral people, and I like spending time with them. But at the end of the day, they just don't have the same values and goals that I as a Latter-day Saint have. Their focus is no longer on enduring and reaching the tree of life and receiving eternal glory.

There was a time in fall of 2019 where it seemed that about every week some apostle of God was saying something to inflame the LGBT community. OK, they weren't surprised when it came from President Oaks, but included in their outrages were President Nelson, Elder Holland, and Elder Bednar. They felt particularly betrayed by Holland. My Facebook feed was filling up with suicide prevention posts and inquiries of how I was personally doing. (Suicide prevention help numbers and wellness checks also regularly get posted each General Conference.) I was confused and started looking around to find out what had happened.

A good place to start is on Facebook with several groups that purport to bridge between the LDS and LGBT communities. I could never see how anything they did actually created meaningful dialogue or relationships between the two sides. They are always so negative and adversarial about the Church. And when they defended the posting of a meme of white, old men in dark suits beating a gay man to death on the ground with scriptures was a final straw for me. The meaning and message were all too clear, and I'd had enough. These weren't Mormons I wanted to be associated with.

But they are still good places to find out why this community is setting its collective hair on fire. I'd find out who said what where, and I'd track down the video or the transcript and find out what was really said. Usually, parts were taken out of context, or exaggerated. I learned to never take what was being reported by these groups about Church leaders as true.

I always start from a position that these men are prophets, seers, and revelators. And what I usually find is that they never really said anything inflammatory at all. All they said is what is widely known to be the established doctrine and policies of the Church. That's it. How can hearing the same thing that's been said a hundred times cause such an outcry?

It's rather easy. What I've seen is that the LGBT community will take comments and actions that they see as demonstrating progress or love towards LGBT members as a change in direction of the Church, and as a harbinger that better times are ahead. They then forecast that the Church is changing, and the days are soon coming when gays will marry in the temple, etc., etc. They build up a dream world with false hopes. And then one of the apostles gives a talk espousing the doctrine and policy of the Church and suddenly their hopes are dashed. They fall back to reality, and they blame this betrayal, and the claimed resulting suicides, on Church leaders and not themselves. Not taking any responsibility for their false narrative that cost lives.

How do I handle when apostles make statements that don't align with how I understand my gender identity? Here are three thoughts. First, Elder Ballard said:

> *As we begin to consider some of your questions, it's important to remember, I am a **General Authority**, but that doesn't make me an **authority in general**. My calling and life experiences allow me to respond to certain types of questions, there are other types of questions that require an expert in the specific subject matter. This is exactly what I do when I need an answer to such questions.*[22]

This to me says that general authorities speak generally. They speak to a worldwide audience and what is generally applicable in all people's lives. The Family Proclamation is general. Your specific challenges and situations may be different than those addressed. It is a proclamation that speaks to an ideal. If your situation is ideal, then that is great, but most people are not in a completely ideal situation. They are not necessarily less valid. Just don't expect that the Proclamation covers every possibility.

There seem to be exceptions to these general policies and doctrine. I have directly heard of many involving transgender members. Since I don't know the details or what went into the decision of their church leaders on each individual case, I won't speculate, but exceptions do happen. It's possible your situation may be exceptional, but probably isn't.

Second, I take my direction from President Oaks who said:

> *The restriction on the ordination and temple blessings of persons of African ancestry — almost invisible to me as I grew up in Utah — was a frequent subject of my conversations in my life in Chicago and Washington, D.C. I observed the pain and frustration experienced by those who suffered these restrictions and those who*

*criticized them and sought for reasons. **I studied the reasons then being given and could not feel confirmation of the truth of any of them.** As part of my prayerful study, I learned that, in general, the Lord rarely gives reasons for the commandments and directions He gives to His servants. **I determined to be loyal to our prophetic leaders and to pray** — as promised from the beginning of these restrictions — that the day would come when all would enjoy the blessings of priesthood and temple.*[23]

If a young Brother Oaks, decades before being called as a General Authority, in the height of the Civil Rights era, could receive revelation that what the Church leaders were saying about the restrictions on Black saints wasn't truthful and stay loyal, then that is an example worthy of being followed. Whether there is confirmed truth or not in what is said by our prophetic leaders today with regard to LGBT matters, we need to stay loyal. Anything less leads to apostasy.

And third, I love the lesson that Elder Holland taught his son about wrong roads, Elder Matthew Holland said:

Sometimes in response to prayers, the Lord may guide us down what seems to be the wrong road—or at least a road we don't understand—so, in due time, He can get us firmly and without question on the right road. Of course, He would never lead us down a path of sin, but He might lead us down a road of valuable experience.[24]

There are many times in our lives when we pray whether to do something that God says, "Sure. Go and do that. See how that works out." with a bit of a knowing grin. Knowing that it is the wrong thing because He wants us to learn and gain valuable experience. That wrong road could be short or long. You can get into some serious mind games trying to figure out whether your answer from Heavenly Father was for a right or wrong road. We will not know what are wrong roads and right roads at the beginning, and it may be a while before it becomes evident that our journey has been on a wrong road. It may even be decades. The good news is that God knows and He planned for it. If you find you were on a wrong road, don't let that deter you. Don't let that shake your testimony. Thank God for the experience and get moving on the right road.

I think what applies to individuals also can apply to organizations. It's possible that the Church as a whole is also allowed to go down wrong roads. I think that the policy regarding same-sex marriage given in November 2015 may have been a wrong road, which accounts for why it could be revelation, or approved by God, both in its establishment and its reversal in April 2019[25]. I have no way of knowing. However, it was a valuable experience not just for Church leaders but also for the members.

I would pray, and think long and hard, before labeling a policy or remark we disagree with as inapplicable, untruth, or a wrong road. You should let the Spirit inform you. But this is not the takeaway from these three thoughts of mine. What I'm saying is that regardless of whether they are untrue or wrong, you still need to remain loyal, still have faith in our leaders called of God, and pray for the day that we receive truth, the day we reach the end of a wrong road. And perhaps one day we will understand which road we've been on, and the reasons Heavenly Father had for the commandments and directions He gave. Or maybe He might not ever tell us.

But there are people in the community who believe they need to educate the Church leadership to prevent these episodes from happening. The church needs to change. And I'd agree with that in how local church leaders and members treat their fellow LGBT members, but not in doctrine or policy. I don't advocate for changes in Church doctrine or policy. Those things are so far above my paygrade. (But I wouldn't complain if they ever got better.)

Elder Ballard remarked in November 2017:

> *We need to listen to and understand what our LGBT brothers and sisters are feeling and experiencing. Certainly, we must do*

> *better than we have done in the past so that all members feel they*
> *have a spiritual home where their brothers and sisters love them*
> *and where they have a place to worship and serve the Lord.*[26]

The Church does need to listen and understand what we are feeling and experiencing. I think it comes with our baptismal covenant to bear each other's burdens. How can you minister or give charity, or bear burdens, or provide a spiritual home, if you don't even know the people you are trying to help?

Often people are afraid to ask questions to understand. They are afraid of asking the wrong question or saying something that will offend. Well, if you do, you won't have been the first. LOL But the short list to know is:

- If it's not obvious, ask for our preferred name and pronouns. This shows you care. If you misgender, just quickly correct yourself and move on. We'll notice you're trying.
- Don't ever ask about our dead name, or our medical procedures. And don't assume our sexual orientation. We are not your entertainment. We may feel some things are private.
- And no matter how much of a compliment you think it might be, please don't say something like, "I never would have guessed you were a boy." Or "You look like a real woman." While we might appreciate the sentiment, it's just cringeworthy.

I had a three-hour discussion with a member of the Primary general board, and at the end she said, "I can't believe I was afraid to say something to you." I was surprised, too. You can always start with something easy like, "I love your nails!" But more likely her hesitance, my friends tell me, is because I have resting bitch face. Thanks, gals!

President Oaks echoed Elder Ballard's remarks above in saying,

> *This walk requires us to seek divine inspiration on what to support*
> *and what to oppose and **how to love and listen respectfully** and*

> *teach in the process. Our walk demands that we not compromise*
> *on commandments but **show forth a full measure of understand-***
> ***ing and love.*** [27]

How can you show any understanding if you haven't put in the work to love or listen?

In the almost six years since I came out to my ward, I've never been visited by the Relief Society, the elders quorum, or the bishopric. There was one Sunday I thought I was finally going to be visited by the Relief Society. I opened my door after church still in my Sunday dress to find the Relief Society president on my doorstep. In her hands were cellophane bags tied with bright colored ribbons filled with treats and a message. She asked, "Is Valeria home?"

"No."

"Are any of your daughter's home?"

"No."

"Oh, do they live next door?"

"Yes." They hadn't lived here for a couple years.

"Oh." And she immediately turned and walked off leaving me dumb-founded. Apparently I wasn't one of the women of the ward she had a treat for, or was worth talking to. I didn't exist to her.

For years I never had ministers, and then after the bishop talked to my parents (He talked to my parents?) they were finally assigned but rarely came. They would report by reading my Facebook posts. No one in my ward has wanted to listen or understand what it meant to be transgender from me. They are content to talk about me in ward council and elders quorum and congratulate themselves on a job well done without knowing anything about my needs. As David Farnsworth observed, "If we're doing such a great job, why isn't she here?" On the other hand, they flocked to my wife, and invited her out for lunches and dinners to hear her story.

I've encountered in the Church what I call the modern-day Pharisees: the spiritual inheritors of the Mosaic mindset. They get fixated on the legalities of the policies with restrictions and their punishments, and forget to give equal weight to the allowances. They are sticklers for the law by making sure it is followed with exactness. But they also look at the law and reason out additional restrictions where it is perhaps silent or less defined, imposing their own standard to a level that was not implied or intended. Always looking for more exactness and going beyond the mark to make sure people stay within their limits.

I've encountered many church leaders during my TransMission, and in other places, who have made up rules and policies to govern my activity in the Church. I'm an old, endowed woman who has lived many years and have a testimony that is pretty solid. I can handle these situations without too many tears. Sometimes. Others may not. They don't yet have the experiences. Their spiritual foundation is not yet firm. This is especially true for our youth. I was told the story years ago of an eight year old boy who was then in the hospital ICU in critical condition. He had just been baptized the week before, and upon coming to church his bishop told him that he couldn't come to Primary again unless he wore a dress or skirt like the other girls. He tried to kill himself. Eight years old!

These Pharisees also want to create Zion today by making sure everyone is perfect and removing the imperfect. Metaphorically stoning and casting out those who are not good enough, or seen as sinners in their own righteous eyes. They look at other sinners as inferior and unwanted—Publicans.

> *10 Two men went up into the temple to pray; the one a Pharisee, and the other a publican.*
>
> *11 The Pharisee stood and prayed thus with himself, **God, I thank thee, that I am not as other men are extortioners, unjust, adulterers, or even as this publican.***
>
> *12 I fast twice in the week, I give tithes of all that I possess.*
>
> *13 And the publican, standing afar off, would not lift up so much as his eyes unto heaven, but smote upon his breast, saying, God be merciful to me a sinner. (Luke 18:10-13)*

How many have thanked God that they aren't transgender like me?

They want to keep these sinners far away where they aren't an influence; afraid that their uncleanliness will transfer to them, and they'll need to make an animal sacrifice to become clean. To create Zion they think they must begin by removing the tares themselves. But Jesus has answered them:

> 28 *The servants said unto him, Wilt thou then that we go and gather [the tares] up?*
> 29 *But he said, Nay; lest while ye gather up the tares, ye root up also the wheat with them.*
> 30 *Let both grow together until the harvest: (Matthew 13:28-30)*

How much of the wheat have we rooted up trying to remove the tares? How many of the good members of this church have we lost because others couldn't live with the LGBT people amongst them? They needed to remove us instead of working like Enoch and Melchizedek to create Zion one person at a time over decades and even centuries. LGBT people are the weeds in their garden. Similar to how the Zoramites cast out their poor because they didn't wear nice enough clothes.

But I had an encounter in a ward that is perhaps an extreme example of this kind of Pharisee. I had attended a ward for a month and just born my testimony. When I got back to my seat, a man and his two children had taken them, a boy age four, and a girl age six. No problem. I just moved further down and was sitting next to his daughter.

When sacrament ended, the kids left for classes and I had many people come up and thank me for my testimony. A man had thanked me from the pulpit as part of his own testimony. Several women invited me to come to Relief Society. I had to tell them that the stake president had told me I wasn't allowed to attend. They didn't understand. Neither did I.

Eventually I was in the chapel with the man from my row who had been waiting for me to be alone. He stood over me and said, "I will do whatever it takes to stop you from corrupting my children by teaching them about transgenderism."

I was shocked. What did he mean by whatever it took? He was clearly bigger than me. Was he threatening me with violence? In the chapel?

He continued, "Gender is not fluid. You are not a woman. You are a wolf in sheep's clothing. You will not normalize being transgender by attending this ward. I will stop you. I will speak out truth against you. I will do whatever is necessary to make every day you are in this ward as miserable as possible till you leave and my children are safe." For the first time in my life I felt unsafe at my church. That was something I never thought I'd experience.

I'm pretty sure his kids didn't pay any attention to me or my testimony, and I don't think I would ever be these kids' Primary teacher. I can't imagine what I would say about being transgender in a class. But what it really came down to was just my simple existence that was seen as a threat to his kids. Just by being there they would see that a transgender person was normal and had a testimony. The horror.

Elder Uchtdorf addressed this by saying:

> It's that simple. **We simply have to stop judging others and replace judgmental thoughts and feelings with a heart full of love for God and His children.** God is our Father. We are His children. We are all brothers and sisters. I don't know exactly how to articulate this point of not judging others with sufficient eloquence, passion, and persuasion to make it stick. I can quote scripture, I can try to expound doctrine, and I will even quote a bumper sticker I recently saw. It was attached to the back of a car whose driver appeared to be a little rough around the edges, but the words on the sticker taught an insightful lesson. It read, **"Don't judge me because I sin differently than you."**[28]

When challenged by the Pharisees about his communing with sinners, Jesus responded by saying:

> *11 And when the Pharisees saw it, they said unto his disciples, Why eateth your Master with publicans and sinners?*

> *12 But when Jesus heard that, he said unto them, They that be whole need not a physician, but they that are sick.*
>
> *13 But go ye and learn what that meaneth, **I will have mercy, and not sacrifice:** for I am not come to call the righteous, but sinners to repentance. (Matthew 9:11-13)*

Jesus was quoting the prophet Hosea's condemnation of the Jews in his day who were more interested in making their animal sacrifices, and in following the law, than in showing mercy to the poor. Here Jesus was saying that our place is to be with sinners, that it was more important to show charity to the sinners, the publicans and prostitutes, than it was to keep traditions and policies. You can be perfect in keeping the law, but if you don't have charity, a Christ-like love, for others, even sinners, then you are lost.

But how can we have publicans or prostitutes attending our church services? Don't we have some minimal standard of worthiness? We can't be rubbing shoulders with sinners, especially transgender people, while worshipping, right? As Elder Uchtdorf said,

> *The Church of Jesus Christ of Latter-day Saints is a place for people with all kinds of testimonies. There are some members of the Church whose testimony is sure and burns brightly within them. Others are still striving to know for themselves. The Church is a home for all to come together, regardless of the depth or the height of our testimony. **I know of no sign on the doors of our meeting-houses that says, "Your testimony must be this tall to enter."***
>
> *The Church is not just for perfect people, but it is for all to "come unto Christ, and be perfected in him." The Church is for people like you and me. **The Church is a place of welcoming and nurturing, not of separating or criticizing.** It is a place where we reach out to encourage, uplift, and sustain one another as we pursue our individual search for divine truth.*[29]

That sounds a lot like The Inn described by Elder Gong. I had a bishop that was fond of saying to the effect of, "Church should not be a country club for saints, but a hospital for sinners." He hoped we could walk through the halls of the ward and ask each other how we were doing with our sins. That's probably hard to achieve if all you hear is the polite golf clap while sitting in the club house.

Alma ran into this problem of what to do with those members of the church who weren't following the commandments. He went to King Mosiah and found out it wasn't a civil issue. So he went to the Lord and found out how he should handle these situations.

> *32 Now I say unto you, Go; and whosoever will not repent of his sins the same shall not be numbered among my people; and this shall be observed from this time forward.*
>
> *33 And it came to pass when Alma had heard these words he wrote them down that he might have them, and that he might judge the people of that church according to the commandments of God.*
>
> *34 And it came to pass that Alma went and judged those that had been taken in iniquity, according to the word of the Lord.*
>
> *35 And whosoever repented of their sins and did confess them, them he did number among the people of the church;*
>
> ***36 And those that would not confess their sins and repent of their iniquity, the same were not numbered among the people of the church, and their names were blotted out.*** *(Mosiah 26:32-36)*

Alma was instructed to blot out the names of those who wouldn't repent, but then what? What do you do with them then? There must have been a similar contention then as now, because Jesus addressed it when he came to the New World and taught:

> *30 Nevertheless, ye shall not cast him out from among you, but ye shall minister unto him and shall pray for him unto the Father, in my name; and if it so be that he repenteth and is baptized in my*

name, then shall ye receive him, and shall minister unto him of my flesh and blood.

31 But if he repent not he shall not be numbered among my people, that he may not destroy my people, for behold I know my sheep, and they are numbered.

32 Nevertheless, ye shall not cast him out of your synagogues, or your places of worship, for unto such shall ye continue to minister; for ye know not but what they will return and repent, and come unto me with full purpose of heart, and I shall heal them; and ye shall be the means of bringing salvation unto them.

33 Therefore, keep these sayings which I have commanded you that ye come not under condemnation; for wo unto him whom the Father condemneth.

34 And I give you these commandments because of the disputations which have been among you. And blessed are ye if ye have no disputations among you. (3 Nephi 18:30-34)

What an amazing concept! Even if people are unrepentant, and they can't take the sacrament, and their names are blotted out and not numbered with the Church, you still don't cast them out. You don't uproot the tares. You still minister to them, because you never know if they might return, or repent.

And I should point out that, under the policy for transgender members of the General Handbook from February 2020, transgender members are not blotted out, or excommunicated, even if we undergo full medical transition. I could have bottom surgery and I would still be allowed to take the sacrament, attend Relief Society, hold callings, say prayers, and give talks.

One thing I've learned is that people will go where they feel loved. If LGBT people are not feeling love from our church and its members, they will not be sitting in our pews. And if they are not feeling love from their families, they will not stay under their roof. Isn't that where we want them? Don't we want them feeling the Spirit? Growing their testimonies?

Having our association? Sitting in our pews and at our tables? If we don't love them, and we cast them out, then they will absolutely find love in the LGBT community. I guarantee you that. And we will lose them.

I started attending a ward and was so loved and treated well. The Relief Society put me on their weekly email list, invited me to mid-week activities, and even assigned me ministering sisters. During the early weeks, the Relief Society president went to the bishop and said, "I think there's a trans woman attending Relief Society, what do I do?"

"Is she preaching false doctrine?"

"No."

"Then just love her."

This went well until the stake president decided that I wasn't welcome to attend Relief Society. I was suddenly off the list, and uninvited. A friend reached out for help. Sharon Eubank told her that while I wasn't allowed to attend Relief Society there, she hoped they wouldn't just let me sit out in the foyer by myself. Well, that's exactly what they did. I would leave sacrament meeting and sit in the foyer, and everyone in the ward would file by on their way to their classes, and I would be left alone for an hour. How do you think that made me feel? As much as I loved these people, after a couple months, I left and found another ward. I didn't matter anymore to them. I didn't belong.

In your ward councils and presidency meetings are you asking what can you do? One ward I heard of came up with several unofficial Relief Society activities that they could invite their trans women to attend. Are you pushing the limits? Are you being creative? I'll give you a hint: if you treat your trans women the same as your cis women, you won't go wrong.

Is it less energy to keep the sheep in the fold than it is to have to go out and find the lost lamb? Are you working to keep them with the ninety and nine? Or do we shrug that they are LGBT, and our hands are tied? They are self-selecting themselves out of our Zion, right? They don't belong here. We're better off without their immoral influence. Are you losing the coin by not cleaning your own house? Are we always so focused only on administering the things that will drive them out?

As a priesthood leader you are obligated to enforce the restrictions, but are you looking for more restrictions where they don't exist? Are you as focused on the "dos," the permissive allowances, and following them? Are you quicker to enforce the restrictions than you are to implement the allowances, or remove unnecessary restrictions?

In an official statement from the Church given in July 2018 it says:

> God's message is one of hope, and we want our LGBT brothers and sisters to know that they are **loved, valued, and needed** in His Church.[30]

How are we communicating that our LGBT brothers and sisters are loved, valued, and needed? The mandate by God to love our neighbor seems fairly obvious, but did you know that you *need* your LGBT members? How might you need them? Think on that. Need implies that you can't do without them. They are integral. You are less without them. What needs do you have that they are uniquely able to fill?

And are they valued? I thought this to be interesting, and the meaning eluded me for a while till I started searching through the Church resources. What I came across were several addresses by church leaders speaking on how our youth could feel valued.

In "Ministering as the Savior Does" from Jean Bingham in April 2018 she explained there are two ways we can feel valued. The first is when we receive service.

> The woman assigned to minister to her brought a listening ear, produce from her garden, scriptures to read, and friendship. The "missing" sister soon came back to church and now holds a calling because **she knows she is loved and valued.**[31]

And the second is when we give service.

> As Sister Bonnie L. Oscarson shared yesterday, young women

*"want to be of service. They need to know **they are valued** and essential in the work of salvation."*

Are we making opportunities for our LGBT members to feel valued by receiving AND giving service? Are they called to be ministers? Are they given meaningful callings?

In the past 10 years, I haven't had a ward calling even though I'm only restricted from some callings. And I've never been called to be a minister. A few months ago, I received an email that the stake was in need of volunteers to help out with a traveling exhibit of a re-creation of the Israelite Tabernacle, complete with an Ark of the Covenant. (Danger! Don't open and look inside!) I signed up for a couple shifts in the morning. A week before the assignment, my stake president called me and told me he was aware that I'd volunteered to help out. He informed me that in consultation with the area authority that I wouldn't be allowed to volunteer because I was restricted from any teaching calling. That was news to me. (Oh, dear. I hope this book isn't considered teaching. I might be in big trouble.) I thought I was only restricted from gendered callings, but OK. Was reading from a cue card really teaching? Did all the volunteer needs qualify as teachers? Did they think of ways how I might participate and not teach? Here was an opportunity for me to feel valued and needed and a part of my stake. Instead, I felt worthless.

Elder Holland in an address at BYU in August 2021 said:

> *We have to be careful that love and empathy do not get interpreted as condoning and advocacy, or that orthodoxy and loyalty to principle not be interpreted as unkindness or disloyalty to people. ... We are tasked with trying to strike that same sensitive, demanding balance in our lives.*[32]

I've thought, "How nice would it be that I might be shown enough love and empathy that I could mistake it for condoning and advocacy. And that someone I know could be loyal to principle and orthodoxy, but

I'd never think them unkind or disloyal to me."

How many members are afraid that showing any kind of love could be construed as condoning? And how many have no problems advocating their principles even if it comes off unkind? You can't go wrong by preaching more truth, right? Especially if that's how you think you should show love. Wrong. Love should look like condoning.

I remember when I first encountered this condoning conundrum. Over Christmas break in 2015, I decided I needed to finish my attic. When I'd put a new roof on the house in 2010, I'd left drywall and flooring stacked in the attic, but never had a chance to finish it. The attic was where I was stashing most of my new girl clothes so that my kids didn't stumble across them.

I came up with a plan to move my stash to my brother's garage for a couple weeks while I put down a floor and hung drywall and ran some electrical for lights and power; shouldn't take too long. I figured it was going to take a couple hours to get all the boxes moved from the attic down two floors and out to the car and then a few trips in the family suburban. So we planned on a Saturday when the kids could spend several hours with their grandparents.

We were all set. Valeria took the kids to the grandparents, and she came back to drop off the suburban and told me she was leaving. "What? I thought you were going to help me?"

"No, I can't do that. When I die and stand at the judgment bar, I don't want anything I've done to be interpreted that I condoned your behavior."

Huh. This was new to me. I knew she wasn't happy about me owning and wearing the clothes, but how does helping me move them to help the family become condoning? So, if giving me service and being nice could be seen as condoning my behavior, could me being nice to my wife be seen as condoning this non-condoning towards me? Could I ever be nice to my wife again?

If my neighbor has a wine collection and I help them move the bottles, is that condoning them breaking the Word of Wisdom? Suddenly the elders quorum helping a neighbor move in or out of their house becomes a mine field of condoning. Who knows what might be in their boxes? Maybe we can only move some of them.

As Elder Holland says, it is a difficult balance to strike. This is where some useful, specific examples would come in handy from church leaders. When we discuss keeping the Sabbath Day holy, there are a multitude of activities that are given as worthy things to do on the Sabbath and actions we should try to avoid, but even still there are times we need to get our ox out of the mire.

Elder Holland expressed that the line between condoning and loving is getting harder to draw with the younger generation in a training broadcast in 2019, and I'd add the church in general as the LGBT population grows.

> *They [Generation Z] tend to "[support] gay marriage and trans-gender rights ... [as] part of everyday life. It would be rare for a Z to not have a [close] friend from the LGBT community."* ***Because of this sociability, the thin line between friendship and condoning behavior begins to blur and to be difficult to draw.***[33]

So what is condoning with LGBT? Where does friendship end?

Can you attend a gay wedding? Send them a gift? Go dancing at the reception? Can you buy a trans woman some jewelry? Go with her to get a pedicure? Compliment her style? Teach her how to apply makeup? Share your old shoes? Give her a ride to the endocrinologist? Use her preferred name and pronouns? Call her Sister?

These are questions that people are struggling with today.

Preaching orthodoxy and principles is so much easier. People aren't afraid of crossing a line in preaching doctrine because how could you ever go wrong with that? (Because, you know, no one has ever told me I'm not a woman, or that I'm an abomination before. One more time might do the trick.) That's what the Biblical prophets did, calling people to repentance. But they'd hate to cross the line on showing love and empathy, or charity, if it meant they condoned. Isn't that backward? Isn't it better to give too much love rather than too little?

We don't condone out-of-wedlock pregnancy, but don't we come together to help the young mother with her baby? Or are we afraid we might condone her actions by supporting her? If a neighbor brings a bottle of wine for them to drink with their meal, are we condoning them breaking the Word of Wisdom?

I have lots of friends who are gay and are in same-sex relationships and marriages. I don't condone these relationships any more than I condone unmarried couples living together. I know that Church doctrine says that these relationships are immoral. I voted against gay marriage, and I'd do it again. But I've had straight friends that have lived together outside of marriage. They're my friends. Of course I'd go to their wedding. Of course I'd buy them a gift. Of course I'd dance at their reception. I think that along with mourning with those that mourn is rejoicing with those who are rejoicing. But if any of them asked, of course I'd tell them what I thought of the morality of their choices. But they don't *need* to hear that from me. I don't need to be unkind.

I also have lots of friends who are transgender. I believe that we are all under the commandment to marry and populate the earth, to have children. If you medically transition, whether with hormones or surgery, you're not going to be having children. And also, socially transitioning, you're not going to be able to go to the temple. I believe going to the temple and having children are really important. But it's not my life. I encourage my trans friends to do these things, but when they tell me they are having surgery, I congratulate them. I celebrate their name changes. I celebrate with them what is making them rejoice.

Maybe we need to worry more about if we are feeding and clothing the least of these, instead of standing safe in our self-righteousness of not knowing that we needed to help them at all. Is it better to err on the side of being a sheep or a goat?

So, yes, I believe that as an LDS community we can be doing better in how we treat our LGBT members within the established policies and doctrine. But I think as an LGBT community we can be doing better in how we treat our LDS community. We need to face reality that the doctrine and the policies of the Church are not going to change.

OK, they might. They might change in 100 years, or 10 years, or in a year, or next conference. I don't know. As a member in good standing, how would you react if the Church in the next conference announced that gay marriages would now be done in the temples? Would you freak out? Or would you support the change? Is your testimony built on traditions and policies or on the rock of continuing revelation?

But I think the more likely scenario is that the policies never change, or never change in our lifetime. Because it doesn't really matter to me if they change after I'm dead. What matters to me is whether or not I was obedient to them while I was alive. I will only be judged by the revealed doctrine, established policies, and commandments of today. I won't be judged by if I live by the commandments under Brigham Young. And I won't be judged by the commandments under some future prophet 50 or 100 years from now.

The Black saints for 150 years weren't able to hold the priesthood or attend the temple. And yet they were expected to be obedient within that restriction. They couldn't be obedient to some future time after 1978 when the restriction was removed. And that must have been incredibly hard on them. I wonder how the other saints supported them. And I wonder how they took each time an apostle said something about the restriction, and about Black saints in the pre-existence. Did they murmur? They had to endure this for about 150 years.

I think as an LGBT community within the Church that we need to endow our children with this kind of legacy of being able to live with the doctrine and policies we have today without murmuring. Even with people who might misgender us; who don't recognize our gender identity; who might just be mean; and we somehow need to not take offense. We need to ignore the arguments and the ranting and raving of the great and spacious building and focus on what is important—eternity.

A seminary teacher showed my class the then current cover of *People* magazine. The cover had this full picture of Princess Diana and in the corner was a tiny picture of Marie Osmond from her temple wedding.

He made the point that one was a princess here and the other was sealed to be a goddess. Are we going to be focused on what the world sees as important? As I like to say, "It's better to be a goddess in eternity, than a queen for day." Let's keep the right focus and priorities.

There are things that the Church can do to make our situation more tolerable and ease our burden and be The Inn, but the responsibility is still primarily upon us to live within the Church, because it may never change. We need to find that delicate balance between the two communities, keep and build our testimonies, stay on the covenant path, and move forward to eternal life.

7.

Girls' Night Out

I
T WAS DECEMBER 2016. MY WIFE AND I HAD SPENT THE LAST
hour negotiating what I could wear to the ward Christmas party. I
loved Christmas and all the cute women's sweaters and accessories. So
much fun. Not the ugly sweaters, though; I don't understand that. With
five minutes to spare we'd found an outfit that wasn't too femme or sparkly
that I could wear, which would express enough of me without outing me
to everyone. Mission accomplished. She left to take the kids to the party.

And then there was a knock on the bedroom door. Shannon came in.
"Dad, would you please not wear anything too sparkly or Christmassy,
because my boyfriend is coming to the Christmas party, and he doesn't
know yet."

"Yet??? So, you're going to tell him?"

"Yes."

"And then what?"

"Well, if he isn't ok with it, then I guess he's not the one." Woah! My daughter was going to tell her boyfriend, and she would dump him if he's not good with it? Cool. So, I then had to figure out what I was going to wear again, and it was time to leave.

My oldest daughters, Shannon and Cathryn, had been told earlier in August. Their mother had broken it to them. I don't know why she did, but they hadn't believed her. A couple weeks later, when I decided they needed to know—because I was going to have surgery—I came out to them. They then knew it must be real. They listened quietly to what I had to say and didn't have any immediate questions.

A week or so later the four of us got together and they shared what they had been thinking. I think it's fair to say they weren't thrilled by the disclosure. Shannon was upset that she felt like her whole life had been a lie. I'm not sure how *her* life was the lie, but it highlights that keeping this sort of thing a secret is not good. Wives and children don't like this news being sprung on them late in a relationship. However, I think they better understood the tension they were seeing between their parents, and they said they didn't want to take sides. They wanted all future discussions to include all four of us. And their top worry was if I'd be able to be at their weddings in the temple. I explained to them that I wasn't doing anything wrong, I wasn't unworthy, and I'd certainly be there in the temple for their weddings. All in all, it seemed they handled it pretty well and I thought we could move forward as a family. I was wrong.

Any thoughts of neutrality or acceptance didn't last long as they spent hours talking with their mother each day and I barely got a "hello." They began plans to move out for Christmas. They didn't want to live with their trans father who wore skirts and dresses around the house. They didn't tell me where they were moving, and didn't want my help. I was cut off.

It was weird not having all my kids under one roof. I was not looking forward to having an empty nest. But by then my wife and I had been separated for over a year. I'd been sleeping on the living room couch that whole time. Now I could have their bedroom.

A year later in December 2017, I was waiting outside the bishop's office for church to end. Back then, if you remember, there was a three-hour block. I had spent the third hour at home as directed by my priesthood leaders. Shannon had announced at Thanksgiving that she was engaged and getting married in May 2018. Yay! But my temple recommend was expiring in January. It was time for a renewal.

At my last renewal in January 2016, I wasn't publicly out yet. However, my bishop and stake president knew what was going on with my transition. They knew I was on hormones. So I wasn't sure what was going to happen then. It could go badly, but I didn't know. I met with the bishop, answered the questions, and I walked out a few minutes later with a recommend. No problem. I then went to the stake offices. The stake president saw me waiting, called in his counselors, and shut the door. A few minutes later they began doing the interviews. The stake president was picking and choosing who he wanted to see. I wasn't one of them. I met with a counselor, answered the questions, he signed my recommend, and I was out of there.

I went home and showed my wife my new recommend. I saw it as proof that I was still worthy despite being on hormones and wearing women's clothes. She however was furious. She thought that after all her discussions with our church leaders that I'd been blacklisted; that there was no way I could get a recommend with all the unholy things I was doing. This was to be my day of judgement. Today I was to receive my comeuppance and learn that I was unrighteous; that what I was doing was wrong and I'd have to change my ways. And frankly I expected there was a good chance she was right. But when that didn't happen she felt betrayed by church leaders and was disappointed. And I understand her frustration. On one hand the leaders were telling her I was unholy, but then now they were validating I was worthy to enter the temple. Which was I? The unholy, or the worthy? Did they know?

I sensed this time wasn't going to go as smoothly. The bishop arrived and invited me into his office and inquired what I needed. I told him I needed to renew my recommend. He leaned back in his chair against the wall. That was not a good sign. He hadn't reached forward for the white binder of recommends in the top right drawer.

"I can't do that," he said, matter-of-fact.

"What?"

"You need to talk to the stake president."

"Why?"

"There's something he needs to talk to you about," he answered vaguely. Confused, I asked, "You don't know?"

"No, I know. I'm just not comfortable about talking to you about it."

Well now I was getting frustrated. "I don't understand. My bishop can't tell me something? And I can't get a recommend? With the policy you told me earlier this year you said I'd be worthy of having a temple recommend, and I haven't done anything wrong." I was regularly attending the temple weekly and doing initiatories every Friday morning.

"Oh. That. That policy was for visiting cross-dressers." I walked out without another word.

Earlier that year in January 2017, my stake president had invited me to lunch. You have to understand, when your priesthood leaders know you're LGBT there are no good meetings. But I figured I might as well get this new unpleasantness out of the way as quickly as possible.

The president told me that he was concerned for my welfare and wanted to help. He contacted a friend in the legal department of the Church to find out if there was any policy for transgender members. There had to be one, right? He was told there was a soon to be official transgender policy that he could pre-release with the permission of the Area Presidency. It wasn't final, but it wasn't expected to change before its release. Permission was granted. The policy was as follows: (1) The first two hours of church were non-gendered, and I could dress however I wanted, but the third hour was gendered. I could not attend Relief Society at all, but I could attend elders quorum if I was presenting male. He suggested I just go home and have a 2-hour church block. (2) I could attend the temple if I was presenting male. (3) I was to use a gender-neutral bathroom. If there wasn't that kind of bathroom in the building, then I could use the women's bathroom after someone went in and made sure it was empty and then stood outside preventing others coming in while I was in there.

I had not been expecting this policy. It was almost everything I could have hoped for! I was expecting something much, much worse. Sure, I couldn't go to Relief Society, but who knows, maybe that would change. This was completely contrary to what I'd been told in the past two years through my wife: that I was unholy and unrighteous, and that I'd broken all my temple covenants and lost my priesthood. She told me I was unworthy, and she no longer needed to harken to me. Yet I still had a temple recommend and I didn't think of myself as unholy. I was still going to church and attending the temple. Could I still be all those things?

I was thrilled. I left work early and raced home and told my kids, my parents, and my wife the good news. None of them saw it that way. They were shocked. There was no celebrating. This was not what they wanted to hear from the Church for policy. How could the Church support me transitioning and be temple worthy? Doesn't the Church care about the children? It was another betrayal, and Valeria didn't believe me. We had a group meeting with the stake president and bishop the next night.

My bishop explained to me that even if I came to church in a dress that I was still temple worthy and still held the priesthood, and that there was no higher certification of worthiness by the Church than holding a temple recommend, and I was worthy in all ways to have one. Wow. Because of this soon-to-be official Church policy and endorsement of worthiness and righteousness under the direction of my Area Presidency, stake president, and bishop, I came out to all my kids and socially transitioned in all areas of my life. I could now be out as Katherine. I had the approval of the Church. I was so rejoicing.

When I showed up to the ward the next week in a dress, it was without my family. My wife took the kids to her sister's ward. I was met with smiles and humor. I must have lost a bet, or someone triple-dog-dared me, or something. After Sunday School, I went home as I'd been instructed. Then the bishop met with each of the adult classes the third hour and explained what was going on without me. When I learned this I was humiliated. Why did everyone need to know my restrictions? It was like sharing my personal, private sins with everyone. I was betrayed. I started feeling like

I needed to leave the house, and I started thinking through my list of all the conveniently-placed solid objects along the freeway I could drive into. Yes, I have a list. I knew if I got in my car that evening I'd soon be dead. I crawled in bed with my estranged wife and told her to not let go of me till morning. This was unexpected for her, but she must have noticed something about me and she did as I requested.

The next week at church I was met with scowls and scorn. The Relief Society sisters continued to ignore me as I was still not one of them. And the elders quorum president would invite me to attend with the men like I wanted or needed some guy time. That'll surely fix me. Did they not understand the concept of transgender? I was avoided. People wouldn't talk to me. They didn't like to call me Katherine. When I would sit on a pew for Sunday School, people would get up and leave. And if I sat on an empty pew, no one would sit with me. I didn't know who my friends were anymore. In a ward where I'd known people for nearly 40 years, I was the new girl in school. I was sitting alone for lunch and felt like a stranger.

I asked the bishop about having a fifth Sunday or fireside to talk about LGBT issues. I thought maybe it might help to explain. He said that the ward had good people and to just give it time. I knew who he meant. I'd been in a bishopric. They were the former bishops and councilors, high councilmen, elders quorum and Relief Society presidents, all the A-listers that kept the ward going. However, none of them were among the few who were showing me love and support. It was the other marginalized members of the ward who cared, the ones not in the country club. After 18 months of "giving them time" I moved on.

With this policy a lot of anxiety and guilt of attending the temple was released. I was worthy even with everything I was doing. I had a reawakened interest and began attending the temple weekly, going every Friday morning for initiatories. It was easier being the only female with all the men than the lone female in an endowment session sitting with the men not being able to be with the women. I wore my best menswear, but I kept getting stopped in the men's locker room and told I was on the wrong side. I silently agreed with them, but I wouldn't risk that. I finally figured out it was because my bra was showing through the back of my shirt. Easily solved. I started wearing a camisole. But I still got reported to the temple president who talked to my stake president. They decided it was better for me to keep attending. However, when I got my ears pierced I stopped going until they healed. And when I got acrylic nails, I made sure when I went that I had a nice French Tip or I would paint them with a subtle nude color so that they didn't draw unnecessary attention. I was supposed to be presenting male after all. I was trying to be good.

And now I'm being told by my bishop that the so called official "transgender policy" given to me by the Area Presidency was the completely wrong policy for me. Ruh-roh. I was neither cross-dressing nor a visitor. One wonders how many cross-dressing men were visiting wards and expecting to attend Relief Society that the Church decided they needed to make a policy. And how would bishops know these were men cross-dressing?

I would later learn from Elder D. Todd Christofferson, and confirmed by the Church General Counsel's Office and the Presidency of the Seventy, that the Church did have a long-standing policy that transgender members could attend whatever meetings they identified with as long as they weren't a distraction or a disturbance. I always could attend Relief Society. For some reason, I wasn't told this policy, which is still the policy of the Church today. My local leaders are still enforcing the wrong policy they were told 6 years ago, and I'm still not allowed to attend Relief Society in my home ward.

Well, I didn't see the stake president to find out why I couldn't get a recommend. That wasn't a conversation I wanted to have at that time. I continued to attend the temple to the very last day of January. And one morning while I was waiting for my turn for initiatories, I prayed if I should get the women's temple clothes, and I was told to go ahead. So I visited the distribution centers and found what I liked. I finally had the ceremonial clothes that I'd wanted from the very beginning. I just don't know when I will get to wear them. In the temple? Or in my coffin? I've left that for God.

My recommend expired. I disposed of my male temple clothes. By then

I had a new bishop and stake president, and there was a new prophet. My new bishop would explain to me that the new and old bishops and stake presidents had met and were all on the same page about me. How could that be bad? He told me that a new policy from the First Presidency had come in about September. It said that because I'd been on HRT that I'd changed my body from male to female, which was the equivalent of an elective transsexual operation, and I was now banned from the temple for life.

Huh. That's bad. That's really bad. But apparently not bad enough to cancel my recommend. They waited months for it to expire naturally.

I was raised my whole life, like many other members, that you always live your life to be worthy of going to the temple. We are told to live worthy to hold a recommend even if there's not a temple close by. You stay on the covenant path.

I had a testimony the Church was true. I'd never broken the word of wisdom, not ever even drinking a caffeinated beverage. I never did porn; I always paid my tithing; and I was honest to a fault in all my dealings. I had attended my meetings and magnified my callings. And now I was banned for life?

So now what? I'd been on HRT for 3 years. The gender dysphoria was gone, and I never felt better mentally and emotionally. But now I find out that it is equated to having bottom surgery. And my body is now female? That'll be news to some people. If I had traded having a female body for a lifetime ban from the temple, I wanted a much better body! OK, Heavenly Father, it doesn't have to be the body of a super model, but maybe just a bit better, right?

What was so awful about it was that I had no warning. This was a new policy. There was no way to repent. I could pay 20% tithing, say prayers 24 hours a day, go to 6 hours of church on a Sunday, read scriptures for hours, and become a nun and say the rosary, and it wouldn't matter. No matter how good I lived my life, I was still banned.

So then I had to confront the hard questions. Did it matter? Should I keep paying tithing? Should I keep the word of wisdom? Should I keep the law of chastity? Should I keep going to this church? I had some heated discussions with God. I admit I used some rather unladylike language at high volume. I wanted to die so I could see my Savior in person and instead of giving Him a hug I wanted to flip Him off, with both hands. This was not my proudest moment, either.

The question I get asked most often is, "Why do you stay?" They hear about this event with the Church and many, many others and question why I'm not all offended and have left. I know many of my friends have left for less. Sure, I could go to another church. I was continually recommended to the Universalists, the Episcopalians, the Community of Christ (aka The Reorganized LDS), who would all love and accept me for who I was.

At a TOFW in Layton, I met Mary Ellen Edmonds (her and my mom were friends growing up in Cedar City). And after hearing some of my story, she asked me this same question.

My response? "John 6:68." And she smiled.

> 67 Then said Jesus unto the twelve, Will ye also go away?
> 68 Then Simon Peter answered him, **Lord, to whom shall we go? thou hast the words of eternal life.**
> 69 And we believe and are sure that thou art that Christ, the Son of the living God. (John 6:67-69)

Did these other churches have the priesthood? Did they have prophets? Did they have temples with saving ordinances? Were they God's restored church on the earth today? Did they have our Lord and Savior, Jesus Christ, literally at the head of their church? No, they weren't and they didn't. Going to them would be false. While they might preach of Christ, they didn't know Christ. I could never believe what they were teaching. I'd just be using them. And I couldn't do that.

But it was really rather a tempest in a teapot. I knew that I wasn't going to be breaking any of my temple covenants. I had a testimony. I knew what was true and that wasn't who I was. It was a rather short, ineffectual revolution. I figured if Black saints could be in the Church for 150 years and not be able to go to the temple, I could too. The important thing was still to always be temple worthy. God would know my heart and desires and my obedience. I also learned that where there is no law given, there is no condemnation.

So I wouldn't be able to see my kids married in the temple like I'd told them. Huh. Well, now the tables had turned, and my wife and kids were vindicated. I was now finally the sinner and heretic they wanted me to be.

The wedding proceeded, but I wasn't a part of it. My wife and I were in the middle of getting divorced. My daughter didn't want to be with me. We had hardly spoken in the past year. So I was left out of all the wedding planning and preparations. I wasn't sure of the exact colors, but I bought a suitable dress in a blue color, just in case, as the father of the bride.

In April, Shannon had a meeting with me and my therapist. She had an ask: for me to attend her reception I'd have to present male as the father she'd always known, otherwise I wouldn't be allowed to attend, at all. It's a typical request, and I guess I wasn't surprised. But it was that last part that shocked me. I wouldn't be allowed to be anywhere at the wedding or reception. I'd thought maybe I could sit in the back and not be part of the formal receiving line. Nope. It was all or nothing. I loved my daughter from the first moment I looked into her eyes. If I loved her, wouldn't I do anything for my daughter, even this? I told her I wouldn't. It'd be a lie.

I decided I needed to stand firm and be me. Katherine was not a costume to be taken off and be put back on. The precedent would be set that anybody could ask me to detransition so that people in my life are not uncomfortable or embarrassed. Be it for church, or for school, or other activities. They could choose to love me for who I am. I'm not going back in closet, ever, not even briefly.

My feeling was and still is that weddings are a big party for family. Everyone else is extra. You don't get to choose your family. You get the good and bad together. I thought she was fine with it. Shannon said her husband was OK with it, otherwise he wasn't the one. I don't know where this idea of how I looked mattered. We're family. When did it matter what other people think? Or how we looked?

So still living at home, and not being invited to the bridal shower, wedding breakfast, wedding, or reception, I decided it was best to not be home that weekend. It would just be too hard seeing all my daughters getting ready and being so beautiful and I wasn't allowed. I began looking for someplace to retreat. I finally found a place with my friend Brooke.

After work on Friday, I went to Brooke's house. We talked late into the night. In the morning I went out running along the Jordan River. I rounded a bend and had to stop. I had déjà vu. I'd seen this place before.

I've learned that déjà vu is a way that my Heavenly Father communicates with me. It tells me I'm where I'm supposed to be. He knows what's going to happen. Sometimes I know part of the conversation. Sometimes there's a feeling that goes with it.

My first one that I know of was in the 1970s at Kimball Junction, UT, looking out the window at a river going through the meadow and how it made a loop in my cousin's backyard. A more recent time, I had one driving to work. There was a feeling attached to it. I was going to lose my job that day. I went to work and had a good day. It was time to be heading home and I thought that I must have been wrong when my boss came and called me into a conference room with HR. Sucks to be right.

So I was where I was supposed to be. Where my Heavenly Father knew I would be. This was unexpected, but comforting. I pulled out my phone and checked the time. I knew my daughter would be leaving soon for the temple. I sent her a quick message. "I hope you have a great day! Love dad." She responded that she loved me too.

Brooke and I went out for lunch and a pedicure and that's when I learned a new way of God communicating with me.

We were enjoying our lunch when this woman, Julie, came up to our table. Julie said to Brooke, "Did you speak at BYU Women's Conference?"

Brooke replied, "No, I didn't this year, but I have in the past."

"Oh, thought I recognized you."

"You might know me from the Church's website. I have a gay son," Brooke responded. I watched their interaction politely.

"Oh, that's probably it. I have a father who came out as gay. I didn't talk to him for many years after. But we eventually did before he died."

Brooke unexpectedly brought me into the conversation. "Oh, that's what is happening with my friend Katherine. Her daughter is getting married today and she's not allowed at the wedding." Then Julie shared some personal advice to me and for Shannon; I was amazed. She then had to run to catch her flight to Arizona and left.

After she left, Brooke said to me, "That was a tender mercy of God."

"A what?" I wasn't really familiar with that term. It's the first one that I've come to recognize. I see them in my life more often now. They are those things that seem like coincidence but aren't. I've come to realize that there are no coincidences. Things are usually happening for a reason. Nephi said,

> *But behold, I, Nephi, will show unto you that the tender mercies of the Lord are over all those whom he hath chosen, because of their faith, to make them mighty even unto the power of deliverance. (1 Nephi 1:20)*

God gives tender mercies to those he has chosen because of their faith to make them strong. Look for the tender mercies in your life. Have faith for them.

Julie wrote about the experience on her Facebook page. Basically, the Spirit was telling her to come over and talk to us, but she was uncertain. She remembered from one of her BYU Women's Conference classes that she needed to have faith. So she decided to come by us on her way to dump her trash. Well as soon as she stood up the Spirit dragged her over.

I'm so grateful for Julie and the Spirit for making this such a foundational moment in my life that I will never forget. I learned that my Father knows where I am and what I need. Even while I'm missing my daughter's big day, my Father is taking care of me. He loves me that much.

The next day I put on my father-of-the-bride dress that I'd bought back in January and went to church. Brooke's husband Steven was the bishop of a BYU YSA ward. Because I was there, a girl decided to come out as gay while bearing her testimony. She said I inspired her.

I don't have any ill will for my daughter, and I'm not sharing to embarrass her. But these are experiences that many fathers who come out as transgender encounter. How families deal with them vary in acceptance.

Strange as it may sound, I'm somewhat grateful that I wasn't able to go. These experiences that occurred because of her decision were formational in my life. Sure, I would have liked to have partied with family and friends in celebrating her marriage. But God actually had other things I needed to learn. I'm glad He took the opportunity to teach me.

A couple months later in July 2018 was my daughter Allison's baptism. My bishop said, "As the previous bishop told you, you won't be allowed to baptize Allison." The previous bishop had told me no such thing last year. I wasn't given any reason why I couldn't perform these ordinances, but Valeria, who was planning the event, was told to make sure I had no part in the proceedings. However, she did leave a place in the program for a to-be-announced speaker that allowed me to bear my testimony.

After baptizing six children, this last time I would not be allowed to participate. I'd failed as a father. My new son-in-law would baptize her, and my father would confirm. I'd been kicked out of my house a couple months earlier and now wasn't feeling part of the family. I hid in the back of the chapel while the talks were given and preparations were being made. While we were waiting for the other families, and not wanting to have everyone walk past me, I left early to sit in the Primary room with the font. No one was there and I sat in the back.

Another family started filing in. One of the men looked at me. I looked at him. He looked at me again and came over. He said, "Don't I know you?"

"Yes, Alex, you know me." Alex is a trans man that I've known. "What are you doing here?"

"My nephew is getting baptized."

"Oh good."

"What are you doing here?" he asked.

"My daughter is getting baptized." We talked a little bit more until they were ready to perform the ordinance. But I sat there thinking how this was another tender mercy from God. What were the odds that there would be someone I knew, and they would be transgender? Having Alex be there briefly was something I really needed. It let me know yet again that my Father is aware of me and what I'm going through. God is so amazing.

It was the influence of Julie that put me on another path. I really wanted to experience this BYU Women's Conference and other programs for women in the Church, the other being Time Out For Women (TOFW).

That fall I went to the TOFW in Salt Lake City with my friend Jeni. I met Tom Christofferson and Mercy River; Brooke and Laurie were also there. I had an amazing time. It was so much fun with good music, wonderful speakers, and the Spirit was so strong. It was nothing I'd ever experienced before.

It was there in talking to Tom that I said, "You should write about transgender people."

He replied, "That's your story to tell, not mine."

After my experience at General Conference with Symphony a month earlier, I then realized that God wanted me to write a book about my life. Yeah, it's taken a while. I'm sorry. But the next year I went to TOFW in Layton and met Calee Reed and the Sistas of Zion. And then was a volunteer in Salt Lake City in 2019 and 2022, and a volunteer in Layton for 2020 and 2022. I just can't get enough of it. I have a new dream, which is to be a speaker at TOFW. How crazy would that be? I wonder what I'd talk about? LOL

So when BYU Women's Conference was announced for Spring 2019, I was so excited to go. Julie said she was coming, and I went with Brooke, and we all met in the Marriott Center. It was good to get to spend some time with Julie and learn more about her experience with her father.

I went to a class on divorce, and a class on LGBT given by two gays. (When will transgender get to speak for itself?). Then I went to a class on having black sheep kids. Sitting next to this woman, I asked if she had black sheep children. She told me she had a daughter that had left the Church. There were things they couldn't talk about at home. She asked if I also had black sheep children. I told her that all my children were wonderful and strong in the Church. So, she asked why I was there. I told her, "I'm the black sheep."

"But you're the one here at Women's Conference?" I know.

But another reason I came to the conference was that Elder D. Todd Christofferson was the Saturday afternoon keynote, and I knew I was going to meet him. But I didn't know how. I just knew. I'd been going through so much crap in my life; I knew that I needed something. Meeting the apostle would be like touching the hem of a robe, just a small miracle that would give me strength. So I was going.

I reached out to Tom Christofferson and asked if he was going to be there. He told me that he unfortunately wouldn't be able to make it. He had stuff to do in Arizona. OK, so Tom wouldn't be there to help me in meeting his brother. How was this going to happen? I didn't know, but I knew it would.

So Saturday came, and Brooke and I were sitting on the lawn having an ice cream. She asked how it was going to happen. I told her I still didn't know, but it was. I had faith. She said, "Why don't you ask Tom?"

"I couldn't do that. Just too much of an ask. I wouldn't want to infringe. Plus, he's not even here."

"Yes, he is." What? "I had a friend who wanted to meet Elder Christofferson because he's her all-time favorite apostle. So I had her contact Tom and he set it up. Tom is here for the keynote."

But I still couldn't ask. He wasn't my favorite apostle. (Apologies. That honor would go to President Oaks. I know. Highly ironic.)

Well, we went into the Marriott Center for the keynote. There was no way to get to the floor. I saw Tom come in and sit down. I sent him a message from our nosebleed seats. He smiled and waved back, and I still knew it was going to happen. But as the program started, I really came to understand that…it wasn't. It really wasn't. But the Spirit was still so strong, and it said to me, "All you had to do was ask." And that was really powerful.

It was so simple, but I was afraid to do it, and I missed out on the opportunity that day. But the interesting thing was that because it could have happened it was as good as having happened. It was enough. I got my miracle. Maybe not the tender mercy I was wanting, but it was the one that I needed. Ask.

Six months later, it was September 28th, I got to meet Elder Christofferson in person. It was still a certainty, just delayed. My plans got canceled for that Saturday evening, and 30 minutes later I walked into the post office and ran into my parents. My father asked if I would like to go with them to a fireside that evening. My transphobic uncle invited my prodigal parents to attend a fireside in his stake with Tom Christofferson. I just looked up to heaven, *Really? Are you going to make it that obvious?*

I told them of course I would go, but I would meet them there. I arrived early and secured a bench near the front for my parents. Five minutes before the fireside was to start, Elder Christofferson walked in and sat on the bench right in front of us. There are no coincidences. I got to finally touch the hem of the robe.

Even with that experience, my life was still a bit in turmoil. It'd been over a year since my divorce was finalized. I'd gotten the house refinanced; my car replaced; and I'd begun dating and had met Harmony. But my boss was giving me grief at work. I had a fireside to speak at and a presentation at the Encircle One conference. There was a lot going on, and I was trying to figure it all out, but I didn't have many answers to these life questions. OK, I didn't have *any* answers.

I was a volunteer for TOFW in Salt Lake City. During training they told us to be mindful of the women who had come. We didn't know what they were going through. We were told to listen to the Spirit and follow promptings. For some that might mean a kind word or a hug. For others it might mean getting a priesthood holder for a blessing.

My job was to stand at the front of the hall and regulate access to the premium seating. Have you ever seen hundreds of women come running down the aisle in order to get a seat as close as possible to see Nathan Pacheco? It's frightening, but I survived. As I stood there with my clipboard, I was dancing to the musical stylings of Mercy River. I became aware that people were taking pictures of me and posting to Instagram.

This woman got up from 10 rows away and walked up to me and said, "I hope you're at the gates of heaven to welcome me."

"Why?"

"Because you have the smile of an angel." Wow. I gave her a hug and she wandered back to her chair.

The next morning was Saturday. It was too early for a Saturday, but I had to get ready and drive to the venue early for volunteer training. As I was driving, the life questions began to hit me one after another. Each time I would respond with, "I don't know." The questions came faster and harder. It wasn't just raining, it was pouring. "I don't know, I don't know, I don't know!"

Finally, in a fit of desperation I yelled out, "I don't know! I don't know anything!" And the questions stopped. It was quiet, and I realized I'd gone too far.

I immediately prayed, "Father, I'm sorry. That's not true. There are two things I do know. The first is that I know this Church is true. And the second is that I know you live and love me. But I'm having a really hard time. I could use some help. Not much. Just a little bit. Just the hem of a robe."

I drove on in silence. I got to the venue and through my duties and the opening keynote. At the first break I got up and wandered around the exhibits to clear my head.

That's when I turned and found two girls standing in front of me. I didn't recognize them, but that's not unusual for me. I'm terrible at remembering people. I'm so much more recognizable. They weren't all that old, probably early twenties. Maybe. I expected the closest one to say something like, "Hi Katherine. Remember me from some ward or event." I had had that happen a couple times the night before. But she didn't say anything.

I looked at her and realized that her lips were moving, trying to form words, but not able to. Something was happening. So, I waited. Finally, after a little while, her face brightened up and she looked right at me and said, "I'm supposed to tell you that your Heavenly Father loves you and that you are brave." Wow. I wasn't expecting that. I thanked her and gave her a hug. She turned and I watched as the two of them wandered off and disappeared into the crowd.

I turned and made it about two steps before I realized what had just happened. I got to a nearby chair and started crying, frantically trying to recall what she'd said. Her words were fading like fog on a hot day, they were slipping through my fingers. She might have said more than I've kept, but the rest are gone. I have great sympathy for Joseph and the First Vision.

What had I asked for? I desperately tried to remember what I had asked for that morning. Just a little help. A little. And what had my Heavenly Father done for me? In the matter of a couple hours, he'd found a vessel, a messenger, who could convey what I needed to hear. He loved me. I had received another tender mercy. He's amazing. Here I was at TOFW supposedly to help the women who had come, but I was the woman who was being ministered to.

How do I know my Heavenly Father lives and loves me? Because He tells me. Over and over, He does things to tell me. And I can't deny them. No more than Joseph could deny the First Vision. Here was yet another woman who was inspired and obedient to come into my life—a willing angel. How can I be more like her?

8.

Single White Female

WITH MY 31-YEAR RELATIONSHIP WITH MY WIFE ENDED, it was just natural for me to continue with that and look to find another woman to marry. It really didn't occur to me to date men. I still didn't find them attractive after several years of HRT. And even so, the Church would not be happy with me dating men as they would see it as two males having a romantic, homosexual relationship. I didn't need more awkward conversations with priesthood leaders. The Church *is,* however, good with me dating women. I think.

As an LDS trans woman should I not date women if I'm really a woman? Good question. Maybe I might ask: do you now any LDS lesbians who wouldn't date a woman if the Church would let her, regardless of reason?

It would put me in the awkward position of not being able to date men because the Church sees me as male, but not able to date women because I see myself as female. I'd be putting myself into a position of not being able to date anyone of either gender. Lesbian members at least have a choice between celibacy and dating men. I'd have no legitimate choice but celibacy. So why would I force myself into celibacy? For the sake of authenticity?

It's a complicated situation and I'm a pioneer. The answers are still being figured out. But I will tell you now that I have made a petition of the First Presidency to have my gender marker changed to female, and was willing to live with all the ramifications of that change, even dating and marrying a man. But it's not yet time for that story.

After a year of being divorced, I decided it was perhaps time to see about getting married again. Why did I wait a year? I don't know. It just seemed like the right amount of time. I didn't want to seem too anxious or eager, right? I guess it seemed like I needed to wait a respectable amount of time of mourning. Why? I wasn't a widow. Maybe I just needed the time to get my life back together.

Prior to getting divorced, I started hanging out with the lesbians at North Star. They were honestly much more fun than the transgender group. The transgender group was always so depressing, doom and gloom. I was sitting in a transgender session at the North Star Conference and the constant laughter through the wall was so distracting and I had to go check it out. I never went back.

I was also curious to know, if my marriage did end up in divorce, what the LDS lesbian community was like. Was there any possibility of me finding someone to marry in this group? It was a community that I didn't know anything about.

Most of them were the same age as my kids, and most of them my age were already married to men. I wasn't attracted to those that were butch. I'm a lipstick lesbian. However none of them ever seemed that interested in me. They didn't really understand why I was with them. I had to explain that I was a woman who was attracted to women. I'm not sure they were convinced it was the same.

I went on activities with my new lesbian friends. We'd go out to dinner. The conversations would usually revolve around the usual feminine topics of guns, cars, sports, weightlifting, and, of course, girls. Quite often the busty waitress who just took our order. All subjects I had a passing familiarity with.

They would also have conversations like, "I wore lingerie the other night." Now for them, sexy was ordinarily something plaid and flannel.

Or "I wore make up the other day."

"Did your husband like it?"

"Yeah. I think he did." They were all genuinely surprised. Madison Avenue has clearly failed to reach this demographic.

I went with them on a getaway to Brian Head Resort near Cedar City, UT. We rented a condo for the weekend, and over a dozen lesbians came from Idaho, Utah, and California. I learned from them that there was not a single good lesbian movie. They'd seen them all. And it's true, some are better than others. I've probably watched some I shouldn't have, but I can only watch so many Hallmark movies where the guy gets the girl. It's nice to see some girl get girl drama on occasion.

The condo only had a king, a queen, and several twin beds, but not enough for everyone. We would have to share. So on my arrival I was shown to this closet of a bedroom with a single twin bed. It was not entirely surprising; I guess I'm not like the other girls. But then I was told that all the married women had to tell their husbands I was coming and get permission from them to come. What?

OK, that seemed kind of sexist to have the women do this. Can't they make their own decisions? But did they not understand this lesbian thing? Or do I not? Because here we had cis women who were going to be sharing beds and bedrooms, and they're worried about the trans woman with a penis? Why would they even think these LDS women would have an affair? And who do you think these married lesbians are more likely to have an affair with this weekend? Why would they choose the lesbian with a penis, when they can get that action from their husband already, and when there's a lesbian with a vagina next to them in their bed? Right? Does that make sense? SMH.

Yes, I was offended and hurt, but not enough to get in my car and leave. But it was clear I wasn't really part of their group. The friendships just never really healed from that weekend. I think the fact that I could date women sat wrong with them. I would always be the outsider

The next year, I scheduled a lunch with a lesbian friend while I was in Los Angeles. I arrived at the restaurant and she introduced a female friend she'd brought along who worked in PR for her stake. She said she'd never met a trans woman before. "You never forget your first," I said. Our 20 minute lunch lasted three hours as her many questions got answered.

But I didn't really know why she was there. Apparently my friend's husband didn't trust his lesbian wife to go to lunch with a "man" unchaperoned. He told her she needed to bring a woman along. Am I the only one confused? He trusts his lesbian wife to go to lunch with another woman, but not with a man? It's so nice of him to not just judge me but also to misgender me as well.

But we're dealing here with a long-held social convention Christian women are raised with that when they are married they aren't supposed to be alone with a man, married or unmarried. Other women are presumably fine, since it is assumed that two straight women won't have an affair with each other. But how does this social convention work with lesbians and trans women? Is your lesbian wife safe with a straight woman, but not a gay woman? Or safe with a gay man but not a straight man? And are trans women considered men or women in this set of rules? Does *their* sexual orientation matter?

I've noticed with my married straight female friends that they can get weird on me. They get nervous at the suggestion of car-pooling with me, or they always turn down invitations to come to my house. I always have to meet them at some place public, or with their husband. Ever been purse shopping with a friend while her husband waited in the car as chaperone? They are worried about being alone with a man when anyone looking from the outside would just see her with another woman. It's a sign to me about how they truly see my gender. Do they treat me as the single man? Or single woman?

And I should point out that even though my many lesbian friends are married to men, they are still lesbians. They aren't straight or bisexual.

They are attracted to women and their husband. We once had two girls from BYU who were roommates join us for dinner. They were attracted to guys and each other. They would go on dates with men and then share a bed in their dorm. They thought that's what all roommates did. Who you love doesn't always define your sexual orientation. That's why things could work with Harmony.

But I've often wondered if that wouldn't be a perfect solution to the whole SSA/LGBT problem for us saints? Instead of having mixed-oriented marriages, you get the gay and the transgender members appropriately matched up?

One lesbian friend would tell me how her husband was a bit overweight and had a good A cup. It was enough for her to fantasize with. Well, come on then, why wouldn't one of these lesbians want my D cups? Right? And they can pay for more if they want. However, it just never worked out. I was never one of the girls. Amazingly, many of them ended up in relationships with cis women and leaving the Church.

So after my year of mourning, I went online and created a dating profile with recent pictures. Within minutes I started to get a lot of likes and messages—from guys. Ugh. This was not going to work. I realized that for LDS dating apps I'd have to suck it up and create a male profile so that the enforced heterosexuality would match me up with the other women. Swiping through the men's profiles was just ewwwww.

I wasn't going to hide who I was. I was going to be upfront and honest, unlike other trans women who apparently were presenting male. It was a bold strategy. Hide nothing and lay it all out there. Call it the Nigerian Prince scam of dating. Sure, almost no one will fall for it, but it only takes one. It's so crazy it might work! Yeah, there's a reason I'm not in marketing. This definitely was going to be a different experience being on the other team. But I'd found a wife before, right? However, I hadn't been out as female back in college, and I don't have my youth and great looks working for me now. Nor do I have extreme wealth to compensate.

Well, let's just say I wasn't anywhere near as popular with the ladies. But within a few days I had messages from women telling me that I clicked on the wrong gender, and I needed to contact tech support to get it fixed. "OMG. Thank you. I'm so embarrassed. I'll get right on that." I had messages from women who had LGBT kids or were allies who told me I was courageous, but they didn't want to date me. They are apparently attracted to manly men. "Thank you! Oh, that's Ok, I'm only attracted to feminine women." LOL. And I had messages from women telling me how ugly and disgusting I am. I was an abomination and caused all sorts of unnecessary pain on my family. "Thank you for your kind words. I love my Savior too." It became quite common to see that a woman had looked at my profile and almost instantly had blocked me. This was not going well.

I'm not sure what I expected. I knew straight women were more fluid and weren't always 100% attracted to men. The women at the salon have told me that they don't find men all that attractive, and I agreed with them. But they found their chemistry with men. Go figure. And I thought there might be some closeted lesbians trying to still do the right thing. Nope.

I thought maybe there would be some disaffected women who could appreciate my being female. Who through their experiences with men in dating and marriage had had enough of toxic masculinity. They might enjoy being with someone who understood them. Who knew what it meant to be a daughter of God. Someone with whom they didn't have to fake enjoyment of sports, hunting, fishing, or the outdoors. Who they could go shopping with and see chick flicks and have a pedicure. Who wasn't gross and smelly; kind of a girlfriend with benefits.

Apparently not.

Harmony told me that women were much more interested in how they were treated by men than the man's appearance. Even if any of that were true, none of these women were at that point of giving up and settling for someone like me. It was a hard, "NO." They were still swiping through the hundreds, and maybe thousands of men in these apps, and there would be more tomorrow. How could I ever be their best match, or any match? Any guy would be better than me.

It is often suggested to me that I'd have an easier time dating outside the Church. I'm sure that's probably true. But why would I do that? I want to be with someone who has my same beliefs and values, but ironically, it's those same high values that prevents these women from ever considering me.

I still have profiles on the LDS dating apps, but I think all the women have seen it and made up their mind. I only ever found one woman who would date me and that required an act of God. Literally. Maybe He'll act again.

But maybe there were some in-person church singles activities? Maybe I could connect to someone in-person with my fabulous personality. I knew that after age 46 that the Church didn't have singles wards and kicked you out to be in the family wards. So I Googled. I eventually found that there were some senior groups in Utah County, which was great because that's where my work office was located. I decided to check out a group called Mt. Timp FHE.

Mt. Timp met every Thursday evening at 7pm and had an hour potluck dinner, followed by an hour fireside, followed by an hour dance. No time like the present, so I went that Thursday. Well, dinner was a bust. No one wanted to talk to me. There was a guy at the table who would spontaneously spout trivia about Montana regardless of what was being said. "Billings is the capital of Montana" or "Montana is called the Big Sky state." Thanks for that. For the fireside there was a woman who had written many books. She was divorced and told her journey of living in a tent in her brother's garage and living in an old RV in Montana and having to put alcohol-soaked cotton balls around her neck so the mice wouldn't run across her face while she was sleeping. Ewwwww. I think all the women greatly appreciated their circumstances in comparison.

And then there was the dance. I'd finally get a chance to talk to someone! I saw a woman at the back of the dance standing alone, so I stood next to her. We introduced ourselves. She asked if I was new. (A lot of people wanted to know that. I hear the men like the fresh meat, and women hate the new competition.) I told her I was, so she started to give the 411 on all the men. "Don't dance with that guy. He'll grope you." Apparently, that is really a thing even at my age. I've heard some men will even unhook your bra while slow dancing. Don't men grow up? We're long past junior high, right?

"And don't dance with that guy, he's a polygamist." What? Well, it is Utah County. I was never going to remember all those details, and I didn't really care, because I wasn't interested in dancing with or dating any of the men.

And that's when this man walked up to me and asked me to dance. Yikes! He had grey hair and a beard and looked like my grandfather. (Seriously, how old was I? Is this really my age group?) He was wearing a Hawaiian shirt and a Santa Claus hat in August. I was shocked. I honestly wasn't expecting this, and I wasn't interested so I politely said, "No thank you." And I watched as his face collapsed, crushed by rejection. OMG. That was horrible to witness. What had I done?

As parents we'd instructed our daughters to always dance with a guy unless there was a real reason not to. It was just a dance after all, it wasn't a marriage proposal. And here I wasn't following our own counsel. Fine. I'll say yes the next time. Please don't be a next time!

If I can just interject, there was this guy who asked me to dance in Bountiful a few weeks later. Yeah, he was super creepy, alarms were going off, but I didn't have a reason to say no. Like, what's he going to do to me, right? He danced fine and as he led me back to my chair he says, "How tall are you?"

"I'm 6 foot 1."

"What size shoe do you wear? 11? 12?"

Feeling cautious of where this is headed I answered, "Uh, I usually wear an 11."

"Oh, I love tall girls with big feet." Ewwwww.

There was something about how he said that that just caused this gross feeling to go through my whole body like a barrel of sewage was dumped on me. What the heck did that mean? Was that supposed to be a compliment?

"I suddenly feel a need to take a long shower," I said to the girls nearby who'd also heard him. Gross. I think guys really don't understand how creepy they can be. And I don't think they realize that women can sense that creepiness. Yeah, we know, and I probably should have said no.

Well, it wasn't 30 seconds later at the first dance and another old man with grey hair who reminded me of my grandfather came up and asked me to dance. Aren't there any young men? I faked a smile and said yes. He put out his hand and I took it for him to lead me out on the dance floor. This was very new and weird. He then proceeded to try and swing dance with me. I'd never swing danced in my life. I went to the University of Utah where swing dance was not a required class. And during the 80's we hadn't particularly paired up and danced with anyone. It was usually a group dancing, a mosh pit slam dancing, or just dancing by myself as Billy Idol intended. This was very new outside of dancing with my wife in the kitchen. But I did my best and he was talented and good at leading.

Well, he was the first of many. I guess I was the fresh meat that night. I didn't get to meet any of the other women. Over the years I've gotten used to dancing with men. They can be fun. I still don't find them physically attractive or romantically interesting, but I noticed with some guys that there is something I feel, something connects, something deeper than outward appearances, when I'm being held next to them. I'm not even sure how to describe it other than security—physical, emotional, mental, financial, spiritual. Sometimes there's just something about them that says I'd be safe in all ways. Maybe it's a feeling opposite of creepy? Maybe I need to read more romance novels? But it's a feeling that I'd want to get lost in that I can't have.

I also found that men are really not all that great at small talk and getting to know each other. And I found I'm a bit of a flirt. OK, I'm actually a big flirt. Who knew?

Some would ask questions like, "Are you divorced?" Yes. Men want to know because if you are widowed they will conclude that you won't be interested in being sealed to them in the temple. There are a lot of men who feel that they must be sealed to someone when they die, otherwise they won't make it into the Celestial Kingdom. So if they've never been married or their ex had the sealing canceled, they are worried and desperately seeking a sealable spouse.

They'd also ask where you live, and how many kids. They rarely ask if you work. I guess they don't think it's very important. One time at dinner, a man made himself in charge and went around the table having everyone introduce themselves. Of the men he would ask where they worked, and of the women he would ask how many kids you had. How sexist. Those questions are just as valid and worthy for both genders. But it showed what he felt was most important about each.

Having conversations about my children is always fun. Inevitably a man will sit next to me and begin asking questions, "Are you divorced?"

"Yes."

"Do you have kids?"

"Yes, I have seven. Six girls and a boy."

"How old are they?"

"They are 13 to 27 years old."

"How many live with you?"

"None. They live next door with my ex."

With a bit of growing curiosity, "Their father lives next door?"

"No, their mother."

The look on their face at that moment is priceless. At that point the questions really begin. One man, a lawyer, spent twenty minutes trying to figure out how two women had seven children without adopting, IVF, surrogacy, sperm donation, or prior marriages. All of which I would obviously deny. He somehow thought if he asked the same question again or differently he'd get a different answer. Nope. They all eventually run out of ideas of how me and Valeria could have children except for the oldest and most obvious way.

"And they are your kids?"

"Yes."

"Are you sure?"

"Oh, definitely."

"How could you have kids with a woman?"

"In the usual way."

About then I make an excuse and leave them wondering. I'm so mysterious, and a tease.

On the occasions I was asked if I worked and what did I do, I found there were two potential answers with very different results. I could proudly say, "I'm a principal software engineer/architect at ENCOM." Or I could mumble something simple like, "I work at ENCOM." They would then assume I was a secretary or worked in the call center. The difference was that if I said the latter, I would get asked to dance again. And if I said the former, I'd get some comment about how I was so smart, and I'd never see them again. I found that men were intimidated by women who are smarter and potentially making more money than them.

What's wrong with smarter women? The woman I married was taking Math 500 classes in partial differential calculus as an electrical engineering major. She was way beyond my math skills. But she tells how all the guys in her engineering classes were dating blond girls as dumb as a box of rocks. I don't understand that. Why wouldn't you want to marry an intelligent woman?

Except there was one guy who was an engineer working at Hill Field on their fighter planes. He found my engineering background to be a positive. He danced with me more. It got awkward when he wanted to ask me on a date and started following me to my car. I finally told him I'd see him at the next dance. I didn't. Another guy persistently asked me to go on a date each week, I finally told him I was seeing someone. "Is he here? I don't want him to hit me!" Well, actually, Harmony was there and dancing with a guy who was telling her "See that woman over there? She's a dude!", but he didn't need to know that. I think he was safe from her.

It's interesting being a woman at a dance. I've done the thing of sitting or standing along the wall and waited for a man to ask me to dance. You're probably shocked. Yes, they actually do. I figure they are nearly blind at our age, or the dance hall is darker than it should be, or both. But it's interesting to watch the men walk around the perimeter looking all of us over and then choosing someone else to dance with. They're like sharks seeking prey. It's literally a meat market. And then you stand there and think, *What was wrong with me? Is it my hair? My outfit? Do I really need to be blonde with big boobs?* Don't answer that. I've found that for the swing dancers they really like a woman with a skirt that will twirl.

But for me, I think my problem is mostly that I'm tall. At one dance a man came up to me during a slow song and asked where everybody was?

"Who?"

He rattled off a bunch of names of my friends. I told him why they each weren't there,

"But I'm here."

"Yes, you are."

Waiting… "You could ask me to dance."

"Oh, I don't dance with tall women. My ex-wife was 5 foot 9."

"Well, Lynette is 5' 10."

"Oh." A man after a fireside came up and introduced himself and told me he was sorry he hadn't talked to me earlier, but he was intimidated by my height, and then he turned and walked away. What? Thank you for telling me that. Harmony told me that she didn't know why short men didn't want to dance with me when my boobs would be right in their face. They wouldn't even need to look down. Who understands men?

Yeah, there's a reason why there are groups of girls dancing together. They are just tired of waiting for men to ask them to dance, or just tired of all the drama and being sexually assaulted. A girl friend told me she came to a dance in Utah County, danced with two men, and was groped by both of them. So she went home and hasn't come back.

In three years, I've never been groped. Which leaves me thankful, but also wondering—is my body really that bad? But I do have to think of my safety. OK, it is Utah, and these are Mormons, what are they going to do?

Well, I danced a couple times with this guy. He was sharp and well spoken. He was on the singles committee. He later told me that he felt something so slightly off dancing with me, and if he'd figured it out at the time, he would have punched me. Woah! We're friends now. He doesn't ask me to dance anymore, but I had to start thinking of trans panic. Trans panic is a common defense used by men when they assault or murder a trans woman after finding out "she is a dude." There are laws against this defense in most states. But men still find it valid in these cases that they can just go crazy, violence is acceptable, and they shouldn't be punished for it. They simply couldn't help themselves.

So that became part of my calculus in my dancing. I was dancing with a guy having a great time, but he was from Montana and had me by about five inches and a couple stone. He probably could punch and knockout a cow. Well, after three or four songs, I could tell he was hoping for a slow song, and I just thought it might be better to end this now and I begged off to go to the bathroom. Bathrooms are a great excuse. I was dancing with another guy, and he seemed alright. And then he started telling me how he was a black belt and he used to work out with all these movie stars. Oh, how many ways could this end badly for me if he comes to the wrong conclusion. He probably doesn't hit like a girl. Time for a bathroom trip. He told me he'd wait for me. Great. I sat in the bathroom for a long time. When I came out, he'd luckily moved on.

So my first night at Mt. Timp went fairly well, and there was a big singles dance the next Monday up American Fork canyon at Mutual Dell for Labor Day 2019. Huh. What could go wrong? I didn't know anyone, and you had to carpool up the canyon. Great. How do I leave if I really need to?

Well, I parked and made it up the canyon. The people in the car all knew each other and didn't say more to me than to ask my name. I paid my money and got a name tag. And then this debonair man wearing a fancy, official name badge says to me, "Are you new?"

"Yes, I guess I am."

"Then save me the first dance." Wow. Not sure what to think about that. I'd play it by ear.

I explored the campground to kill time till dinner. Dinner was a bust. The people around me were even less interested in who I was than the people in the car. Finally, they cleared the tables and made a dance area for the live band. And sure enough, for one of the first songs there was Dennis. His arm was outstretched inviting me to dance with him. So I took his hand, and he led me out onto the dance floor. He was about my height, bald, and very overweight, and he pulled me tight against his belly. I was uncomfortable.

He said to me, "I'm not like the other men here."

"Really?"

"I'm ready for commitment. I want to get married."

"Oh, well that's good. What kind of girl are you looking for?"

"Oh, it doesn't matter what she looks like, as long as we're mutual friends."

"Good thing we're at Mutual Dell then." He looked at me quizzically. I guess the reference went by him. I have a weird sense of humor.

He continued, "But there are two requirements."

"What are these two requirements?" I was curious.

"Well, the first is that she must be a natural born woman." A sudden weird feeling erupted in my stomach. Why is he telling me this? Does he know? Does he suspect? If so, where is this going, and why would he be dancing with me if he did? Am I in danger?

It was about then that my ears told me that he'd finished the second requirement, which I didn't listen to because I was internally panicking. It was now my turn to say something. What do I say? I don't even know the second requirement. Uh... In a split second my brain came up with what I thought a reasonable response, "Has this been a problem for you?"

Now I've since learned by sharing this episode with my girl friends that the proper response for this insult would have been to perform one or more of the following actions: slap his face, stomp his foot, knee his groin, or simply walk away. Yeah, none of those had occurred to me. Lucky for him.

He looked at me with this odd expression and said, "That was meant to be a joke."

"Oh, right." And I gave my best fake girl laugh. Very useful in conversations with men who think they're funny. He then proceeded to explain to me how later in the night that it was going to get very romantic. He'd brought lanterns to put out in the forest when it got darker.

"Oh, won't that be interesting." And not a chance in this life. We danced a couple songs and again later that evening. There was thankfully no romance.

But I realized that spending my time dancing with men was at times fun. It also gave me validation as a woman that I wasn't completely hideous. It was good to know I was attractive on some level. But it was doing absolutely nothing for my dating life and getting married. I needed to do something different. So I looked around for any potential ladies to meet. And in the back on the far side was a woman standing alone. She stood right out to me. She seemed like an opportunity.

I walked around the dance floor and stood next to her. We introduced ourselves. Her name was Melody. Usual stuff about divorce, kids, and work was exchanged. She told me she came to this dance to be a lighthouse. A lighthouse? I didn't understand. Then she said to me, "You see that man up there leaning against the pole?" Yes, I could see him. "In 10 seconds, he's going to leave and we're going to move up there." That seemed unusually rather precise.

"Why?"

"Because you need to get asked to dance more." Oh. Um. Actually, I was enjoying the conversation till it got weird. But I looked at the man, and back at her, back at the man, and in what might have been exactly 10 seconds he did in fact walk away. Wow! She took my arm and walked me to the pole. We had come from the back of the end zone to the 50-yard line of the dance. And we got asked to dance more. A lot more.

Well, I tried talking to her again, but we almost never were standing by the pole at the same time for long enough. But then the committee woman who had been working the welcome table walked up to Melody and whispered in her ear. Melody got this odd look, and they walked off without saying a thing to me. That was curious. After several minutes, Melody came back alone. Again, with the odd look. "Are you alright?"

"I'm fine. It's you that is in trouble."

"Oh?"

"There's a girl going around the dance saying that you're really not a woman and that you have a web page that says that you're a man who wants to marry a woman. You're a woman, right?"

Oh, right. My dating profile. What were the odds that one of the many, many LDS women who'd looked at my profile in the past couple weeks would be at this very popular dance in Utah County? Apparently much more than zero. Ok, the jig is up. Time to come clean, right? I was about to answer her question when she provided her own answer for me. "Well, of course you're a woman! Anyone can tell by looking at you. You don't even have an Adam's apple. So, what if your voice is a little lower than other women? You tell anyone that you got your voice from your father, but you got all your best parts from your mother." Wow! I'll be sure to tell people that. My mom will be sooooo proud.

I didn't have any idea what to say then, so I just went with it. We continued to dance, and my curiosity got to me. "Do you see the woman who was spreading that rumor?" She looked around and didn't see her immediately, but a while later she pointed out a woman. Yup, she looked familiar. And Melody strode over to her and had an animated discussion and walked back. "I told her that that was mean to be spreading lies like that about another woman." Oh great. Now I'm going to go to hell because this woman is spreading the truth. Don't I have to say something? I didn't. But I felt really bad.

The evening came to a close and I carpooled with Melody down the canyon. I tried to think of a way to ask for her phone number, but I came up blank. I figured that I'd see her soon at another activity. Well, I was wrong. I went to Mt Timp every Thursday and every Friday night was a dance somewhere from Farmington to Orem. And I danced with men, and I tried to make friends with the women.

Problem was that someone was sharing my secret with the men. A man would dance with me one week, and maybe the next, and then the next week I didn't exist. Or if I did, I got silent glares. I was off limits. They wouldn't speak to me. Some would shield their eyes to not see me. One man when he saw me walking towards him turned and strode straight through the middle of the dance floor to keep away from me. Word was getting out. The only men who would ask me to dance were the new ones. Luckily there were always new men, too. Men had such fragile egos. They couldn't deal with the thought of having danced with me. It was better forgotten. I ceased to exist even though we'd had a great time getting to know each other.

I have met some great guys and danced with them, especially Tim and Sam. They both know I'm transgender and what that means, but they will still ask me to dance, even a slow dance. They don't care what others think, and they know what it means to me.

But they are also telling the women that they see me talking with. I don't understand. Why would the women need to know? Why do they feel a need to out me to everyone I come in contact with? And I've met some great women like Lynette, Heather, and Wendy who will dance with me, too. Lynette got to lead for her first time. That was exciting.

The funny thing is that no one seems to have told Dennis from Mutual Dell. He continued to dance with me for weeks and even months. Oh, he figured it out fairly quickly that I wasn't interested in a relationship with him, and he spent his attention on other women, till I only got a hello and a piecrust promise to dance with me later. It wasn't till the pandemic that he found out and blocked me. Today, years later, some of these men, even Dennis, will sort of talk to me or at least acknowledge my existence.

But it also was raised up to the committee in charge of the activities. Something had to be done. One evening at Mt Timp I was called into the nursery room to explain myself to two men and a woman. Good thing there was a woman there as chaperone. At least they recognized that of me. They wanted to know who my bishop and stake president were. I had no intention of telling them that. How would that go? Then they asked me questions essentially wanting me to out myself. I wasn't going to do that either even though it was obvious. They wanted to know if I knew what was on the website. I told them of course I knew, I wrote it myself. We got nowhere.

This led to a meeting with the stake president that oversaw the group. Fortunately, my friend Brooke knew him, as he was in their stake when her son came out gay. A meeting was scheduled.

I gave him a quick overview of my life in 10 minutes. He then asked, "I understand that you are attracted to women, so why are you dancing with men?"

"Because they ask me." I know, I'm still shocked. And I've made it a rule to not ask them.

"Isn't that sort of homosexual?"

"We're not doing anything, we're just dancing. So can I dance with women then?"

"NO! That would look homosexual." And here I learned that perception is more important than reality.

"Ok, but you can't have it both ways."

"What do you mean?"

Here I was facing the duality of being both male and female. I was growing frustrated. I was afraid that he would decide that I couldn't dance with anyone.

"You can't say that I can't dance with men because I'm male, but I can't dance with women because I'm female. Don't you have to pick one?"

The easy answer would have been to pick that I was male since that was church policy and what was on my records.

"Maybe I should just ban you from coming."

I didn't expect that answer.

"Well then the haters win."

"What do you mean?"

"People are uncomfortable. The easiest and quickest solution is to ban me so everyone else is fine. But it doesn't teach. They don't learn to understand or to love. What they learn is that their prejudices were valid because I'm the one that's gone. You teach them that their hate is right."

"Well, we don't have to decide this now."

That is one of the frustrating things about being transgender is living in this duality. People will choose whether I'm male or female based upon what satisfies their ends. In the Church that usually means what affords the most restrictions. "You can't go to Relief Society because you're male. And you can't go to Elders Quorum because you're female." Now it affected who I can dance with. I know a couple who had church leaders tell the husband, "You can't go to Relief Society because you're male, and we're thinking of excommunicating your wife because she's in a same sex marriage." What? How does that work? Not female enough to go to Relief Society, but enough to be in a same-sex marriage?

At the Christmas dance, I was asked into a classroom and my new friends told me that the presiding area authority had decided that I was banned from attending any Utah County Single Adult dances. If I was found in the building, I would be asked to leave. These dances were held in Orem and Lehi. But the Mt. Timp dances and the Farmington and Spring Lane dances I could still attend, since they were under other priesthood leaders. No explanation was given.

This was disappointing and hurtful. Sure, I might have understood a policy of not pair dancing with men, or women. But why couldn't I dance alone, or in a line, or in a group? Why couldn't I come and talk to friends? Have refreshments? Why was I banned from the building? That seemed a bit extreme. Would they call the police? I could attend a dinner or a fireside, but not a dance?

I felt like a foolish virgin all over again. In 2017 I was righteous enough to be able to go through the doors of the temple, but I couldn't go through the Relief Society door, in a ward building where supposedly everyone was welcome. I could only stand or sit outside, or preferably just leave. That was really disheartening. It makes you feel different and other-ed. You don't belong. How long could you do that?

The next March I would be finally banned from the Mt. Timp dances after it was reported that I was seen holding hands with a girl. I was stopped in the middle of the dance floor and told that we would have to leave the building. "Why?"

"It's not LDS standards."

"You know that I'm male on Church records and she's female on Church records, so since when is it not LDS standards for a man and woman to hold hands?" I'd seen numerous other examples that night.

"We don't know. We're just telling you what we were told." Sigh. Good thing they didn't see Harmony and me kissing in the car earlier. Their heads would have probably exploded.

Last year I finally had an opportunity to learn why I was banned from the UCSA dances. The area authority thought that because of the unique nature of dances, and because there was the possibility of contact between me and others, that people had a right to know that I was transgender so that they could make an informed decision of whether they wanted to interact with me. Of whether they wanted to talk to me or even be near me.

He said that the only way he could think for this to work was for me to take the microphone and announce to everyone at the dance that I was a trans woman. Since he thought that would be really embarrassing for me, and he was right, he thought it was just better to ban me. Well maybe I'm more creative, but historically lepers had to ring a bell to warn people of their approach. Or maybe I could embroider a scarlet T on the front of my dress. Seriously? Is that how I should be treated? People have to know I'm transgender in order to decide if they want to come near me?

But we're back to the simplest solution: the outright ban. It doesn't teach correct principles; it just supports those who have the lowest compassion and understanding. The Church wants me to marry a woman because they see me as male, but they make it near impossible to have a relationship with a woman because I'm a woman, too.

I would join several LDS Singles Facebook groups through the pandemic, and I met saints all over the world. But I would run into similar situations. What's the point of being in a singles group if only the men are interested in you? I would have to come out as transgender eventually. I would make an introduction post much like everyone else with a picture and a description of who I was. This would bring out the supporters and the haters, if it got posted at all. This was sometimes when my group membership suddenly ended. The admins would decide that I wasn't someone they should have in the group.

For one group, I was told that it was the first time in years that all seven admins had met to decide anything. I lost two to five. One of them was the owner of the group. He hoped that in time he might convince another two admins to let me in, but that hasn't happened yet. Though I heard he found a third. The group was for worthy LDS singles. Since I couldn't have a temple recommend, there was no reason for me to be in the group. The owner sheepishly admitted that he knew of several in the group who weren't even members of the Church.

But one thing I kept hearing over and over was, "Isn't there someplace better where you can be with your kind?" My kind? Who is my kind? Am I some alien? I'm no longer human? But what they were saying is that shouldn't I be with the LGBT people? I'm not welcome in this LDS community. This was interesting because I'd always considered the LDS community to be my people.

They also thought there must be better Facebook groups for my dating. Like there's the group, "Straight LDS women who want to date gay trans women" out there. Is there? I'm sorry, how many people do they think would be in that group besides a lot of trans women? Why would someone even look for that group? It makes no sense. I've given up on Facebook groups as a way to get dates as well.

So in the past three years, I've tried the LDS lesbians, LDS dating apps, LDS online groups, and LDS in-person events. And I've met a lot of nice men and women. I'm not really interested in being friends with the men, which seems to be fine with them. I'm not one of the guys, and I'm not someone they want to date. I've met a lot of women and tried to make friends with them. It's difficult, because their attention is mostly on meeting men. I don't want to have to come out to everyone. Why can't I just be me? I just want to be a woman. I don't want to be the trans woman. Why can't people just recognize who I am, and women be naturally attracted to me? Yeah, let me know if you figure out that puzzle. LOL. It's so frustrating.

Making new friends at this age is next to impossible. They all have kids, grandkids, families, jobs, school, church callings, and friends and best friends. They've got friends that they've known for decades. They have a life, and they don't have time for one more person. And even if they do have a spare moment on occasion, all it takes is some guy to walk in and smile and all her free time is gone. So I don't chase friends. I've learned not to invest more into a friendship than what I'm getting in return. If I reach out a few times and nothing happens, I move on.

I've tried asking women out, even just as friends, not a date, who know I'm transgender, but I usually get some excuse. I think it's the duality. As a male, I'm not someone they are interested in dating, but as a woman, I'm not really someone they want as a girl friend either. They have plenty of girl friends who are, well, girls. So they don't want to lead me on. They don't think it's appropriate. They are just not interested. They're seeing someone. They need to think about it. So many excuses. So much rejection. I just don't even try anymore without some positive sign.

I'm so very grateful for the few women I've met who are able to get past all that and have allowed me some time out of their lives and treat me as someone who matters.

But the story of Melody is not finished. You thought I'd forgotten her, right? Well, she did finally come to a dance at Spring Lane a month later. We chatted a little. We both were busy dancing, but something was different. Before she left, I asked for her phone number so we could go do something, and she gave it to me.

A week or so later we got together for dinner at Chick-fil-a. We talked for hours about our divorce, our families, and our lives, but the T-word never came up. I just didn't feel a need to. We were just two women getting to know each other.

A month later in November 2019, I was at the Mt. Timp FHE. Someone had forgotten to reserve the building for that Thursday evening and some audacious bride booked it for her reception. Oops. So we had moved to another building in Traverse Mountain. As the fireside was about to begin, I got a call from Melody. She wanted to know where I was. I told her. She asked me to give her directions. I told her I could get her the address. She said that Google maps didn't work on her phone and could I please guide her there. Ok, that was strange, so I went out in the hall and gave her directions through the streets of Lehi to the chapel as the fireside was ending. She made it just in time for the dance.

It was an odd night. I'd recently had the meeting with the stake president about my dancing with men, and I'd decided I would try not dancing that evening as a test to find out whether I could do it or not. So I sat in a chair on the sideline the whole night. There were many men who came and asked me to dance, and I declined. Some asked why. I told them I wasn't allowed. But that required the follow-on question of who said so and why was I not allowed. I didn't want to talk about that, since I wasn't really banned. This was just kind of a dress rehearsal for what I expected to eventually happen. It was a miserable night, but Melody was having a great time.

At the end Melody and I walked out together. Her car was far away since she arrived so late. I offered to drive her since it was snowy and cold. As we got in my car, she asked how I was doing. She could tell I was having an off night. "Do you remember what I was accused of up at Mutual Dell?"

"Yes."

"Well, it's actually true."

"I know."

"How do you know? When did you find out?"

"The next morning as I was praying. God told me that you were transgender, and I was to treat you as the woman that you are."

She then shared a bit about her life. She said that every morning she asks what God wants her to do that day. Woah! I've heard this before from Symphony. Ok. She said that she had committed herself to being obedient to God. That she would do whatever He asked. After a while she learned to get inspiration of where she needed to go, who she needed to see, and what she needed to tell them. She was sort of a delivery messenger service for God. She lived in American Fork, but worked in Ogden, so she delivered these messages all along the Wasatch Front.

That is an amazing gift. I'm doing good just to know where to go to church each month. But knowing what to say to some random person somewhere? That's out of my league right now.

She said that other times Heavenly Father just wants her to go somewhere and be a lighthouse and shine her light and help those it attracts. I've heard this before. She said something about being a lighthouse the night at Mutual Dell. "So, were you at Mutual Dell for me?"

"Yes."

"And why are you here tonight?"

"I have a message for you." She shared with me what my Heavenly

Father wanted me to know. We talked for about 3–4 hours, and I got home very late. I was lucky to remember anything of the message, but I've tried to implement what I recalled into my life. I've never seen or heard from Melody again.

But here again, my Heavenly Father has shown his love for me by bringing women into my life, angels. A new way He speaks to me is through these messengers. On a night when I was alone, up a canyon, and the night was probably going to take a turn for the worst as a distraught woman was upset about my presence at the event. He provided a woman to protect me and give me support, someone the committee knew and respected, who would shield me. So amazing.

And she was the first to confirm to me who I was. God told her to treat me as the woman I am. So she did. She treated me like every other woman she knew. That's a pretty big deal. He didn't say to treat me as the woman I was pretending to be.

These women just amaze me. They just inspire me to do better, and be better, so I can be an instrument in God's hands like them. I want to be a willing angel to help others. And maybe my TransMission is like that. Maybe it's a start.

9.

Ring Wild Bells

THIS IS PERHAPS THE HARDEST CHAPTER TO WRITE, BUT also it's the most important. I've been dreading writing it. It's why this project has taken so much longer than it should. And I'm not sure I want to write it. I've been putting it off for a long time because I'd like to believe it hasn't finished. Only time will tell. Know that I'm literally crying over my keyboard. So here it goes.

September 29th will always be known to me as Unicorn Day. It was the day I met Harmony. It was the day after I'd met Elder Christofferson at his brother's fireside. It was the day I first bore my testimony as part of my TransMission. It was a weekend of miracles.

She later told me that she had briefly seen my profile come up in the chat bar for just a second or two before I went offline and then she had spent over an hour trying to find me.

I got a message on an LDS dating site while I was at a Dennis Schleicher fireside that said something like, "Do you mind if I send screenshots of your profile to the trans woman I'm dating?" I saw her picture with her long dark hair, but it was her eyes and her smile that lit the room and my heart. It was her. I knew she was the one.

But, hold on! She's dating a transgender woman? What? I sent her a message back like, "Of course. So you're dating a trans woman? You wouldn't happen to have a likeminded sister, or a friend, or a neighbor at all? Where can I find my own unicorn?"

She responded saying, "Well, I was dating one, but apparently we just broke up." What? Why would some trans girl break up with this woman? I don't know a lot about her yet, but she's obviously gorgeous. Are they so easy to find for her? What is wrong with her? Is she crazy?

"Women! Gah. Who understands them. What are they thinking? The world might be better off without them, right? Oh wait."

"Thank you for making me smile."

"I guess you're probably not looking for a rebound trans woman right now, but maybe we can be friends?"

"Yes, I'm not looking to date another trans woman. But we can be friends."

So I kept it as friends; at least publicly and superficially. In my heart and mind, I was praying and hoping that it would become more. I would send a message every few days till we were eventually texting every day. And then I got up the nerves to call and hear her voice—the sound of an angel. After a month, I was trying to figure out how to see her in-person. She lived in another state. She was living with and taking care of her 80-year-old mother as her health deteriorated.

As Thanksgiving approached, she realized she had to meet me. Great minds. She hatched a plan to fly to Utah. She had a daughter living in student family housing at the University of Utah. She could bunk there if I could give her a ride. Could I? I'd carry her if I had to.

She came that Tuesday and spent the day with her daughter and grandkids. I was freaking out to know she was so close. *Patience,* I had to keep thinking to myself. The next day her daughter left with her family to spend Thanksgiving with her out-of-state father. I arrived after that to pick up Harmony.

To see her in person was a million times more moving than to see her picture. We hugged and she got in my car, and we had a full day. I showed her the Lone Cedar Tree monument, the Gilgal Sculpture Garden, and the Great Salt Lake. We went to Fashion Place Mall and shopped. She picked out clothes for me at Ann Taylor. And we went to a private Bachata lesson.

The instructor asked where we were from. When it was evident we weren't from the same state, she asked how we met. Harmony said, "This is our first date." It was decided I would lead, but holding her hands while we danced sent chills through my whole body.

We then changed clothes and went to dinner at The Roof on top of the Joseph Smith Memorial Building. I'd reserved a table overlooking the Salt Lake Temple. The server asked where us ladies were from and then how we met. Harmony said, "This is our first date." Surprisingly the server congratulated us—on Church property!

Afterwards we went to the production of "Savior of the World" at the Conference Center Theater. It was a magical day.

The next day was Thanksgiving. I picked her up and we went to my house for a dinner feast comprising of turkey sandwiches. I showed her around my house, but her favorite place was in my unfinished attic. There were skylights that we could lean against and watch the sun go down in the West. And we talked about everything. Really, everything short of our banking PIN codes. There were very few details of our lives and past marriages that we didn't share.

The next day we spent time talking more and cuddling on the couch watching movies. At some point I said, "I feel like you might want me to kiss you. Do you?"

"Yes, but not at this time. I don't know where this is going, and I don't want to complicate it." So we waited.

The next day I picked her up and took her to the airport with a rose.

While she was home, she told me how she and her friends had gone to a Christmas light event, and there was an igloo made of pink lights and how it was so romantic inside. Hmmmm.

Well, she decided to come back for Christmas. I took time off work, and we spent 10 days together. She stayed about a mile away at Straight Heather's house and drove my car back and forth. We went Christmas shopping, spent Christmas with my kids, went dancing at Mt. Timp FHE, had New Year's Eve, and spent a lot of time talking and kissing in the igloo. She just had to learn to keep her hands off my chest. Not something she was used to doing in her prior dating experiences with men.

The igloo? Well, before she came back, I emptied my attic of all the boxes. I finished the drywall and painted. Covered the floor in white husky fur, put in a huge red bean bag couch (her favorite color), and hung pink fairy lights and snowflakes. Yes, I'm that kind of girl. I remember things. It was our own romantic pink igloo.

She came again in January, and we went to a Midge Ure concert. But here it had been four months and she had yet to say she loved me. She struggled because she wasn't sure if we were really meant for each other. Maybe this was a wrong road. Maybe she or I needed to go down this road so we could find the right road. And as we sat in the igloo, she told me that she had a premonition that she was to marry someone else.

How could that be? How was this not a right road? We were perfect for each other. Strangely we had both moved to Utah in our youth within months of each other. We both met our spouses the same year; although she got married quicker. And we both confronted our spouses the same year that ended up in our divorces. We both got divorced within a month, and we both started dating the same month a year later. All a coincidence?

We had about the same number of kids, and we shared very many common interests in life, fandom, and music. We had such great chemistry. And importantly we both had strong values and a testimony and love of the Lord. On paper our families were very compatible.

How could it not be right? She told me how many years earlier she was taking an online class at BYU Idaho, and she had to write a paper on a social issue. While the rest of the class was doing immigration and abortion, she was inspired to write a paper only on transgender women. This was very odd, since she didn't know anything about LGBT and had no one in her family who was. A year later she was supposed to write another paper. This time she was inspired to write about Caitlyn Jenner. Again, very odd.

So when she was dating just a few months earlier, she was going out with this guy. On the third date as she was leaving the house to meet him at a restaurant, she got a text message. "Hope you haven't left the house yet. Just wanted to let you know that I'm transgender and I'm waiting at the restaurant as Cassandra. Hope you still come!" Wow. That was a surprise. (Has this happened to you?) Her dates had been with a tall man who was completely bald.

She said a quick prayer of "What do I do?"

And the answer was, "Go ahead. It'll be fine." So she did.

She learned a lot more about the LGBT community and transgender people over the next several weeks. Sometimes she went out with the man and sometimes the woman. But it all ended the night she found my profile. Without those directed experiences over several years, she wouldn't have been in a place, like most straight, conservative LDS women, to have ever considered reaching out to me when she saw my profile. God had prepared her to date me. And, yes, she's straight and only attracted to men, but for some reason she didn't understand she found me beautiful, attractive and even sexy.

I'm sorry, I don't want to make this about her, since this is my story. She should really get to tell her own incredible story, but you kind of need some background for what will happen.

She explained to me one night in the igloo how she had spent years learning how to flow energy and to heal with it. Flowing energy was something she and her kids had a natural talent for doing.

She *healed* people with energy? You're probably thinking the same things I was thinking. Mind blown. This was completely new to me. I didn't know anything about this energy healing. I'd never heard about it. And if I had, I would have categorized it with all the spiritualism, mysticism, and occult things which are taboo and off limits. But apparently this is a big thing in Utah that even has conferences.

I wasn't sure what to do with this disclosure. She was naturally hesitant to share these experiences, because she realizes how it might put some people off and not want to date her further. Really? You don't say. I was wondering myself now about where this relationship was headed. I was in love, and wanted to marry this woman, but was this something that I as an active believing LDS woman could accept in my life? I needed to know more.

I went to the source of truth. I searched the Church website and approved sources and found that women did perform healing for the first 100 years of the Church.

> *Joseph Smith endorsed women's participation in healing. "Respecting the female laying on hands," Joseph said, "it is no sin for any body to do it that has faith." For women, blessing the sick was a natural extension of their work as the primary nurses and caregivers in times of illness. In particular, Latter-day Saint women often anointed and blessed other women in cases of pregnancy and childbirth. ...*
>
> *With respect to women's participation in healing blessings, a 1914 letter from the First Presidency affirmed that "any good sister, full of faith in God and in the efficacy of prayer" may bless the sick. But the Presidency emphasized the priority of priesthood blessings.[34]*

This was part of our LDS history that I had never heard about in all my many callings as a teacher. I'd been taught in priesthood quorum how to consecrate oil and perform blessings, but the only healing I knew of by a woman was Mary Fielding Smith blessing her oxen.

OK, so Harmony, as a good sister and full of faith in God has blessed the sick and they were healed. It was solidly grounded within Church doctrine, but it took a couple days to adjust and wrap my head around it. It further confirmed to me what an amazing woman she was.

But what was this thing about energy flowing?

She told me how she was led to the library to find books on ancient and eastern mysticism. She'd grab a large stack from the shelves and take them to a table. She'd hold them up and ask God if she needed to read it. If He said no, she set it aside. If yes, she'd ask what she needed to read in it. Sometimes the Spirit would say the whole book, or a chapter, or as little as a paragraph, maybe even a sentence. She read only what God needed her to learn.

In some way, I understood this process. Many years earlier, I'd taken an interest in understanding the *Book of Revelation*. It's fascinating with all the symbolism and mystery. Joseph Smith said,

> *The book of Revelation is one of the plainest books God ever caused to be written.*[35]

Really? Challenge accepted. I wanted to understand this plainly-written book.

I spent years reading and re-reading the chapters. I bought books— dozens, even a hundred books—by scholars and theologians from all kinds of religious backgrounds. I scoured the used bookstores around Salt Lake City, buying books from LDS authors. And in practically every single one was a different idea about the meaning of the beasts and the cryptic signs.

But what I learned was what Joseph Smith said about the Apocrypha.

> *1 There are many things contained therein that are true, and it is mostly translated correctly;*
>
> *2 There are many things contained therein that are not true, which are interpolations by the hands of men.*
>
> *4 Therefore, whoso readeth it, let him understand, for the Spirit manifesteth truth;*
>
> *5 And whoso is enlightened by the Spirit shall obtain benefit therefrom;*
>
> *6 And whoso receiveth not by the Spirit, cannot be benefited.*
> *(D&C 91:1-2, 5-6)*

There is truth in it, but these truths are mixed in with misinformation and the philosophies of men. You need the spirit to help you sift through everything and find the truth in order to benefit from it. And there is an ever-present risk that you might be wrong and lay hold upon falsehoods. These falsehoods could begin to undermine a testimony. For most people it isn't worth the effort or risk, because it's not necessary to know for salvation. The truth is out there, amazing truths, but are you willing to risk your exaltation? You have to stay grounded in the gospel and Church.

Donald Parry in his book *Angels* makes a similar observation:

> *I have approached this topic with caution. Many teachings regarding angels must remain tentative and provisional because there is so much we do not know; we must ever remain humble and teachable. Perhaps the Lord's revelation regarding the Apocrypha can apply to teaching about angels. (D&C 91:4-5)*
>
> *Some statements and accounts of angels, even though they may have been published and widely distributed, are not doctrine. ... How should we understand such teachings? If they are not aligned with the teachings of our prophets and apostles, they do not belong in any meaningful discussion of angels.* [36]

If you're curious, I was enlightened on what all the beasts and signs were about. But that's another book I've been procrastinating to write. I know. You're now wishing I'd written that one instead of this snooze-fest, right? That one is the e-ticket ride and worth the price of admission.

So in one book I'd find a thought that rang true about one thing, and in another 800-page book that covered only half of Revelation, I'd find a single idea that would spark thoughts that led to understanding something else. Harmony was doing the same thing with all these books about near eastern and far-east mysticism. Something that I'd largely stayed away from with its mysterious chakras and meditation. But here and there she was sorting through all these philosophies of men with the help of the Spirit to uncover truths for her benefit.

The culmination was that after seven years of this study and practice, a woman terminal with cancer came to her, and after a period of time of energy healing sessions she was completely cured of her cancer. Harmony would say that it's not her doing the healing. That she is simply the conduit for Christ's love to pass through her to the woman, or something like that. And following that miracle, Harmony hasn't done much healing since. That part of her life was largely over.

When talking about this with my mother, she told me that when I was a little kid that she gave me a woman's blessing. She said it was similar to a priesthood blessing, but with slightly different wording. This perked my curiosity. I'd never have suspected my mother of doing something like this. With my follow-up questions, she quickly realized she'd said too much. She refused to explain why she would give me such a blessing and left the room. My father said he knew nothing about this. I'd had several blessings from my father when I'd been sick as a child. I'm at a loss of what could have been happening in my life that my mother would feel this was necessary. Why not involve my father? Later that evening my father called to tell me that she simply meant that she gave a prayer for safe travel like when I went to scout camp. Uh-huh.

In December 2020, long after these events, the church added this statement to the General Handbook in section 38.7.8 Medical and Health Care:

> *Church members are **discouraged** from seeking miraculous or supernatural healing from an individual or group that claims to have special methods for accessing healing power outside of prayer and properly performed priesthood blessings. These practices are often referred to as "**energy healing**." Other names are also used. Such promises for healing are often given in exchange for money.*

That hit a little close to home. I find it interesting that the Church only discourages these practices, while encouraging consultation "with competent medical professionals who are licensed in the areas where they practice." The Church also discourages vasectomies and transgender transition. Discouragement is not a ban. I think we all know good members who have had vasectomies and are transgender, right? It is not forbidden like abortion, or pornography, or practices of the occult. Energy healing does not seem to be considered by the Church to be Satanic, but they do seem to be indicating that it might be quackery.

Read another way, "You are encouraged to seek miraculous or supernatural healing from individuals or groups who access healing power through prayer and properly performed priesthood blessings that are done without charge." Which is essentially the policy given in 1914 by the First Presidency quoted above. While many energy practitioners would not qualify under this policy, Harmony would.

I couldn't imagine Harmony was somehow evil or bad. She told me that maybe all the years of preparation to meet me was just like all the years preparing her to heal the woman. It had a singular divine purpose, but then the purpose would be satisfied, and she would move on. I rather didn't like the sound of that.

But Harmony wasn't done yet with her disclosures. She also shared with me that her family had another gift. She could see dead people. Not in some *Sixth Sense* way from the movie of seeing fully-formed people. She could see the blobs of light, or energy, of those who were good spirits and also those who were bad spirits.

How often had I read the Book of Mormon and how Moroni listed the numerous gifts of the Spirit of which one was:

And again, to another, the beholding of angels and ministering spirits; (Moroni 10:14)

Ever wondered what having that gift was like? Harmony was one of these "anothers." Here we should probably remember Brother Parry's caution about statements and accounts of angels or spirits, but also remain humble and teachable.

Harmony explained they could hide from her view, but she could also tune them out. She told how when she was a child, a grouchy old woman energy blob would sit next to her on the bench while she practiced piano and just point out every tiny mistake she made and wanted to make Harmony feel bad and discourage her. She also learned how to protect herself from the bad spirits.

This explained why Harmony never, ever has misgendered me. Even the best of my friends, even those well-grounded as allies in the LGBT community, occasionally have failed my pronouns. But she always saw me as female, because, well, she could "see" that I was a woman. She told me that all the other trans women she'd met were only pretending to be women; however, I *was* one.

So Harmony was concerned that the bad spirits would go to war against me like they had with her husband and family. She'd learned that having this gift brought unwanted attention from spiritual forces to herself and those she cared about. She was concerned that since I couldn't go to the temple that I wouldn't have the ability to protect myself. The temple was a source of renewal and power for her as it is for others. I'd had spiritual attacks since I was a teenager. They were scary, but I'd so far managed to get through all of them. I noticed that they were greatly reduced after I went through the temple and received my endowments, and also when I had a spouse with me and wasn't alone. But now I was alone.

She was also worried about how her family would react when they found out about me. I've since learned that she would tell her family that she had a boyfriend "Kevin" and friend Katherine that she would visit in Utah. No, Kevin is not my dead name, though Harmony did learn it from my parents, and respectfully never used it.

Well, this was a problem. Actually, two problems.

I didn't know how to solve these two concerns of hers. What did I know about spiritual warfare? Or her kids? I'd never even met them. And I could feel our relationship falling apart and ending. So for Fast Sunday in February 2020, I thought we should make it the focus of our fast and prayers. She agreed.

I cried unto God that if He intended for us to be together, that it wasn't going to happen if He didn't solve both of these concerns. I couldn't do anything about the spiritual warfare, and I couldn't do anything about how her family would react to me. So if He intended for us to be together, and I believed He did, then He had to do something, and do something soon. I needed a mountain moved.

I began the fast Saturday afternoon and by that evening I was under attack. The spirits attacked all that night and into the morning. I got very little sleep. There was an overwhelming, malevolent force telling me that I needed to break up with Harmony and I needed to forget all about her. And each time I would think that maybe I should never see her again, they retreated and I had some peace. But then I didn't want to leave her. I loved her. I rejected their will, and they would try to break me again for my disobedience.

For Sunday I went to a ward with my friend Straight Heather as part of my TransMission to bear my testimony. When I stood up and went to the pulpit the attacks ended abruptly. A couple hours later, Harmony called me, "What did you fast and pray for?!?!" So, I told her. I got the sense that she had prayed for something different. She never told me what that was.

She said that a couple hours earlier that God told her that she didn't have to ever worry about the people she cared for being spiritually attacked again because of her. Wow! She said that if anyone could have a mountain moved, it would be me. God came through and removed one concern for me. Didn't that mean something? Like He did want us to be together? If we weren't going to be together, if we were just going to break up, why would He do this?

But things still felt tenuous. So I jumped on a plane and flew to see her at her home. We spent several days together. She took me to all the local tourist sites, and I got to meet her mother. Her mother had dementia, or she might have wondered why we spent so much time in her daughter's room. (We were always good Mormon girls.) But before I left, she finally said, "I love you."

Well, the emojis in our texts raised to a new level of romance. (Don't be gross.) And we planned for how she was coming in March for the

North Star Conference. I would be speaking in a session. She felt that Heavenly Father wanted her to come. We also had more serious talks about marriage. It was something we wanted to do, but we couldn't until the situation with her mother was resolved and she could move to Utah. And that wasn't happening for many, many months or perhaps even longer. We might not get married for months, or even a year. There was time. I always thought there was time.

For Valentine's Day we were long distance. I sent her a huge bouquet of red roses. Deep red conveniently being her favorite color. Her ex-husband never celebrated Valentine's Day. This was a new thing for her. And I spent the day recovering from surgery. I had an orchiectomy, or for those who didn't go to med school, I had my testicles removed. Surgically castrated. It was an extremely ironic thing to do for the holiday. I thought it was funny.

My urologist had told me that I needed to get off my antiandrogens. They weren't intended to be used for years and could cause liver or kidney failure. Yay! Glad to get that good news. For cis men they usually stopped because they died from prostate cancer, for trans women they usually medically transitioned. I was doing neither.

I'd gone to my bishop years earlier to get permission. I didn't expect to get it, but it was worth a shot. Surprisingly, he agreed with my urologist. He didn't see it as an elective transsexual operation, but a required surgery to keep me alive. I told him my wife would claim it was and try to get me excommunicated. He told me not to worry about her. And, she did try.

I remember going into the surgery wondering if this was a good thing. I'd been suffering testicular pain for years, nearly a decade, with no relief. And I wanted the testosterone gone and to not need anti-androgens. Two birds.

As I awakened, I expected to be overwhelmed by a huge sense of "Oops." You know that guilty feeling that the Spirit gives you when you've totally screwed up, and then I'd know I was toast. I mean if this wasn't completely and totally wrong, what is? But nope; I felt nothing of the sort. My conscience was completely clean. That's good, because it'd be really hard to repent from. Not sure how I'd do restitution. I have to say that it's honestly one of the best things I've done. Having the testosterone factory gone and my skinny jeans fitting right has been amazing. I highly recommend it for all my male friends. LOL

Harmony came out for the North Star conference in March, and we went to Mt. Timp FHE. We held hands and I didn't care who saw because she was my girlfriend, we were in love, and we were going to get married. Well, apparently peopled cared and we were thrown out, and I was banned from any future dancing. My talk went great at the conference. She got to meet everyone, and we had a long discussion that night about what she heard from spouses. There were no concerns when we finished.

She flew home on Sunday. It was her Mother's birthday. At the house were two of her sisters and her brother. They all wanted to know why she'd gone to Salt Lake City. "I went to see Kevin and Katherine. And I went to the North Star conference." They wanted to know what that was and then they wanted to know why. Why would she go to an LGBT conference of all things? She then came clean and explained that Kevin and Katherine were the same person, and that she was in love with me. They wanted to know if she was thinking of marrying me. She told them yes.

Well, they freaked out. They didn't think that their sister marrying a trans woman was exactly marrying up. I have a feeling that they would have been happier with the man who was unemployed living in his mother's basement; at least he was a man. She had lost the respect of her mother and siblings. And having respect in her family was a huge deal to her. She was the only one who didn't have a college degree and was divorced. She had fallen in their sight.

It didn't get better. She told two of her daughters whom she thought might react best. One called her every night crying and begging her to dump me. Her other daughter, after consulting with her husband, informed Harmony that as long as we were together, she wasn't allowed in her home, and she wouldn't see her grandchildren ever again. They didn't want my influence on their family. OUCH! The interesting thing to me was, what about her influence? Her views of LGBT didn't come from me. They had come through Heavenly Father. But they were clearly uncomfortable with a transgender person, for whatever reason.

We decided to make it a matter of fasting and prayer for the next Sunday. I told my Heavenly Father that there was just this last concern, and I still couldn't do anything about it. I again needed His help for us to figure out how to work this out with her family and kids. We weren't going to be together if something didn't happen. The inspiration I got was that I should make some videos that her family could watch to learn about me and about being transgender. I started writing some scripts.

The next week we were supposed to have a remote FHE together. She didn't make it. Her kids had called, and she spent the evening with them. No problem. The next night was Tuesday, March 17th. We talked for a couple hours and then she said, "I have something to tell you. We need to break up."

Well, I wasn't expecting that. My heart fell. "God told me Monday that if I didn't break up with you right now, we would end up getting married. And He still had things for me to do. I needed to meet some man and help him, and I can't do that if we are dating."

How can I argue with that? I know of her connection to Heavenly Father and her angels. I totally believed her. I expected nothing less than for her to be obedient, and I supported her 100 percent, even though it meant we were done. But I took comfort in that we were going to get married. It was a done deal according to the Lord, but it took Him intervening to stop us. How cool is that? We talked some more, and we agreed that we would try to stay friends, but she said our safe word was "goodbye." If either of us said that magic phrase it was really over and there was no contact, no calls, and no messages.

The next morning, I woke up to an earthquake. Have you ever been in a house made out of rock? It makes noises that are terrifying as the rocks grind. I sent her a text about the earthquake. She responded that she was glad to hear from me and that we were still talking. She said she had a message for me. The text read something like, "Your guardian angel wants you to know that he did everything possible to stop the breakup. You need to move on and let her go." What? (I do that a lot.)

Having a guardian angel is a concept we have in the Church, but it really isn't concrete. We know there are angels, that is, resurrected beings and spirits of those who are still in a pre-mortal existence and of those who have died. But we don't usually know who they are, and we don't talk to them like we would our friends and family. Harmony does. It's a little disconcerting.

She once told me that she had had a female guardian angel, but she was just too emotional, so she requested having a male guardian angel instead. You can do that? Most of us we have no idea what our guardian angel is doing at any given moment, or their gender.

President Holland spoke of angels in a conference talk *For A Wise Purpose*:

> *One of the things that will become more important in our lives the longer we live is the reality of angels, their work and their ministry. I refer here not alone to the angel Moroni but also to those more personal ministering angels who are with us and around us, empowered to help us and who do exactly that. ...*
>
> ***I believe we need to speak of and believe in and bear testimony of the ministry of angels more than we sometimes do.*** *They constitute one of God's great methods of witnessing through the veil, and no document in all this world teaches that principle so clearly and so powerfully as does the Book of Mormon.* [37]

So my guardian angel was now a reality in my life and helping me. And I had no idea how important in my life my angels would become.

The story I finally learned from Harmony was that after God had instructed her to break up with me that she heard a commotion. She asked her guardian angel what all the noise was. He responded that there was an angel insistent on speaking to her who claimed he was Katherine's guardian angel. She gave permission for my angel to approach. She said my angel's personality was a lot like me, so she allowed him to address her. He told her that she had to marry Katherine as soon as possible, without delay. She explained to him that Heavenly Father had just told her we needed to break up right then. He began to then negotiate and try to bargain with her about marrying me. She was firm in doing what God wanted. (That's my girl!) So he left.

She said that he was now standing with her and had dictated to her the message she just sent to me. Uhhhhh. I was completely unprepared for this. I had been coming to terms that Harmony regularly had angels in her life. I'd not considered the angels in my life. This was not stuff talked about from the pulpit. There was nothing in a Sunday School lesson or even the fabled high priests group to cover this.

I didn't understand. Why wouldn't my guardian angel know what God wanted her to do about the breakup? She explained that our guardian angels only have stewardship over us. They don't receive guidance for others. I never learned what the bargaining was about, or why he thought we needed to marry ASAP. The only thing I could think of was that it was a test for her to prove her resolve to obey the Lord. Otherwise, I don't know. I don't have the ability to talk to him like she does.

We texted every day. But gone were the hearts and the kisses, though there was the occasional hug. The pandemic came down a week later and the world stopped. I continued to work on my scripts for the videos. She shared that she had fasted and prayed that I would be OK when we broke up. Wow. I guess we weren't on the same page. She explained to me about *Quantum Touch* by Richard Gordon and *Emotion Code* by Bradley Nelson. How they were similar in principle to what she practiced, but she had been guided by the Spirit into her own methods. And she even performed her emotion code on me even though we were very far apart. She said it was easy. That everyone was connected, and she could find me simply by following my energy link to her. We were all just energy. Of course, that's how she saw all the spirits.

Aaron Franklin wrote a book *The Spiritual Physics of Light* for BYU. In the Preface he says:

> *I propose that all forms of light have spiritual significance and are influential on every person's soul; hence, a study of light that*

includes both physical and spiritual attributes is warranted.
Whether or not you have been—or have yet to become—inundated
with the same depth of wonder regarding light as I have, I hope
this book will provide an opportunity for you to see this power in
an entirely new...light. [38]

Light was a form of energy. I was a mechanical engineering major in
college and had taken a lot of physics courses. The implications of the
relationship of energy, matter, and light in a spiritual sense could probably
fill volumes. From what Harmony had shared had me thinking in all kinds
of interesting directions with scriptures from the *Doctrine and Covenants.*

Harmony said that there were always these women angels watching
over me when she did her coding. She explained how emotion coding
released bad built-up energy from experiences in our life. She had spent
hours each morning after the divorce coding herself to get rid of all the
bad energy. It was why she was so happy. Well, after an hour of coding,
she would be exhausted, and honestly, I didn't feel any different. I couldn't
tell that she was doing anything. But we would have rid maybe a half
dozen bad experiences from my life, and we were dealing with events from
high school. When do we get to the bad energy from my divorce? Or the
breakup? Painful events that were more relevant in my life? This seemed
grossly inefficient. Wasn't it possible to release more than one experience
at a time? She said no there wasn't and that the best way was through the
Atonement. The Atonement of Jesus Christ can do more for us. Huh. Not
an answer I was expecting in this context.

I was still trying to understand the breakup. In my morning scripture
reading I came to the chapter about the people of Alma. Heavenly Father
had decided to test them, so He brought them into bondage to find out
if they would be obedient and have faith.

21 Nevertheless the Lord seeth fit to chasten his people; yea, he
trieth their patience and their faith.

22 Nevertheless—whosoever putteth his trust in him the same shall be lifted up at the last day. Yea, and thus it was with this people.

23 For behold, I will show unto you that they were brought into bondage, and none could deliver them but the Lord their God, yea, even the God of Abraham and Isaac and of Jacob.

24 And it came to pass that he did deliver them, and he did show forth his mighty power unto them, and great were their rejoicings. (Mosiah 23:21-24)

Then when He removed the bondage they would know that only God could have done it, and their testimony would be strengthened. Something about that resonated with me. God had put me into bondage. One day this bondage would end, and if I had faith Harmony and I would be together again. OK. It's a plan. I will wait for the bondage to end and we will rejoice.

A couple weeks later, I went out into the pandemic and bought her a birthday present. When I got off the freeway and checked my messages at the light, there was just one. "Goodbye." Wow. Apparently, we had unbroken up the breakup and had in a way gotten back together because of our platonic messages. She hadn't let me go either, and she needed to if she was going to do what God needed her to do. I wasn't expecting this, or so soon, but I abided by her wish, and sent her a short note in reply. I'd have loved to have known that we'd gotten back together, right?

So, what do I do now? Well, I finished the scripts and made the videos and put them on my Facebook page. I know she watched them because only she could see them, and the view count went to one. I hoped she would share them with her family. She didn't.

This period of time was hard. Very hard. And something very special happened that April, but that is a story I'm going to come back to at the end. Remember that.

It was the pandemic. Everything was shutdown, even church. I received an email from the ward saying, "With the receipt of this email you are authorized to administer the sacrament in your home. Please wear a white shirt and tie." Huh. See this is why the Church should move trans women to the Relief Society list. Nobody had told me what I could or could not do with the brand new Church policy on transgender members that came out just a couple months earlier. So I administered the sacrament to myself every Sunday. I would put on a white shirt, a floral tie, and a skirt to match. I'd sing a hymn, read a conference talk, and bless the sacrament. I didn't sense any problems.

What I was sensing was the spirits around me. Since the breakup, I was more attune to things I couldn't see. I went to the graveyard after Memorial Day to put flowers on the graves of my grandmother and great-grandmother. I got out of my car, and I could feel all the dead. Thousands and thousands of them. And when I got to my family graves I could specifically feel them there, too.

I became more aware of my personal angels that watched over me. I had at least my guardian angel, and my mother's mother, and a granddaughter. I wasn't ever as good as Harmony, but I learned some rudimentary communication. I know through which of my children my granddaughter will be born.

One evening in May, I could sense my angels really wanted to tell me something. My granddaughter wanted to talk to me about the bondage and Harmony. I learned that the bondage would end before the end of the year, but it would last longer than six months, and I would see her again. Even get married. Great, I just have to make it to the end of the year.

Over the summer, I did all the Zoom and Facebook groups as everyone else, I suppose. I sheltered in place. It was great to work from home. I read my scriptures religiously, and said my prayers, and had such a great spirit in my home. I hardly ever watched a movie or television. And I listened continuously to Mercy River, Calee Reed, and Cactus Jack. I did some emotion coding on myself and tried to flow energy. I felt the Spirit continually.

I also started remodeling my house. I was told that I needed to remodel my house for the one who would come, the one I would marry. I was really hoping the one would be Harmony. So I demoed two small bedrooms to make a large master bedroom, the bathroom, and part of the living room, and began working to put them back together, upgrading the HVAC, electrical, and plumbing.

The remodel became a continuing exercise in faith and following inspiration. I got schooled by my Heavenly Father. I did so many things I'd never done before and it put me out of my comfort zone. It was near impossible to find contractors during the pandemic. My remodel job wasn't large enough, and everybody on the planet was remodeling. I was able to do a lot of the work myself, but one thing I wanted was to upgrade the 100-year-old drafty, non-standard windows in the new master bedroom. That was beyond my skills. I couldn't make an energy efficient vinyl window.

I called everyone that sold windows and got bids. They were all far more than I had in my budget. Then one morning coming home from running, I passed a guy installing windows at the old firehouse. *Go talk to him.*

What? I'm supposed to talk to that guy? I'll just get the name off his truck. Oh, there's no company name on the truck. Oh well. And I kept driving home. *Go talk to him.* So I turned around and drove back. He was still working. But I don't want to! I'm hot and sweaty and just wearing a sports bra and shorts, and I drove on by again. *Go talk to him.* Urg. I turned around and drove back. His truck was there but the guy was gone. Now what? So now I'm stalking the guy? I parked and waited. He finally came out, and I walked over and said hi, startling him. He didn't drop the window. Long story short, they came that day and measured my windows, gave me a bid for half the price of anyone else, and the windows arrived and were installed just in time. One of many miracles related to the remodel.

This project filled my time till it was Unicorn Day.

She had said goodbye, and we did try to abide by that. However, I did send her a video message on Facebook for her birthday. She didn't reply, but I know she watched it. And for my birthday, she left a GIF in the comments. But now it was Unicorn Day, our first anniversary, if we were together. Weren't we? There was just this bondage thing that was supposed to end soon.

I arranged to have a bouquet of flowers delivered to her. Unicorn Day was on Monday. I spent Sunday fasting and praying that the bondage would end and that there would be deliverance. And I received an answer. I was searching through the Gospel Library, and I came across the talk "The Immediate Goodness of God" by Elder Kyle S. McKay about being in bondage:

> *The immediate goodness of God comes to all who call upon Him with real intent and full purpose of heart. This includes those who cry out in earnest desperation, when deliverance seems so distant and suffering seems prolonged, even intensified.*
>
> *God also gives immediate hope for eventual deliverance. No matter what, no matter where, in Christ and through Christ there is always hope smiling brightly before us. Immediately before us.*
>
> *Moreover, He has promised, "My **kindness** shall not depart from thee."*[39]

That last part was a quote from Isaiah:

> *For the mountains shall depart, and the hills be removed; but my kindness shall not depart from thee, neither shall the covenant of my peace be removed, saith the Lord that hath mercy on thee. (Isaiah 54:10)*

That really struck me like a 16-ton weight, because Harmony and I did have pet names for each other. I was her Sweetness, and she was my Kindness. Every night as we signed off, I would text "sdK" for "Sweet dreams, Kindness." God would move mountains, but Kindness would never depart. Deliverance was immediately before me.

The next day I was calm and had peace. I didn't know what was going to happen or not happen, but I was fine if nothing happened. Late in the afternoon, I got a text from Harmony. She briefly thanked me for the flowers. There were some awkward messages and I could tell the conversation was dying and about to end. So I fought back and we texted for a couple hours, and then switched to a phone call for a couple hours, and then we switched to FaceTime for about 7 hours. We didn't stop till about 4am and we caught up on everything. She still thought of me daily. She missed my kisses. She had gone on some dates. She still loved me.

We texted every day after that. Things weren't back to how they'd been. We weren't together, but we were at least friends, and we agreed it was good to be talking again. And then her son announced that they were going to be blessing their new baby in Utah County in a couple weeks. The whole family was going. She was coming to Utah at the end of October. The bondage would end just as foretold, longer than 6 months, but before the end of the year. I worked to have a house that was somewhat accommodating. It wouldn't be finished, but it would be livable.

She would come and spend a few days with her son and family, and then a few days with her daughter and her family, and then she'd spend some time with me. She'd arranged to stay in a hotel in Salt Lake City. I wasn't supposed to see her till Sunday, but on Friday she was coming up to see her daughter. She sent me a message asking if I wanted to meet her in Salt Lake. Seriously? Of course I did. My new bedroom windows had just been installed earlier that day, a miracle, along with new floor joists and subfloor. There would be something to stand on and wind wouldn't be blowing through the rooms when she came. I threw the tradesman out of my house and raced to meet her train.

She was as beautiful as ever, and that light in her eyes! I couldn't see her smile with the Covid mask. I was supposed to drive her to her daughter's, but those few minutes became an hour, and then a couple more hours, as we went to the mall and had dinner. She held my hand and I put my arms around her, and we basked in the warmth of just being together again. She would borrow my car and spend as much as time as possible at my house in all the commotion with contractors.

And it was there one night that I asked her to marry me, and I gave her a ring. As I've explained, I'd learned that for some blessings you need to ask. So I did. She wasn't sure. She would need to think about it. Nothing had changed with her family. But she wore the ring on another finger. We had a great time. We still had chemistry. And then she went home. A couple days later she told me that she couldn't marry me. She couldn't because of her family. She needed to move on. There was still this man she was supposed to find. She asked what to do with the ring. I told her to keep it.

That was devastating. We didn't talk for a month. And then we didn't talk for another month. And then in the middle of January, we talked again, and we were soon talking every day. She loved me, but it was an asymmetrical love. It wasn't as much as I loved her, but I could be patient. We planned for a grand adventure. She loved to go on trips with no pre-planning. Just get in the car and go and get lost. We did agree to do this at the start of April. She would come for 10 days, and we tentatively thought we'd head toward Nauvoo.

During the past year, I was praying that the bondage would end. I was praying that Harmony and I would get back together, and we would marry, but if not? I remember a conference talk about "But if not…" by Elder Simmons:

> *Our God will see that we receive justice and fairness, but if not. …*
> *He will make sure that we are loved and recognized, but if not. …*
> *We will receive a perfect companion and righteous and obedient*
> *children, but if not, … we will have faith in the Lord Jesus Christ,*
> *knowing that if we do all we can do, we will, in His time and in*
> *His way, be delivered and receive all that He has.*[40]

Sometimes, or even often, Heavenly Father doesn't answer our prayers like we want or might expect. I fully expected for Harmony and me to see each other. My angel had told me we would. Why would she lie? And I had faith that we would get back together and even marry. But what if that wasn't the plan? I wanted to be open to whatever plan God had for me. Maybe Harmony wasn't my future, and I wasn't hers. So I prayed, "But if not, please help me find another woman you've prepared that will love me as she does." And hoped it wouldn't need to come true.

During the pandemic, I really came into my space internally as a woman, as being female. There was now this connection, this place in me that felt the Spirit almost continuously. I'd met another woman, Rhapsody, who also lived out of state, that I was friends with. She had died several times and come back through the veil. She hasn't shared much about these near-death experiences with me, but the result is now that the veil is very thin for her, and she sees things. She always sees me as female. Add this to what Harmony sees, and what Melody was told, and I had another three witnesses confirming who I was, along with all my other experiences.

So, I had to wonder about this. Maybe my future isn't having a female spouse. Maybe Harmony will marry a man, and might I marry a man? Ewwwww. But I added that to my prayers. "But if not another woman, help me find a good LDS man who will love me???" And I really hoped that wouldn't come true either. I'd have to talk to my friends to learn what they find so appealing about men. But for it to come true it would mean that the First Presidency would have to change my gender marker. And I didn't see how that would ever happen. I felt safe.

Then in December while Harmony and I weren't talking, the Spirit said, "It's time." Uh-oh. I knew what that meant. I was supposed to make my petition to the First Presidency. It was time for the Church to recognize me as female. Yikes! I spent December finding out how to even make this petition and then write it. Elder Christofferson told me to put in all the details I thought were needed. I also tried to keep it to a few pages, like 16.

I finally had my petition all written and ready to mail to Church headquarters in early January 2021. I was going to mail it Monday, and I prayed that weekend for confirmation that I was doing the right thing and that I had written what I needed to write. On Sunday I went to church for my TransMission, and I realized when I arrived that I didn't have a face mask, not in my car, or in my purse, or coat. I was screwed. Since I couldn't enter the building without a mask, I went home. Where do I go to church today? I remembered I didn't get to spend any time after bearing my testimony in the previous ward. So maybe I could go back today. It was a plan.

They remembered me in that previous ward. As I was leaving the building this woman was waiting. She told me that she and her husband had been praying for the past two weeks that I would return. Wow! Because they needed to tell me what happened to her husband the night before I bore my testimony. That sounded intriguing. We arranged to have dinner at their house that evening.

After dinner, her husband, who was the elders quorum president, told me that he'd had a dream while he slept. She interjected to say that happened to him often. OK. And in this dream, he decided he wanted to be a woman.

What? I wasn't expecting this.

So in his dream he went and talked to his bishop, and the bishop sent him to the stake president, and he went up the whole chain of area authorities and seventies and apostles till he was finally talking face-to-face with the First Presidency, even President Nelson. They asked why they should grant his request, and he explained to them. But they didn't understand. So they asked more questions, and he answered them, and they didn't understand. They just couldn't understand why he would want to do this. He finally said to them, "It's just a dream."

President Nelson said, "Oh, well, since it's just a dream, then no." And they left the room and the dream ended.

He told me what was evident in the dream from their many questions that the First Presidency had no understanding why he wanted to be a woman. And he felt I needed to know that they won't understand me either. I then explained to him what I'd been doing and what I was praying about. How amazing is that? No coincidences.

I went home and began again. This was clearly something I'm supposed to be doing, but apparently I wasn't addressing the most important question. Why? Well, I had no proof of being intersex other than my father's vague answer to my brother when I was 18. So that wasn't going to work.

But what I had was fruit. Alma talked about planting a seed and nourishing it and determining if it is a good seed or a bad seed, and what kind of fruit do you have? Well, what fruit did I have?

30 But behold, as the seed swelleth, and sprouteth, and beginneth to grow, then you must needs say that the seed is good; for behold it swelleth, and sprouteth, and beginneth to grow. And now, behold, will not this strengthen your faith? Yea, it will strengthen your faith: for ye will say I know that this is a good seed; for behold it sprouteth and beginneth to grow.

31 And now, behold, are ye sure that this is a good seed? I say unto you, Yea; for every seed bringeth forth unto its own likeness.

32 Therefore, if a seed groweth it is good, but if it groweth not, behold it is not good, therefore it is cast away. ...

42 And because of your diligence and your faith and your patience with the word in nourishing it, that it may take root in you, behold, by and by ye shall pluck the fruit thereof, which is most precious, which is sweet above all that is sweet, and which is white above all that is white, yea, and pure above all that is pure; and ye shall feast upon this fruit even until ye are filled, that ye hunger not, neither shall ye thirst. (Alma 32:30-32, 42)

Over the past couple years, I'd gone from a closeted, miserable trans woman with family, friends, and a ward. And now I was a socially transitioned woman with no family, no friends, and no ward, but I was happy. Maybe that was a wash, but what I had that I never had before were all these spiritual experiences that had grown my testimony. I'd had the three witnesses at the conference center. I'd had the tender mercy of Julie for Shannon's wedding, and Alex at Allison's baptism. I'd had some woman at TOFW. I'd had Rhapsody and Melody. And I especially had Harmony and all the things that I had learned from her. I'd had my angels. And I'd had a remarkable experience and many other miracles and tender mercies.

Those kinds of things never happened in all the decades of my other life being "male." Why would God do these things for me now? Why would all these miracles and tender mercies and visitations happen to someone like me, a socially and medically transitioned woman? I was supposedly doing things that are counseled against and getting all kinds of restrictions from the Church. I couldn't go to the temple ever again. Why was the Spirit still in my life? Shouldn't I be in spiritual darkness? Everyone treats me like I've strayed far from the covenant path. If that's true, why are these spiritual experiences happening to me? Satan? Really? Show me the scripture that says that Satan does all these things to strengthen our testimonies in the Church and our Lord and Savior.

> *12 Wherefore, all things which are good cometh of God; and that which is evil cometh of the devil; for the devil is an enemy unto God, and fighteth against him continually, and inviteth and enticeth to sin, and to do that which is evil continually.*
>
> *13 But behold, that which is of God inviteth and enticeth to do good continually; wherefore, every thing which inviteth and enticeth to do good, and to love God, and to serve him, is inspired of God.*
>
> *14 Wherefore, take heed, my beloved brethren, that ye do not judge that which is evil to be of God, or that which is good and of God to be of the devil. (Moroni 7:12-14)*

All these things happened when I started living for who I am: a daughter of God. And I've received witness after witness that that is who I am, as impossible and unlikely as that may seem. I don't know how else to explain it. That is my fruit from my tree.

> *Then, my brethren, ye shall reap the rewards of your faith, and your diligence, and patience, and long-suffering, waiting for the tree to bring forth fruit unto you. (Moroni 7:43)*

I mailed off the petition at the start of February and waited for a response. A week passed, and another, and then February ended. I looked up online how long it takes the First Presidency to handle petitions for marriage approvals, sealing cancelation, and mission calls. It's usually about 2 weeks or less. So how long does it take to reject a petition for gender marker change? Maybe they were still reading it. I should have kept it shorter. I was praying every day that the First Presidency would be inspired, have understanding, and grant my petition. That may seem odd, but I didn't know why else God would want me to make this petition. They had to grant it. But I realized that in doing so my life would change. I would be able to go to the temple again, but I wouldn't be able to have a romantic relationship with Harmony or marry her. But I would have validation for everything I'd said in my life about who I really was to show my family. Wasn't that worth not marrying Harmony? She could still be my maid of honor, right?

Well, it got to the end of March. Harmony was coming the next week, and I got a message from my stake president. He and the area authority wanted to meet the very next week, right in the middle of our Nauvoo trip, right when Harmony was in town. There are no coincidences.

It was so good to see Harmony again. It had been almost 6 months since she was last in my arms. She hadn't been dating. She had no desires to date anyone. She stayed at my house in the guest bed. The new master bedroom was now dry-walled and painted. She loved what I'd done with the house and the other future changes. I really wanted her to feel like it was her house, too. You want to talk about the one who would come; well, she's the only one so far who has come. There's never been anyone else.

We lounged together Saturday and Sunday and watched General Conference. And we went out dancing at a non-church dance. She didn't want to cause anyone to be uncomfortable, so we didn't slow dance. But it should have been pretty obvious that we were only dancing with each other. And, yes, we still had fabulous chemistry. She still loved me, but it was still asymmetrical. And she was still wearing the engagement ring.

So, Wednesday night came, and we met with my stake president and area authority. It was good to have her there. They were a bit surprised to see her and wanted to know how we knew each other. I told them about that. We talked for about three hours. I probably did most of the talking. I wanted them to understand, because it was really evident early on that they didn't understand. I couldn't even tell that they had read my petition.

In short, while it wasn't explicitly stated, the inference was that the First Presidency had rejected my petition. They were supposed to refer me to the policy in the handbook. I also learned that they had received the reply from the First Presidency after one week. Did a member of the First Presidency even read my petition? Or did it get rejected by a senior missionary in the mail room? I don't know. So why did it take 2 months to make this appointment? They didn't say. I asked about callings and didn't get any better answer than before. I asked about attending the temple if I presented male like I had before. I was told that wasn't possible, either.

What they were interested in was that since I had such a strong testimony and that I 100% sustained the leaders of the Church, wouldn't I like to detransition? Huh. I wasn't expecting this, but maybe I should have. I started thinking about this. Maybe it had some validity. It's not like I haven't considered this at times. And shouldn't I heed the counsel of church leaders? Shouldn't I abstain from what is discouraged? Didn't I want to go to the temple again?

But the problem I always come to is this: I wouldn't know how to desist even if I wanted to. They probably thought it would be easy to just change my clothes. Like Katherine is a costume. I'd have to change my name and gender on all my legal documents again? And have a double mastectomy? And cut my hair? And take testosterone? And after all that the problem is I still am Katherine, and I'm female. I am a daughter of God and always have been. That can't be changed. I still couldn't ever be the man that they wanted. It'd be a lie. I don't know how to go back to that life. And I'd be a miserable wreck with the returned gender dysphoria raging, if I stayed alive long enough.

I was thinking about how to respond to their question, when I heard, "No. She won't be. That's not who she is." Harmony had given them my answer.

They were shocked. So was I. It clearly wasn't the answer they were expecting. And certainly not from her. Maybe they had more faith in me, or maybe they thought the two of them could double-team me, but obviously they hadn't really read my petition. They didn't understand the fruit in my life. And they certainly didn't expect the girlfriend to want to be in a same gender relationship. Wouldn't she want to be with a man? Wouldn't she want a normal relationship? Wasn't this the push needed to straighten me out? How could she not go along with that? They probably figured that their odds had gone from 2-to-1 to 3-to-1. Nope. Yet again, my Heavenly Father provided me with help and protection from a woman to defend me as a woman. With not much else to say, it was a stalemate; the status quo held, and the meeting soon ended.

Harmony and I had talked many times in the past about the temple. I was effectively banned for life, but I'd told her that I would detransition so we could get sealed in the temple. She meant that much to me. She wasn't sure if she wanted to be sealed again. That was fine. I just wanted to spend the rest of my life with her. I figured people would seal us together after we were dead, and then it'd get figured out in eternity. She knew my heart. She knew my desires. And she knew why I couldn't go to the temple. She knew who I was, and she didn't want me to be someone I wasn't for her. She told me that in her reasoning of who to marry she would never hold it against me that I couldn't go to the temple.

The next day we went on an adventure to Goblin Valley. I hadn't been since I was a babe in my mom's arms; I only knew pictures. Harmony had never been. We got to Green Valley and found all the hotels were booked. It was Spring Break for BYU. But we did get the last room at the last hotel. That evening Harmony flowed energy on me starting at the top of my head down to my feet. When she got to my lower abdomen, this huge spike of energy filled my body and then went away. I didn't say anything till she was done.

"What was that when you got to my stomach area?"

"I don't remember... Oh, right. Your spirit was sad that it didn't have the right genitals, but I told her that it was OK."

Well, I didn't think it was OK. They were the wrong genitals. During the night she woke up from a bad dream; she looked over at me and ran over and we cuddled for a few seconds and then realized where she was and went into the bathroom. When she came back, she said, "Were you looking at your phone earlier?"

"I don't think I was, why?"

"Because when I woke up, I looked over at you and you were bathed in light." When she took pictures of me at Goblin Valley there was this stream of light coming down on me. Sure, it maybe could have been a lens flare. But was it?

We had an amazing 10 days together and she went home. She told me, "You don't need to do anything special for my birthday. My family will be all out of town and my friends are busy, so I'm just going to spend the day by myself." Huh. I wasn't stupid. I immediately booked a flight and got a hotel. I also had flowers delivered.

When I got to her place, there was this huge bouquet of red roses on the kitchen counter. Her family told me they were from Kevin. I teased, "Kevin? You're dating someone? Who is this guy? When do I get to meet him?" We spent most of the time because of Covid at her brother's house by the pool. He and his family were on vacation. We went night hiking with her friends, and we sat outside the temple. I went to church in her home ward and sat on the stand since she was the chorister. It was also Fast Sunday, so I did my TransMission in her ward. But the highlight was when she took me to her special place. It was up on top of a mountain where she could park and listen to the wind and the coyotes, look at the stars, and eat her special snack. (Wheat thins with pepperoni and cheddar cheese.) That was amazing. But while she loved me, and the chemistry was still great, the love was *more* asymmetrical. She said many things that caused me concern. I was losing her.

After I got home, she said, "Would you like me to come out for your birthday next month?" Does she need to ask? Really? Duh. So we made plans for my birthday. She told me she had this dream that she was asleep in my bedroom and my dog Credence wanted to go outside. She knew that I'd had a hard day, so she got up to take Credence out. I didn't ask which bed she was in. I just assumed. LOL. I liked this dream.

About a week before she came, she sent me a message. She said she had

had a dream that night and she needed to tell me about it. OK, another dream. In this dream she was wearing her wedding dress. It was her wedding day, and she was finally going to marry the love of her life, Katherine. She was so happy. People came in and told her it was time and she needed to get going. So she looked around for her shoes and couldn't find them. Someone else came in and told her to hurry. She looked around for her shoes, but she still couldn't find them. She then realized she wasn't going to ever be able to find her shoes, because she wasn't going to be able to marry Katherine. She asked for someone to get me so she could tell me the bad news. Wow!

That dream started out really well, but the ending... She couldn't marry me? She asked if I still wanted her to come out for my birthday. Because after she left, it would be goodbye again. Well, of course. If I was never going to see her again, then I wanted these few days to be with her as much as I could. So she came.

We drove to Logan to get some cheese curd and we walked around the temple. Patrons were unsure what to do with the two women holding hands, but we found a nice bench on the west side to watch the sunset. We drove to the top of the mountain above my house and looked at the stars and had her favorite snack. No coyotes. We went dancing and celebrated my birthday. We went up into the High Uintas and hiked up a mountain. And we went to church.

Her son-in-law had graduated from the University of Utah. So her daughter was moving back home. She wanted to spend some time with them, so I drove her there. There was some hope that maybe her daughter would meet me, and we could talk. Nope. They wanted nothing to do with me. So I sat in a lawn chair in the communal area and read a book for hours while Harmony played with the grandkids in their apartment.

The next day I dropped her off. We hugged, we had a last kiss, and she disappeared around the corner. The last thing she said was, "I'm not saying it." We had agreed that the safe word would not be said. I sent her a text message that night. I didn't get a reply. It was goodbye again. She deleted all her accounts on my streaming services. That's a modern breakup.

Ultimately, she couldn't marry me because of what it would do to her family. She couldn't tear them apart. And really, how could you expect a mother to do that? Plus, she still felt like there was this man out there that God wanted her to find for some reason; a stake president or Seventy or someone. And how could she marry a woman?

It was hard. I still loved her. I went back to my angels and asked if I'd ever see her again. They said yes. I asked when. They said end of next year. I'd have to wait nearly 18 months this time for the bondage to end. Well, I sent her flowers for Unicorn Day. I didn't get any response. I wasn't surprised.

By February, I was going nuts. A month earlier, Harmony's Mutual profile came up in my feed. It was good to see her. I guess she'd decided to start dating again. It was a little hurtful that she'd used pictures that I'd taken of her or that she'd taken for me. Such memories came back of these times. I swiped down. I'd spent these many months relentlessly going to all the LDS singles activities I was allowed to attend. Dinners, firesides, and parties, and I went to some alternative LDS dances. I'd met lots of women, danced with lots of men, and I had some friends. But for all my praying, the bondage hadn't ended, and I still hadn't found any other woman who would date me.

So I decided I was going to go to Mt Timp again. I hadn't been during winter. I thought I'd make a splash. I'd never brought food before, so I ordered six dozen bags of breadsticks from Olive Garden.

I was out driving running some errands getting groceries and things, and while I was driving, I was praying as I've done before. I was crying to God. I let him know of all my frustration, my loneliness, my hurt. What was I supposed to do? So I asked. I asked for a hint. Nothing big, just a hint. Was I supposed to continue waiting for Harmony till the end of the year? Or was I supposed to find someone else? Or was I never ever going to meet someone, and I'd spend my life alone till I died? Just a hint!

I got home in time to let Credence out one final time and got ready quickly to leave for Mt. Timp. I checked my phone and there was a notification from Facebook. It was from Harmony. She had commented on a post I'd made earlier in the week. It was a post that only she could see. I would do that sometimes. We were still Facebook friends, but I didn't know if she still followed me or read anything I posted. I had hoped she was. (She, on the other hand, never posts anything.) I didn't think it was breaking our code.

It was a simple comment. "Yes, that is interesting." After 8 months of complete silence, she broke protocol and sent a message just an hour after I asked God for a hint. So, what do you think I was thinking? No coincidences, right? This was my hint.

I wrote back a quick reply. She didn't respond. I left for Mt. Timp to get my breadsticks and a woman turned left into my driver door, totaling my car. I posted about the accident. A week or so later, Harmony posted a comment about the accident. I made a reply. She didn't respond. This was interesting progress. Months ahead of what I was expecting, but I wasn't going to complain. A week later, there was another post I made just for her. She later commented on it. And I commented. She commented back, and soon we had a long trail of comments over the next few hours.

We got caught up. There wasn't much to tell. Nothing had changed. We still loved each other. We still missed each other. But nothing had changed. The next morning, I sent her a text message suggesting maybe we should use text messages instead of Facebook comments to communicate going forward. She texted back that she was at a conference, and we'd talk that night.

And we did text that night. It was going well, till she said, "I need to tell you something. I have to break up with you. I can't keep doing this. It's just too painful each time. I can't do this to my family. We can talk tonight, but at the end it's over. It's goodbye."

I looked at the clock. It was 10pm, March 17th. It was exactly 2 years to the hour that she broke up with me the first time. Coincidence? We chatted a while longer but there wasn't much to say. The next day I posted on Facebook and didn't realize that the privacy was still set for just Harmony. Oops. As soon as I realized the accident, I tried to fix it, but she had unfriended me. Ouch!

The next month I had a stroke. I climbed off my bed to play with Credence, and I realized that I couldn't sense my left arm. It was like it didn't exist, but I could move it if I watched to see where it went. I had no proprioception.

I didn't know if I was having a stroke or a heart attack, and I didn't much care. It was just so peaceful, and I was ready to go Home. I wanted to go Home. I pray every single day to go Home. I wondered how long I had to live, and I made a quick mental list of the three most important things to do with what remaining time I might have left. Interesting how impending death focuses your priorities. And they were as follows:

1) I got out my laptop and I ordered flowers to be delivered to Harmony for her birthday that was in a couple days.
2) I sent a text message to Rhapsody to let her know why she might not get her daily message.
3) I called my ex-wife to make sure someone came and took care of Credence.

I wasn't even thinking of going to the hospital or calling for medical help. I knew that my company wouldn't do a wellness check for at least three business days, but since I worked remotely it could be longer. I probably wouldn't have visitors for weeks even though my kids lived next door. I didn't want Credence to be stuck with my dead body all that time. My ex-wife sent my daughter Raechel over to take me to the hospital. I guess I had to go now. Six hours later, they still had no idea what happened, but my arm was normal again.

I got no response from Harmony for the flowers or her birthday gift. And I didn't hear from her for my birthday. Today as I'm writing this is actually Unicorn Day 2022, and I didn't send anything, and I haven't heard from her. Why didn't I send anything? Because I'm still learning from her, I think.

Harmony really cared about other people's feelings and didn't want to hurt or offend anyone ever. She wouldn't slow dance with me in public because she didn't want other people to be uncomfortable. I was less worried about that; maybe they needed to be uncomfortable.

But I was thinking how she's said goodbye now a few times, and I respected that to a point of feeling like I had carved out exceptions for these two days of her birthday and Unicorn Day. But really, I probably hadn't.

I was worried that maybe in all this time that she'd moved and who would receive the flowers. So I prayed that I could find out where she was living and I went to her Facebook page for the first time in many months. She only posts a couple times a year, but I found that she'd updated her picture just a couple days earlier sitting in her mother's living room. Prayer answered. She was so beautiful and with a huge smile. I tried to imagine why she had decided to make this profile update and why she was smiling. I'm not sure I liked any of my answers. It was unlikely because of me. But I knew I didn't want to dim that smile.

I've had an order of flowers ready to go for a long time, but I just can't seem to click on purchase. It hasn't felt right; in fact it gets really spiritually uncomfortable, which has just been hard for me.

I remember the first time she flew to see me that I gave her money to cover the cost of the flight. I had a job, and she didn't. It wasn't fair for her to have to pay to come see me. The next time she wouldn't take the money, so I put it in her suitcase. And the next time she wouldn't, so I slipped it into her coat pocket. I thought I was being clever and was doing the exact sort of thing I've seen my parents do many times. It was how I was raised, and maybe there was a little chivalry. But I didn't understand that it wasn't about false modesty on her part, but there was actual hurt from my lack of respect. She didn't want people to think she was taking advantage of me. I don't know who those people would have been, but it was a real concern of hers and I wasn't being mindful. Am I now? Was this about me or her happiness? I decided to let it drop. I didn't want to hurt her. I'm hoping it was the right thing. Always.

So it's getting toward the end of the year. Will the bondage end again like I believe my angels said? Will the hint work out as I thought it would? Or is this the "But if not…"? Was this God not signaling the first option, but removing it from the board? I don't know. And I'm afraid to ask my angels. I don't want my fears to be confirmed. I'm going to keep the faith and find out what she does. It won't be Unicorn Day, but I'll be keeping the hope till New Year's Eve, if necessary.

Waiting for her and trying to find someone else to love looks a lot the same. I'm still alone. In three years, she's been the only one; the only woman who would date me. The only one who truly saw me as female and not some mentally ill man. How will I ever find that again?

I don't have the problem of sorting through many suitors and dating and watching for red flags. Or trying to figure out who I have better chemistry with, or who is better for me. I have faith that God can as easily bring Harmony back into my life again as He has in the past. He just has to tell her. But He can also just as easily bring another woman into my life that He also has prepared. I know He loves me, and I trust him. He's not going to leave me alone. I just have to be patient with His plan.

Why would God bring us together if it wasn't to be together? Why would he prepare her for years to date me? Why were our lives so similar? Why did she, against all her nature, find me beautiful, attractive, and even sexy? Why would God tell her not to worry about me being spiritually attacked? Why did God want her to come to North Star? Why would God end the bondage and have her come when was promised by my angels? Why would God have her come for my meeting with the area authority? Why, with all of that, after months and months of no contact, did she still obviously love me? Why can't we be together? Who will love her more than me? Who? Who will love me as much as her? Will I ever find someone again?

Well, I can tell you why. I know at least one reason why God did all those things.

After the first break up and goodbye, I was understandably devastated. (She says she was too.) I spent a lot of my time in my white room.

What is a white room?

I got the idea from our Stake Patriarch, President William O. Nelson. He had set apart a room, minimally furnished, in his house that was solely for giving patriarchal blessings. So, I'd taken one of the old bedrooms. It was painted white. And I put a white lace bedspread on the futon that I kept in there. It worked as a couch or a bed, but mostly a couch. I put in silver lights with white shades, and I hung pictures of Jesus in the Garden and of the Salt Lake Temple. It was where I kept my scriptures. It was where I had sacrament meeting during the shutdown. It was where I listened to conference talks and good music. It was a place that I kept clean from the world. Since I couldn't go to the temple, it was my Celestial Room. Harmony loved my white room.

I would read scriptures and I would cry unto the Lord. I was in pain, and the feelings of loss and loneliness and hurt did not subside. I couldn't let Harmony go, despite what my guardian angel had said. I was in bondage. Though the bondage would end, I didn't know yet when.

They say time heals all wounds. Mine weren't healing. They weren't fading. I couldn't sleep. I would lay on the futon and listen to music, and I would cry for relief, for an end. And I would lay there till I eventually fell asleep.

After many days, one evening I was hearing this song "How Gentle God's Commands" sung by Paul "Cactus-Jack" Le Mar, and the lyric, "Come cast your burdens on the Lord" really stuck out to me. Can I do that? I would hear from time-to-time people in church talk about how Jesus had suffered not just for our sins, but that he'd experienced everything that has happened to us. He knew what it was like to hurt, to feel lonely, and sad. And he could take that from us.

I was raised that the Atonement was about repentance for sins. And in Seminary they drilled into us how to repent. Something about being a teenager makes those a weekly church lesson. So I knew how to repent, but how does God take these pains from us that are not caused by our sinning?

Alma said faith is like a seed. You have to plant it and nourish it. We use this metaphor all the time, but in the next chapter the people are like, "What does that mean? How do we do that? What do we plant?" And then Alma tells them. Metaphors are great until you actually need to implement them.

So how do I cast my burdens on the Lord? How do I put them at his feet? If Jesus were physically standing in front of me, how would I do that? Do I just say, "Take them"? I hadn't a clue. I started searching the scriptures and conference talks. I searched through Deseret Book for books on the Atonement. I read a lot of great talks and books, but they were all 99.8% about repentance, with some brief mentions of what I wanted, but no details.

In *Worth the Wrestle* by Sheri Dew she spoke of an experience she called "the gift."

> *Some decades ago, I experienced a crushing emotional blow that left me adrift in a sea of hurt and loneliness. I didn't handle myself very well during that painful season. I flailed about emotionally and wallowed in anger, including at the Lord for "letting me down." In the midst of that ordeal, however, I received a priesthood blessing in which I was told that this trial was a "gift." At the time, I couldn't comprehend how that could be true.*
>
> *But I wrestled for understanding and for peace. Neither came quickly. During the process, however, I began to understand for the first time that the Atonement, as Elder Bruce C. Hafen taught, was not just for sinners. Because the Lord took upon Himself our sins, weaknesses, mistakes, and agonies, there is godly power available to help His followers deal with all kinds of pain.*
>
> *That "gift" from many years ago altered the trajectory of my life. For the first time, I understood what Malachi and Nephi meant when they prophesied that the Savior would rise "with healing in his wings" (Malachi 4:2; 2 Nephi 25:13). I appreciated Isaiah's prophecy that He would give those who mourn in Zion "beauty for ashes" and the "oil of joy for mourning" (Isaiah 61:3). I believed that the Savior came "to heal the brokenhearted," the "wounded soul" (Luke 4:18; Jacob 2:8), and that He took upon Himself my pain and would "succor," or run to, me (Alma 7:11-12).*
>
> *Since that time, I have viewed the Atonement as the source of all*

healing. The Savior will heal us from sin, if we repent. He will heal us from weakness, sadness, and loneliness; from hurt, fear, and mistakes; from the emotional and spiritual bruises of attempting to live covenant lives in a spiritually hostile world; from the effects of unfairness, abuse, and the sins of others; from disappointment, a lack of courage, or wavering faith.[41]

Oh, good. I was apparently having my own "gift." I was being taught the same things. But how was she healed? How does our Savior heal us from all these things that He's taken upon himself? What happened, Sheri? What happened? Urg. So frustrating.

And then one night I finally found the answer. Or maybe just my answer. I found an Ensign article about a woman who was feeling like me. She was recently divorced from a horrible husband, and she was hurting. She went to her bishop and asked him how she could get rid of all this hurt. His answer was, "You need to forgive." She was shocked. How could she forgive her scumbag of a husband? He had done terrible things. She couldn't forgive all the things he'd done. The bishop's answer was, "Then forgive what you can." There were a couple things she could forgive, so she did, and her pain lessened. In time she was able to forgive more, and more of the pain went away. It was like eating the proverbial elephant. She had to just keep taking bites till it eventually was all gone. Wow.

OK, so I needed to forgive. As I thought about it, this made sense. There was a connection between forgiveness and forgetting. When we sin against God, we hurt Him. And when He forgives us, He forgets our sins and remembers them no more. So, when someone hurts us, if we forgive them, then God can take that hurt on himself, and we can forget as the pain goes away. This is so cool!

So, I needed to forgive, but who am I forgiving? I wasn't upset with Harmony. She didn't do anything but be obedient to God. (Yay!) So that only left God. Was I mad at Him? I didn't think so. But how do you forgive God? How do you *not* forgive God might be a better question. I didn't know how to do this. What I finally came to think was that I hadn't really come to accept what He had done. Maybe I was still fighting it. I needed to surrender my will even though I was accepting of the bondage.

I'm not sure what I did. I can't point to anything in particular, no breakthrough moment when my will was truly surrendered, but a few days later something happened. I woke up very early in the morning about 4am to voices. I could hear myself saying, "Yes." It wasn't just one yes, but many thousands, and they echoed out in a long endless stream. My whole body was buzzing, arms, legs, from head to toes. It was like some electric current was running through it. I jammed my arms under my pillows and my legs under more blankets. Anything to get the feeling to subside, but it kept going. After a while it began to subside, and I fell back asleep.

When I woke up hours later, I went downstairs for breakfast and realized something. All the pain was gone. The hurt, the loneliness, heartache, pain, sadness—all gone. And it wasn't just from the past few weeks about Harmony. It was from my whole life. I could sense parts of my life disappearing, memories being erased. It was like the Great Nothing of the movie *Never-ending Story.* I was a bit worried by not knowing what I was losing, but then I couldn't remember it. It was gone. I suppose I should have felt joy or happiness of this occurring, but I didn't know how to. It was like the song "Opposition" from *My Turn on Earth.* You can't know the happy if you don't know the sad. I didn't know sad anymore. It was all gone. My soul had been emptied.

It was a really amazing feeling to be empty of all of that, to have that blank slate. Don't get me wrong, I'm not saying I was forgiven of all my sins. This wasn't about repentance. At least I don't think it was. This was just about the Atonement working for taking our pains from others.

As the day progressed, I began to feel other emotions. Life happens. And I thought about what had happened. I remembered from my emotion code sessions with Harmony that after she'd identified a bad emotion and she was releasing it, she would always ask, "May I release it?" and "Is it released?" And the answer from my spirit was "yes." She also said that the Atonement was the only way to release more than one emotion. So had I like had the biggest emotion code session ever? Was I hearing myself say

"Yes" to releasing all these emotions? Harmony had told me that when your body feels electrified, it is healing.

I don't know how the Atonement works, or how God works, or if things work the same for all people. And I don't know how emotion code works, or even if it does work from my own experience. I'm not endorsing it or any energy work. All I know is what happened to me. Maybe it happened that peculiar way for my unique understanding from Harmony. I haven't done any emotion code since. Harmony was right. It's slow and not nearly as effective of a treatment as the Atonement. Maybe it's a good thing if you have hours every morning for years to do it for yourself. But probably the easier thing to do is what we find Jesus telling us in the scriptures, "And I tell you to forgive everyone." If we forgive everyone their trespasses then we won't have these bad emotions for long, and we can be happy. I've seen that happy every day from Harmony.

I've found that there's been a long-term change in me. I don't remember things. I used to remember the slightest details of things for years. I used to be able to hold on to things. Now they fade so quickly, I have to write them down. If I don't, I won't remember them later. I rely on my angels to bring things back to my attention. And the things that happen to me because of others don't matter. I've desperately tried to keep a hold of the memories of Harmony in order to write this book. I'm afraid that by writing them down, my mind can finally let go of them, and I'll forget and have lost her. It feels like I've already lost so much.

Later in the day, I was still overwhelmed by this experience, but I was feeling some happiness. I really wanted to tell Harmony about it, but I couldn't. Might this be an exception to the goodbye protocol? No. I was really struggling. I wanted to tell someone; I was sooooo grateful.

And that's when I began to sense that there was someone sitting next to me on my right. I couldn't see them, but I could definitely feel their strong presence. That feeling grew even stronger. A lot stronger. They took my right hand in theirs and this warm feeling grew in my breast. It eventually came to fill my whole body with joy and peace that is just indescribable. I sat and just absorbed this feeling, never wanting it to end. But after what was probably a minute or so, they let go of my hand and departed, and what I was feeling slowly faded away.

I can't describe to you how much I want to feel that again. How much I want Him to hold my hand again, to next time have Him put his arms around me, to see Him face-to-face. I want that feeling in my life every day.

Sometime later I found in a talk by Elder Holland in October 1996 an explanation of what I'd gone through.

> *With time and perspective we recognize that such problems in life do come for a purpose, if only to allow the one who faces such despair to be convinced that she really does need divine strength beyond herself, that she really does need the offer of **heaven's hand**. . . . Those who have never had a heartache or a weakness or felt lonely or forsaken never have had to cry unto heaven for relief of such personal pain. Surely it is better to find the goodness of God and the grace of Christ, even at the price of despair, than to risk living our lives in a moral or material complacency that has never felt any need for faith or forgiveness, any need for redemption or relief.*[42]

I did a video in February 2019 for North Star called "I know."[43] And I thought I knew then that my Savior lives. I had no idea how much my Heavenly Father loves me and how much more I might now. That I could actually *know*. That He would spend years preparing a woman to date me, a woman so perfect for my life, that we could fall in love, only for Him to then rip her away from me and put me into such despair.

No, I didn't have that testimony then, but I'm glad I have it now. I paid the price of despair. I had to be convinced that I really needed divine strength, and I cried unto heaven for relief. I asked, and I was literally given heaven's hand.

Maybe Harmony was right from the beginning. Maybe her purpose wasn't for us to get married. Maybe it was for this one cause of despair. But I'm so grateful to my Heavenly Father that He loved me enough to do this to me, that I had the rich blessing of having her in my life all those months. I was so blessed. And maybe, just maybe, I'll be worthy to have her back again.

Never stop asking. And always remember.

I'm moving that mountain.

And Harmony, if you're reading this,

sdK always.

10.

———

Postlude

Now you know who I am. So can someone like me even have a testimony? I think you now know the answer. Or you should. Or I just wasted a lot of my time and yours.

Today in Relief Society, the instructor spoke of the Samaritan woman at the well. She had been divorced five times and was living with a man in sin. She was flawed, but Jesus knew that. He knew all about her, but He chose her to be a witness of His divinity, and she testified of Him.

> *39 And many of the Samaritans of that city believed on him for the saying of the woman, which testified, He told me all that ever I did.*
>
> *40 So when the Samaritans were come unto him, they besought him that he would tarry with them: and he abode there two days.*
>
> *41 And many more believed because of his own word;*
>
> *42 And said unto the woman, Now we believe, not because of*

> *thy saying: for we have heard him ourselves, and know that this*
> *is indeed the Christ, the Savior of the world. (John 4:39)*

Like her, I'm also flawed. I'm divorced. I'm transgender. I'm an imperfect woman, marginalized, cast out, banned, and ostracized by society and my church. I'm a horrible, awful person. I'm the least of these. But like the Samaritan woman, my Savior has chosen me to be a witness through many miracles and tender mercies of His divinity. If He will do this for someone like me, what will He do for you?

Have you asked? Have you asked to know He is real? Have you asked to know He loves you? Have you asked to know what you should do? How you can serve Him? Will you now ask?

Will you put off your natural man and try overcoming the world? Are you ready to receive "spiritual strength, personal revelation, increasing faith, and the ministering of angels" [44] like President Nelson said? Like I literally have?

Hear my sayings of what I know to be true. But don't believe because of my saying. Go and hear Him yourself.

Gentle reader, I'm glad we've had this time together, but it's time for me to go. So, I will leave you with my testimony.

I know that Joseph Smith was the prophet of the restoration in these latter-days. And I know that this Church is led by prophets, seers, and revelators today, even President Nelson who I support 100%. I know that Joseph saw the Father and the Son in a grove of trees. I know that he translated the *Book of Mormon*. I love reading from it each morning. I know that he restored the priesthood and its holy ordinances that occur in the temple that seal us together as families for all time and eternity. I know that if we keep these covenants that we make there that we can return to our Father and receive all that He has. That is so amazing. Can you even begin to imagine everything that our Heavenly Father has? What wouldn't you do? What wouldn't you give up in order to receive all He has?

I KNOW that I have a Heavenly Father. And I KNOW that I have a Savior, even Jesus Christ, the Son of God, creator of all things heaven and earth. I know that He atoned for my sins; that He suffered for me. Through the power of His Atonement my sins can be forgiven, and all the pain, loneliness, sorrow, heartache, and hurt we experience in this world can be erased, and we can experience a joy and peace beyond our understanding.

And I leave this testimony with you.

My name is Katherine. I'm a Daughter of God. And I was born transgender. And I say these things in the name of Jesus Christ, Amen.

Appendices

Transgender 101

President Oaks said in January 2015:

> *This question concerns transgender, and I think we need to acknowledge that while we have been acquainted with lesbians and homosexuals for some time, being acquainted with the unique problems of a transgender situation is something we have not had so much experience with, and we have some unfinished business in teaching on that.*[45]

SEVEN YEARS LATER, I THINK WE CAN SAY WE'RE ALL ACQUAINTed with the transgender situation. Perhaps too much. The world has gotten to hear about transgenderism daily in our classrooms, newspapers and magazines, TV shows, movies, and social media. It's in our state houses with laws being passed regarding bathrooms, locker rooms, sports participation, legal name and gender changes, hormones, and block-ers and surgeries. You see the transgender flag flying at houses, being worn as a cape, and even used as an emoji. You may be sick of it, or you may still be questioning what it is really about.

Well, I am not a biologist, nor a Supreme Court nominee. I'm not a medical doctor, a therapist, or a lawyer. I don't speak for the trans com-munity, and it is not uniform. I can only share my personal experience as a trans woman.

"Trans" is a Latin prefix meaning to cross over. "Cis" is another Latin prefix meaning on the same side. So transgender means to cross over to another gender. Cisgender means to stay with the same gender.

And "binary" means that there are only two of something.

AMAB is an acronym for assigned male at birth. AFAB is assigned female at birth. Our bodies were examined when we were born by highly trained nurses and doctors and determined to be male, female, or inter-sex. Usually what this meant was they looked between our pudgy legs and looked for a penis or a vagina. As we all learned from the movie *Kindergarten Cop*, "Boys have a penis and girls have a vagina."

But what if the external genitalia are ambiguous? That is a form of being intersex. Additional tests will be performed by ultrasounds and genetic testing to assign a gender as God intended. Being assigned either male or female is the gender binary.

> So God created man in his own image, in the image of God created he him; male and female created he them. (Genesis 1:27)

However, we also have an innate sense of gender. This is the gender we identify as. Some would say this comes from the genetics found in every cell of our body, or it comes from how our brain was sexualized. We as Latter-day Saints would say our gender comes from our eternal pre-mortal spirits. It is not something that is learned.

Bruce Reimer was a boy who tragically had a botched circumcision soon after birth. With consultation of doctors and parents, it was decided to finish the job and raise Bruce as Brenda. This didn't go very well, because Brenda always knew something was wrong despite what she was told and how she was raised. Brenda was told the secret at age 14, and she transitioned to being David. He would later take his life.

The awareness of this identity can come as early as 2 or 3 years old. Or it may grow as puberty progresses. It rarely comes after the start of puberty.

So, cisgender is a person who identifies as the gender they were assigned at birth. A transgender person is someone who doesn't. A cis woman is a woman who was assigned female at birth and who their whole life identifies as a woman. This is the usual case for some 99.997% of the women in the world. And trans women are women who were assigned male at birth, but as they got older didn't identify as male and crossed over to female.

So, when we talk about transgender, the gender and sexual orientation is after the crossing. A trans girl or trans woman are AMAB. And if a trans woman is attracted to men, she is straight. If she's attracted to women, she is gay, or a lesbian.

Cis women and trans women are both women, but they are obviously not the same.

So, I am AMAB, and I identify as a binary trans woman and I'm gay. Meaning, I believe in only two genders, male and female, and I was assigned male at birth because of my body, but I believe I am female, and I'm attracted to women.

So what is non-binary?

Non-binary (NB) means there are more than two choices of gender—that gender is not limited to just male and female. Non-binary says it is possible to be some mix of male and female, and it is possible to be agender and not be male or female at all.

Non-binary people may identify as 100% male and female. They are equally and fully both genders. Or maybe 10% male and 50% female, meaning they are not very male, but only partially female. And how they identify can be mutable and fluid. Their gender may change over time, daily, and even hourly.

There is a long list of labels used by the enbies (NBs) to describe these conditions. I don't experience being non-binary. So I will let them speak for themselves.

How can you be transgender?

Oh, if I had dollar for every time I read, "If you're confused about your gender, look in your pants. And if you're still confused look at your genes." You'd think it would be that simple; and it is for most people, except for the ones it isn't.

This is a subject that the nerd in me would love to dive deep and go into the weeds, but I won't. Well, not too much. But I will share a few things I've learned about for your consideration.

Bodies are very complicated things. Every new parent when they learn they are expecting pray that their baby is born healthy because there are so many ways they might not. It can be terrifying to consider the seemingly endless list of genetic disorders and defects, as well as physical and mental handicaps, that a baby could be born with. But the good news is that we don't really need to worry about these complications happening, because they are usually quite rare—until they aren't.

I believe that being transgender is one of these complications of mortality.

Our bodies are sexualized through an interaction of hormones and genetics during three principal times in our lives. The first is at about 8 weeks in utero to form our genitalia. A few weeks later our growing brains are sexualized. And then lastly, many years later, when we go through puberty both our body and brains are further sexualized.

Our sexualization is not a single event, but an ongoing process.

Genetics

From grade school biology we learned that our bodies are made up of cells. Each cell has a nucleus with our DNA that is comprised of 46 chromosomes in 23 pairs. The 23rd pair is the sex chromosomes of either XX or XY.

Girls are 46XX and boys are 46XY—unless they aren't.

Each chromosome is made up of genes. There are over 26,000 genes in total. Today, scientists only understand what about 4,000 of these genes do. That means there are still 22,000 genes that we don't know how they affect our development. And genes can have a number of variants. That is how we get people with blue eyes or red hair.

Girls and boys have the same 26,000+ genes, except boys have an additional hundred or so genes on the Y chromosome. So, boys and girls don't have completely different genes. Boys have ALL the girl genes. Boys have genes for having a vagina, uterus, ovaries, menstruating, lactating, and even pregnancy. Girls don't have genes for a penis and semen.

However, a human fetus will by default develop as female if the sexualization process is not altered by these additional boy genes. Boys and girls begin development with the same body parts, they just change. One special gene is called the SRY gene. This stands for the Sex Region of the Y chromosome. It is responsible for the development of external male genitalia. And as its name implies, it is usually found on the Y chromosome. So boys are traditionally identified by having a Y chromosome and the included SRY gene.

Except when they don't.

Sometimes the SRY gene accidentally gets transposed to the X chromosome, and you get 46XX boys. They are boys identified by having a small penis and testicles without semen because they don't have all the necessary boy genes. However, there are cases of 46XX boys that don't have an SRY gene—anywhere. Scientists don't yet have an explanation of how this happens. The secret may lie in the genes we don't know.

And while the SRY gene is very important, it isn't the first or only gene involved in the sexualization process. For instance, if the CBX2 gene on the 17th chromosome is bad, or has a variant, and causes the SRY gene to not work or express itself, you will get 46XY girls.[46] There may be other ways as well that we don't know about.

This is not an exhaustive list of genes that are involved in the sexualization process, or how people may be born with genetic variants and disorders of sexual development, but this is only meant to give you a taste of what can happen. It's all still very new. The whole human genome (DNA) wasn't completely sequenced till March 2022. There is still so much to learn about the role of genes and how our bodies develop, even sexually.

Consider that you don't actually know the genetics of any person. You may guess what some of their genes are by their hair or eye color. You may guess what some are because of whether they appear male or female. And you will be right 99.997% of the time, but there will be times you will be wrong. The presence of a penis or vagina doesn't guarantee the contents of their DNA. It's just the result of a complicated process.

Mosaicism and epigenetics

Our genetics is further complicated by the fact that we don't actually have the same DNA in every cell. This is called mosaicism. DNA replication can go wrong, which is why there is a chromosomal pair with a backup copy of our genes. But, even still, your DNA can vary. That's how we have cancers.

One amusing example is that males lose their Y chromosome as they age. It's called loss of Y (LOY). You might say men are becoming women as they get older.

And another complication is that while individual genes may have variants, external chemicals can bond to genes that can cause them to act like variants. So you could have a good gene, but through epigenetics, that gene may not express itself. And epigenetics is replicated and even inheritable.

Consider how a person might have the right genes, but variants through epigenetics and external influences might affect how we develop sexually.

Chimera and micro-chimera

Like the Greek mythological hybrid monster, the Chimera, made up of a lion, goat, and snake, our bodies can be a hybrid made up of cells from other people. The cells of a fetus can transfer to the mother and be found many decades later in her brain. And the cells of older siblings have been found in their younger siblings.

Also, we are familiar with conjoined twins. When babies are sharing a uterus, it's not only possible for their bodies to grow into each other, but it's also possible for one fetus to completely absorb the whole other fetus. You may contain cells from a fraternal twin that grew independently in your body.

I have read many stories of trans women who were functioning males, who were found later in life to have a working uterus and ovaries. One trans woman had a vaginoplasty, and there were complications. When the doctor went in to see what was causing the bleeding, they found the patient had a uterus.

Another example is Lili Elbe. She is the subject of the Hollywood movie The Danish Girl with Eddie Redmayne. When she was having her surgeries in Germany the doctors found a uterus and ovaries shrunken from her earlier radiation treatments.

I know a man who told me that he had gender dysphoria. He chose not to transition after deciding that he knew the source of his female feelings. He had skin on his body that was not the same as the rest. He believed it was from his twin sister. The spirit of his sister was connected to his body through her skin. He kept a diary of her adventures.

This is similar to stories from those who receive organ transplants. These people have found that they begin having unusual cravings, or can speak with an accent, which are tied to their dead donors. One remarkable story was of a woman who had a heart transplant. Afterwards she had dreams of being murdered. When she told the police about these dreams and drew a sketch, the man was arrested for the murder of her donor.

Whether these female cells or organs were from their own genetics, or a very close relative, we'll never know. But consider how having cells—or even whole organs—from a twin sister, an older sister, or your mother in the body of a boy could influence their sexual development and gender identity. There may be connections to a female spirit that is influencing them. And with so many variations and unknowns, it's impossible to say we understand everything about how a body and spirit work.

Brain sexualization and hormones

Our hormones and genes don't only influence how our bodies develop with our external or internal genitalia, but they also influence how our brain is sexualized. Male and female brains have differences. Scientists have found similarities between gay male brains and straight female brains. Our sexual orientation seems to be something that is wired in our brains before we are born.

But what about our gender identity?

The problem is that transgender is relatively new and hasn't been studied anywhere as long as sexual orientation. Also, the population of transgender people is not nearly as large, and it's difficult to study transgender people before they have undergone hormone treatment. We don't have any definitive way to determine what the hormone levels were during the embryonic stage of a person's life.

It is thought that the ratio of the index finger to ring finger is an indicator, referred to as the 2D:4D ratio. Men typically have index fingers that are shorter than their ring finger, while women's fingers are typically the same length or longer. The thought is this has to do with the amount of testosterone exposure in-utero. But this measurement is debated.

Women between the 1940s and 1970s were prescribed DES, or diethylstilbestrol, to prevent miscarriage and premature delivery. DES is a synthetic estrogen. The effect was to jack up a woman's estrogen level 4000%. While it may have stopped early labor, it was also known for many birth defects. One of the health problems was a higher incidence of transgender women amongst the DES boys. Amongst the DES girls was a greater inclination to be feminine and domestic.

There is growing evidence that the brains of women and trans women are similar in some ways. And that the brains of trans women are different in ways from male brains. Studies[47] show that there are as many as two dozen genes responsible for how testosterone is processed by the brain, and that trans women share many of these gene variants.

A particularly interesting study[48] showed that the areas of the brain that activates when we see ourselves will activate when trans women see an enhanced image of them as more female, and they don't activate when they see an image as more male. This is a confirmation that trans women actually don't see ourselves in the mirror until we transition. But I'm not sure we know why this happens. How do we know what we're supposed to look like?

If the root of being transgender is from having a sexualized brain contrary to the rest of your body because of genetics, then it is an intersex condition that is not identified by ambiguous genitalia. It is identified by the person when they are able to understand and communicate the incongruity. We are only beginning to acquire the knowledge to confirm a self-diagnosis of transgender.

Consider how the many factors of gene variants and hormone exposure might not only influence the development of sexual orientation, but also our gender identity in our brain. Is it literally possible to have a girl brain in a boy body?

What is gender dysphoria?

People who are transgender often have a condition called gender dysphoria. It is described as distress caused by the incongruence between your gender identity and your gender assigned at birth. It is incongruence between brain and body. It is characterized by strong desires to cure this distress by being the other gender, living as the other gender, and having the body of the other gender.

A person with gender dysphoria will have at least two of these six conditions for more than 6 months[49]. I'd say they should have more and for longer:

- A marked incongruence between one's experienced/expressed gender and primary and/or secondary sex characteristics.
- A strong desire to be rid of one's primary and/or secondary sex characteristics because of a marked incongruence with one's experienced/expressed gender.

- A strong desire for the primary and/or secondary sex characteristics of the other gender.
- A strong desire to be of the other gender.
- A strong desire to be treated as the other gender.
- A strong conviction that one has the typical feelings and reactions of the other gender.

Some transgender people don't have gender dysphoria. Some feel only a mild distress, while others have severe debilitating distress. For some, the distress is cured or lessened with social transition and/or various medical transitions.

As I said, I believe that the incongruence is caused by biological factors rooted in our genetics and sexual development of our brains and bodies. It may also include causes from epigenetics, chimera, and mosaicism. And the degree to how severe the distress manifests may depend on the type and severity of these complications. So as there may be many different causes, there may not be any single solution for curing the distress.

What is rapid-onset gender dysphoria (RODG)?

Often today there are kids, most often AFAB girls, who are going through the normal anxiety of puberty, the awkwardness of being a teenager, and have been exposed to transgenderism, that convince themselves that what they are experiencing is instead gender dysphoria. Their friends often come to the same conclusion; and there are therapists and LGBT activists who will affirm these self-diagnoses with very little—if any—skepticism or verification and fast track them for social and medical transition.

They are exposed to transgenderism through social media that promises likes, followers, and attention for taking the journey. They also learn from others what to say and do to manipulate parents, doctors, and therapists into approving their medical transition. Sadly, they eventually figure out after taking irreversible actions like taking hormones or having surgery that their problems didn't go away, and they were never transgender. They eventually desist and have to live with the consequences of their choice.

A study[50] showed that amongst children there was a difference between those children who said they *were* a girl and those who said they wanted to be a girl. In following these children, they found that the majority of the "wants" desisted by puberty and were usually gay. However, the majority of the "were" children didn't desist.

It is possible for people to convince themselves after puberty that they are transgender.

I met someone at the North Star conference who thought they were a girl. He was 32-years old, single, living in his mother's basement, had just quit his job, and spent his time playing video games. I asked him how long he'd had gender dysphoria. "About a year." That sent a lot of red flags. I counseled him to get a good therapist and not do anything stupid.

I met a woman distraught that her 23-year-old son had just come out to her as a woman. He had had gender dysphoria for about a year; again with the red flags. He'd seen a therapist who wasn't knowledgeable, and after 6 months had come out at work and started transitioning. This led to divorce.

Soon after my discussion with his mother, he decided he wasn't a woman. His wife had bought a new girly duvet for their bed, and he liked it. He decided that as a man he shouldn't like something girly. But he wasn't manly like his father or stepfather. So maybe he wasn't really a man?

You can read through the online stories of a growing population of teens and adults who have regrets for their transition. In every case I've read, they weren't really transgender. It was something they came to realize long after puberty started and after exposure to transgender influencers on social media, or they had therapists who were overly affirming.

It's my opinion that if your "gender dysphoria" didn't begin until you were older than 12 or 13 years old, you probably don't have gender dysphoria, and you're not transgender.

Please, find a better therapist and save yourself all the future regrets.

What is transmisogyny?

Transmisogyny is the intersection of transphobia and misogyny. It is a bias against trans women.

Men coming out as women in our society is seen as emasculating. It is losing power, prestige, and privilege. Why would any man in his right mind want to do that? Why would he want to be weak? Whereas we celebrate women who act manly to gain power, prestige, and privilege; it is based in our historical and cultural view of the worth of women. Women were property, so trans women are an easy target for comedy, humiliation, and ridicule.

Other forms of transmisogyny center around authenticity.

A simple example is when someone says, "That a trans woman really isn't a woman, because she is just living as an extreme stereotype." If a trans woman is very feminine by wearing dresses, heels, and makeup, then she's not authentic. She's just copying some idealized view of what it means to be a woman. Even though many women live that way or may want to live that way. My ex-wife was always telling me that real women don't like wearing skirts. I was always hearing what "real women" do and don't do as a way to invalidate my existence.

Then there is the converse example when someone says, "A trans woman really isn't a woman, because she's looks or acts too manly." If a trans woman just wears jeans and a t-shirt, likes motorcycles, sports, guns, or playing video games, or is too assertive, then she's just really a guy. Even though there are many women who like those things, too.

Natal women can be femme, tom-boyish, or somewhere in between and it's no problem. But for trans women it can be a minefield living according to expectations.

Our authenticity is also not dependent upon how well we pass. There's a t-shirt that says, "I survived testosterone poisoning." Most trans women didn't get to skip male puberty, many trans girls won't either. Most won't win any beauty contests, but neither will many women. Comparing the worst of the trans women with the best of the cis women is not fair. There are cis women who will fail to pass as women.

Forcing trans girls to go through male puberty and then making fun of them because they aren't dainty, petite girls with their broad shoulders, square jaws, and facial hair is rather unsympathetic. It's not like we wanted this transformation. And many trans women have had to provide for their families through very physical and labor-intensive jobs.

Many women have had to put off careers and hobbies to have a family. Other women had to put off family for careers or working two, three, or four jobs just to make ends meet. Women have always had to make sacrifices for the needs of their family and spouses. Many trans women also had to make a similar sacrifice in not being able to live their life as they wanted to and did what was necessary for their family.

If you're treating a transwoman different than you would any other woman, femme or tom-boyish, then ask yourself, why? Are you looking for reasons to invalidate her existence? Are you just being catty? I think the opening to the church policy on transgender members sets the right expectation:

> *Transgender individuals face complex challenges. Members and nonmembers who identify as transgender should be treated with sensitivity, kindness, compassion, and an abundance of Christlike love.*

Start with compassion and show an abundance of Christlike love.

What about female safe spaces and sports?

A TERF (Trans Exclusionary Radical Feminist) is a cis woman who is a feminist that believes that trans women are not women, which is considered a radical viewpoint. Trans women are excluded from women because they weren't assigned female at birth. Many years ago I read a quote on a TERF website that has stuck with me: "If you can't respect the rights of women, then you're just a guy in a dress." And it made sense to me. It's a transmisogynistic view of trans women being misogynistic. Can a trans woman be misogynistic?

Maybe it's my LDS upbringing, or maybe my conservative values, or my female nature, but I can't imagine women treating other women the way that many so called trans women do. Of course cis women have rights. But trans women also have rights. How should they be resolved?

The way I look at it is the same as citizenship. Some people are natively born in a country and have rights from birth. They are natural born citizens. And then there are people who are tourists who visit for a while for a day or a week, and there are those people who may find a job and stay longer, and then there are those who are willing to go through a naturalization process and be granted citizenship. But even those who gain citizenship may not have all the rights of a natural born citizen. And if anyone can enter the country and claim natural born rights, then citizenship and the country is meaningless and there is chaos.

I believe that trans women and cis women are both women. But they are not equal or the same. Cis women have rights because they are the natural born citizens of womanhood. Trans women have rights dependent upon on their commitment to reside and their ability to earn the good faith and trust of the citizens.

There was a time when transgender people had to undergo months and years of psychological evaluation and live as women for at least a year before they could medically transition with hormones or surgery. There are some school districts that require trans girls to live as a girl and be on hormones for a year, and then the principal can make a decision based upon his observations and in consultation with the student's religious leader, parents, and therapist about the sincerity of their transition before they are allowed to play sports, or have access to the safe spaces.

There are, and have been, gatekeepers and processes in place to protect transgender people from ill-considered irreversible and life changing decisions, but also to protect women from nefarious men. Instead today, there too many places that allow self-identification, and misconstrue the non-binary and gender non-conforming with transgenderism. That gives the perverts, autogynephiles, and fetishists the social and legal cover to further take advantage of women. Any trans woman who would parade their junk in front of women should be deported and have their green card revoked.

It's easy to look at a trans athlete like Lia Thomas of the University of

Pennsylvania swim team and determine that she shouldn't be competing with the women. And the fact that she believes that she should and has no respect for her other teammates, and doesn't have their respect, says something to me about her genuineness. She is the 'ugly American' being obnoxious and loud, trampling on their culture, and only caring for her own welfare.

And then I look at a Rebekah Bruesehoff who is a 15-year-old trans girl who started transitioning at age 7, has been on puberty blockers, and never been through male puberty who is hanging out with her girl friends and playing girls' field hockey, and I have no problem accepting her. She has the trust and respect from her friends and teammates. How could I ever see her forced to participate on a boys' team or have to use the boys' locker room?

This is not something that will get fixed overnight, but cis women should feel heard and safe, and have confidence that the trans women that are in their spaces and calling themselves women are validated and have demonstrated their authenticity. But also trans women have rights to feel safe in using restrooms and public accommodations without prejudice.

And in case you were wondering, yes, I've been using the women's bathrooms for many years and there's never been a problem. No one has ever stopped me or said anything. Although, I heard long after the fact that at a singles dance a woman thought a man was in the bathroom. It was probably me. Some days if I'm feeling like I'm not passing well, I might get concerned. But it kind of comes down to that you just need to pee, and which bathroom is going to be safer. And frankly, if you look like you belong, and you act like you belong, you don't really get a second look. I think women are sort of used to trans women and have been willing to cut us a little slack. I think women can tell who's genuine and who's being creepy.

And as long as I'm talking bathrooms—no, I've never been in a women's locker room. But that's mostly because I've never needed to be. If I did, I'd make sure I had a friend with me. But I think I can say that I'm not worried about trans girls in a high school locker room. For those thinking that a trans girl is going to parade around exposing her junk, you're just wrong assuming she's thinking like some stereotypical teenage boy. She's not. She's a girl, having gender dysphoria, and massive body conscience issues. I have six daughters, and they all assure me that teen girls never get naked in the locker room, and they don't shower. It's a comparison issue. The last thing a trans girl would want is to be seen as not having the right genitalia. That would be mortifying. Same thing goes for a trans woman.

And you also need to realize that the earlier a trans girl transitions, the more likely she is to be straight. So more than likely, the trans girl in a high school locker room is going to be attracted to boys just like the cis girls. She's not going to be aroused by any naked girls or wanting to have sex with them. If there's anyone in the girl's locker room enjoying whatever nudity, it's more than likely the lesbians. I have great faith in teen girls being able to sense the authenticity and sincerity of a trans girl and beating the crap out of the ones who aren't.

What is church policy and doctrine?

It might surprise you to know that while President Oaks said that transgender was something that the Church didn't have much experience with, the Church was certainly aware of the issue and had made references to it in the past. As early as 1970 at the Fifth Annual Priesthood Genealogical Research Seminar, Elder Harold B. Lee said:

> *The Lord said: "Let us make man in our image, after our likeness; and it was so. And I, God, created man in mine own image, in the image of mine Only Begotten created I him; male and female created I them." (Moses 2:26, 27.)* **Do you need anything else to prove the falsity of any such hellish doctrine as this so-called "transsexuality" doctrine of some wild dreamer? The Lord created male and female, and He didn't have a woman's soul trapped in a man's body, or vice versa.**[51]

I hear those same beliefs echoed all the time from Christians today.

President Spencer W. Kimball[52] [53] and Elder Boyd K. Packer[54] would make similar statements in the 1970s.

These sentiments were captured in 1983 with an addition to the Handbook 1 policies regarding membership and the planning of or obtaining transexual operations.

> *Transsexual Operations: The Church counsels against transsexual operations, and members who undergo such procedures require disciplinary action. ... Members contemplating transsexual operations should be informed that the Church counsels against such procedures, but any disciplinary action is deferred until the individual has made a decision whether to undergo the operation. A change in a member's sex ordinarily justifies excommunication. After excommunication such a person is not eligible again for baptism. Questions on difficult cases can be forwarded by local priesthood leaders to the Office of the First Presidency.*[55]

Church leaders were taking this situation very seriously. You could be excommunicated for just deciding to have a transsexual operation. You didn't need to actually go through with it. And you could not be re-baptized after excommunication. What happened if you didn't go through with the surgery after excommunication? Wouldn't that make just deciding to have surgery worse than like murder?

Some time later the policy was softened. From the 2019 edition of Handbook 1:

> *6.7.2.3 Transsexual Operation*
> *Church leaders counsel against elective transsexual operations. If a member is contemplating such an operation, a presiding officer informs him of this counsel and advises him that the operation may be cause for formal Church discipline. Bishops refer questions on specific cases to the stake president. The stake president may direct questions to the Office of the First Presidency if necessary.*

6.12.10 Apply for First Presidency Approval (If Necessary)

If the person was disfellowshipped or excommunicated for any of the following reasons: [an elective transsexual operation], or if he committed any of these transgressions after being disfellowshipped or excommunicated, the approval of the First Presidency is required before he may be reinstated to full fellowship or readmitted by baptism and confirmation.[56]

Discipline was not mandatory, although excommunication was almost always the result in practice for actually having surgery, but excommunicated members could now be re-baptized with First Presidency approval.

In February 2020, the Church removed the sections on transsexual operations and included a new section governing transgender members. The consequences of having an elective transsexual operation were once again softened, dramatically.

38.6.23 Transgender Individuals

Church leaders counsel against elective medical or surgical intervention for the purpose of attempting to transition to the opposite gender of a person's biological sex at birth ("sex reassignment"). Leaders advise that taking these actions will be cause for Church membership restrictions.

Leaders also counsel against social transitioning. A social transition includes changing dress or grooming, or changing a name or pronouns, to present oneself as other than his or her biological sex at birth. Leaders advise that those who socially transition will experience some Church membership restrictions for the duration of this transition.[57]

Excommunication was no longer a possible outcome for surgical transition. There would, however, be membership restrictions. But now social transition in your appearance, name, or pronouns was added as a reason for the same membership restrictions.

Can a trans woman take hormones as a remedy for gender dysphoria? Yes. The Church recognizes gender dysphoria and the usefulness of hormone therapy as a treatment for adults and minors with parental permission. From the same section:

> *Some people experience feelings of incongruence between their biological sex and their gender identity. As a result, they may identify as transgender. The Church does not take a position on the causes of people identifying as transgender.*
>
> *Some children, youth, and adults are prescribed hormone therapy by a licensed medical professional to ease gender dysphoria or reduce suicidal thoughts. Before a person begins such therapy, it is important that he or she (and the parents of a minor) understands the potential risks and benefits.*

Can a trans woman attend Relief Society? The short answer is, yes. This section also says:

> *All are welcome to attend sacrament meeting, other Sunday meetings, and social events of the Church (see 38.1.1).*

There is no mention of limitation or restrictions based on gender assigned at birth, or your genitals. If there was, this would be the place to do so, right? All means all, and Relief Society is a Sunday meeting and a social event.

Section 38.1.1 Attendance at Church Meetings of the General Handbook makes note of age but not gender requirements for different meetings:

> *The Savior also taught that Church members are not to "cast any one out from ... public meetings, which are held before the world."*
>
> *All are welcome to attend sacrament meeting, other Sunday meetings, and social events of The Church of Jesus Christ of*

> Latter-day Saints. The presiding officer is responsible to ensure that all who attend are respectful of the sacred setting.
>
> Those who attend should avoid disruptions or distractions contrary to worship or other purposes of the meeting. All age and behavior requirements of different Church meetings and events should be respected.

Elder Christofferson told me in March 2019 that the long standing policy of the church was that transgender members could attend any meetings they identified with as long as they weren't being a distraction or disturbance. He said the policy came from the Presidency of the Seventy. In April 2019, I talked with the Office of General Council of the First Presidency. They said the policy was as given by Elder Christofferson. In June 2020, I talked with President Vinson of the Seventy. He explained that Elder Christofferson was correct except the policy didn't come from them. It came from the First Presidency. In March 2020, people who were involved in the writing of the transgender section of the General Handbook and worked directly with the apostles in its approval said that the policy allowed for trans women to attend Relief Society. In January 2022 I talked with a board member of the General Relief Society. She said, "Of course trans women can attend Relief Society, that's why we put it in the handbook. We push down on this at regional priesthood meetings all the time."

So it is and has been the long standing general policy of the church for trans women to attend Relief Society. However, the question is whether local leaders may decide that their presence or activity constitutes a distraction or disturbance. And that might be a loophole you can drive a bus through.

I find the February 2020 policy to be really accommodating of transgender members on paper. How local leaders choose to administer it is why the term "Leadership Roulette" was coined. Individual circumstances may vary, but the administration will also vary from bishop to bishop and stake to stake.

I would encourage you to read the rest of the policy.

What the church has said as far as doctrine is basically in the Family Proclamation[58]. Gender is binary, and gender is eternal. Our gender, of being male or female, was established in the pre-mortal world and will continue in the afterlife.

In the General Handbook, it clarifies that the gender of our spirit aligns with the gender our bodies were assigned at birth. So, if your mortal body was assigned male at birth, Church policy says your eternal gender is also male.

Except when it doesn't.

The First Presidency will change your gender marker assigned at birth if you can provide proof of a recognized intersex condition. I have met a couple people who successfully went through this process a few years ago as adults. So, if you were born with one of a few well-known disorders of sexual development, usually resulting in ambiguous genitalia, and identify as the other gender, the Church will consider correcting your gender on the records of the church. They will do this once, and only once. They haven't done this for generic claims of being transgender as far as I've heard.

But it does recognize that it is possible for some individuals to have a spirit with an eternal gender different from that assigned at birth. It acknowledges that errors can happen even with all our technology. Since this policy is not public, or publicized, the question becomes—what intersex conditions does the First Presidency formally consider currently? And might they consider others in the future? I don't know.

For many years the church had a policy that if you were a Black saint that you couldn't hold the priesthood or enter the temple. This simple policy was easy to enforce for a long time because the Church was mostly located in the United States and Europe, principally white, and there was little interracial marriage. It was easy to identify those with dark skin as having African descent. As the Church went worldwide the question of who was Black had to be revisited many times. Was it simply the darkness of your skin? Did it have to do with your ancestral origin?

There were members of the Church who were baptized and went to the temple only to find out when they researched their family tree to perform temple ordinances that they had African heritage. They then fell under the restrictions.

I wonder if the simple policy of intersex is not dissimilar. It was easy when there were so very few members of the Church who were intersex, and transsexuals were even more rare. A simple policy based upon ambiguous external genitalia was easy to implement. But as science has changed and we know more about human sexualization, and the world has changed to allow transgender people to come out of the closet, maybe we need a broader definition of intersex. Are there more conditions where a girl spirit might end up in a previously identified boy body?

I suppose it comes down to an understanding of what God's intention was. The idea would be that bodies, minds, and spirits would align across the board in sexualization. So, looking at the body and its genetics, you should be able to know the gender of the mind and spirit. This is the ideal, and this is true in almost all cases.

However, spirits come to bodies with all sorts of genetic disorders, and mental and physical handicaps that do not reflect the characteristics of the spirit. Some bodies are blind and/or deaf, but spirits aren't blind or deaf. Some bodies are effectively missing arms and legs, but spirits aren't. Some bodies have brains that are not fully developed. But spirits aren't mentally handicapped. And spirits have to deal with these circumstances of mortality.

But what was God's intention with a 46XY girl? Does the spirit align with the genitals? Or the contents of the DNA? Did God intend for the body to develop as male, but the fallen mortal world caused the SRY gene to not express so a male spirit is in a girl body? Or did God send a girl spirit to this should-have-been a male body? What is that like?

Does God send a male spirit to a 46XX boy because he knew they would have a transposed SRY gene? Or is there a female spirit with this male body and brain? What would that experience be like? How does that work?

And if God had a choice, knowing a body would be male with a sexualized female brain due to hormones in utero, is the right choice to send a male spirit for the genitalia, even though it would fight the brain? Or a girl spirit who would work with the brain, but fight the body? Which makes more sense? I don't know. It might depend on what our all-knowing Heavenly Parents believe is best for their spirit child.

What I do believe is that our spirits were chosen to come in a time and place, and given a body, and we would have challenges we would uniquely be able to endure, perhaps with the help of our modern medicine.

Not all bodies are born blind, but the spirits that inhabit them were chosen for that struggle. Not all bodies are born physically disabled, but their spirits were also chosen. I see no difference in having challenges with spirits having bodies that develop sexually incongruent from their eternal gender.

Regardless of why we are as we are, the trial is not our bodies; it is whether we will be obedient and do everything that our Heavenly Father commands us. Will we multiply and replenish the earth? Will we be baptized? Will we stay on the covenant path? These are trials that are universal to all our circumstances. Being blind isn't the trial. Being Black isn't the trial. Being handicapped isn't the trial. Being gay isn't the trial. Being a woman isn't the trial. It is this: given those situations, will we still have faith, hope, and charity? Will we desire to be more like our Savior? Will we keep His commandments? Will we endure to the

Timeline

1966 Born
1969 Came out to my parents
1979 Moved to Utah. Taken to a therapist
1980 Cross country family vacation
1984
    Graduated from High School
    Fall: Started at University of Utah
1985
    Fall: Dropped from University of Utah
1987
    Fall: Rematriculated at University of Utah
    Sept: Met Valeria.
    Dec: Dropped from University
1988
    April: Came out to Valeria, got dumped
    Fall: Going steady w/Valeria
1989
    Jan: Started career as computer programmer
    June: Received girl clothes for birthday
1992
    Feb: Tried to get married
    Sept: Tried to get married again
1994
    March: Bought my house and got Ardath
    May: Got engaged
    June: Got married
    July: Wedding reception
1999 Got put in the closet
2002
    Oct: Received patriarchal blessing

2010

Feb: Changed jobs. Cloister Bell

2012

Oct: Talk with wife. Out of closet.

2014

Nov: Started w/therapist

2015

Jan: Cloister Bell. Met with stake president.

Feb: Started cross-hormones

Oct: Separated to living room

2016

Aug: bishop approved orchiectomy. Valeria told Shannon and Cathryn.

Sept: I told Shannon and Cathryn

Dec: Shannon and Cathryn move out

2017

Jan: Given the "official" transgender policy that wasn't

Jun: Valeria files papers for divorce

Nov: Shannon engaged.

Dec: Temple recommend interview

2018

Jan: Temple recommend expired

Feb: Trip to California

Mar: Started attending other wards

May: Shannon married. I moved to rental house

June: Visit by bishop and stake president

July: Allison baptized. I got divorced.

Sept: Moved back into my house

Oct: First conference hugging

Nov: First TOFW. Write a book.

2019

Mar: North Star conference

Apr: Second conference hugging

May: BYU Women's Conference

July: Created online dating profiles

Aug: Started attending LDS singles activities.

Sept: Started TransMission. Met Harmony and
Elder Christofferson.

Oct: Third conference hugging

Nov: Utah Hearth Fireside. TOFW volunteer.
Harmony Thanksgiving.

Dec: Banned from UCSA dances. Harmony Christmas and
New Years

2020

Jan: Harmony visit

Feb: Visited Harmony. Official Transgender policy.

Mar: North Star talk. Harmony visit. The breakup. Earthquake
and Pandemic

Apr: The Event

Jun: Meeting with President of Seventy

Sept: Unicorn Day. Harmony startup.

Oct: Harmony visit, and breakup.

2021

Jan: Letter to First Presidency. Harmony startup.

Apr: Meeting w/Area Authority. Harmony adventure.
Got Credence.

May: Visited Harmony birthday

Jun: Harmony visit. Another breakup.

2022

Feb: Harmony startup

Mar: Harmony breakup

Apr: Fourth conference hugging

Jun: North Star keynote

Oct: Fifth conference hugging

TransMission

Bountiful Utah Stake
    Bountiful 26th Ward
    Bountiful 31st Ward
Bountiful Utah Central Stake
    Barton Creek Ward
    Bountiful Hills Ward
Bountiful Utah East Stake
    Bountiful 21st Ward
Bountiful Utah Heights Stake
    Bountiful 54th Ward
Bountiful Utah Mueller Park Stake
    Mueller Park 1st Ward
    Mueller Park 5th Ward
    Mueller Park 9th Ward
    Mueller Park 10th Ward
Bountiful Utah North Canyon Stake
    North Canyon 4th Ward
    North Canyon 5th Ward
Bountiful Utah North Stake
    Bountiful 10th Ward
    Bountiful 19th Ward
Bountiful Utah Orchard Stake
    Orchard 1st Ward
    Springwood Ward
Bountiful Utah South Stake
    Bountiful 20th Ward
    Bountiful 25th Ward
Bountiful Utah Stone Creek Stake
    Pages Lane Ward
    West Bountiful 7th Ward

Bountiful Utah Val Verda Stake
    Val Verda 1st Ward
Centerville Utah Stake
    Pheasant Ward
Centerville Utah Canyon View Stake
    Centerville 2nd Ward
Centerville Utah North Stake
    Jennings Lane Ward
Centerville Utah South Stake
    Centerville 6th Ward
    Centerville Canyon Ward
Farmington Utah Stake
    Farmington 3rd Ward
    Farmington 12th Ward
Farmington Utah Farmington Bay Stake
    Farmington 6th Ward
Farmington Utah North Stake
    Northridge Ward
    Shepard View Ward
Farmington Utah South Stake
    Davis Creek 3rd Ward
    Farmington 4th Ward
Farmington Utah West Stake
    Burke Lane Ward
Layton Utah Valley View Stake
    Summerwood Ward
North Salt Lake Utah Stake
    Eaglewood Ward
    Ridge Top Ward

North Salt Lake Utah Legacy Stake
  Foxboro 7th Ward
  Woods Cross 18th Ward
North Salt Lake Utah Parkway Stake
  Orchard 8th Ward
  Spring Hill Ward

West Bountiful Utah Stake
  West Bountiful 3rd Ward
Woods Cross Utah Stake
  Woods Cross 10th Ward
Woods Cross Utah North Stake
  Woods Cross 2nd Ward

Honorable Mentions:

Bountiful Utah Stake
  Bountiful 1st Ward
Bountiful Utah Val Verda Stake
  Val Verda 6th Ward
Bountiful Utah YSA Stake
  Mills Park YSA Ward

Acknowledgments

N ORMALLY HERE AN AUTHOR WOULD ACKNOWLEDGE ALL
the many people who helped in the writing of their book. Well,
God gave me all the experiences, the outline of chapters, and
what stories I should put in them. I simply followed His plan. So most
of the credit goes to Him. But it was my editor who had the hard job of
cleaning up my many fragmented sentences, obscure references, and other
crimes against my mother tongue so it looks like I didn't actually fail AP
English, even though I really did. Briana also was invaluable in giving
me suggestions to make it better. I'm indebted to her contributions and
grateful for her participation in this project.

If there are still any imperfections, I blame the reformed Egyptian.

In closing, I'm reminded of *A Midsummer Night's Dream* by
William Shakespeare:

If we shadows have offended,
Think but this, and all is mended,
That you have but slumbered here
While these visions did appear.
And this weak and idle theme,
No more yielding but a dream,
Gentles, do not reprehend:
If you pardon, we will mend:
And, as I am an honest Puck,
If we have unearned luck
Now to 'scape the serpent's tongue,
We will make amends ere long;
Else the Puck a liar call;
So, good night unto you all.
Give me your hands, if we be friends,
And Robin shall restore amends.

I would also like to acknowledge many of the worldly influencers in my life that made this story possible. Thank you for your contributions in making this life worth living:

a-Ha, ABC, Douglas Adams, Neca Allgood, Alphaville, Lynette Austin, B-Movie, Mark Bair, Tom Baker, Bananarama, Margaret Barker, Amberly Bean, Michael Blocker, Becky and Bennett Borden, Brighton (jewelry), Julie Brinton, Marcyne Brown, Steven Brust, Bucks Fizz, Jonnie and Brad Busath, Laurie Campbell, Trina Caudle, Rosanne and Neil and Christian Christiansen, Tom Christofferson, Lisa Cline, Debra Coe, Glen Cook, Lady and Croaker, Jeni Davis, Depeche Mode, Larry Dewell, Devo, Deron Dickmann, Sara Dowdle, Karen Dufresne, Lara and Todd Duzett, Danielle Ensign, Erasure, Amy and Grant Fairbanks, Fancy, Randi Ford, Emily Belle Freeman, Gary Gygax, Debra Ghomy, Lynnette Gipson, David Gittins, Mara Green, Christine Griffin, Barb Guy, Hollie Hancock, Lisa Hansen, Kurstin Hardy, Colleen and Ernie Hewlett, Gaye Hogge, Human League, Apio Hunter, Kris Irvin, Joelle and Rick Jackson, Steve Jackson, JMS,

Steve Jobs, Joy, Lori and Rudy Klopfer, Katherine Kurtz, Adam Lambert, Kate Lee, Paul "Cactus Jack" Le Mar, Becky and Scott Mackintosh, Kez Maefele, Drew Major, Kris and Rob Maxfield, Clifton May, Kelly McAfee, Livier Mendoza, Men Without Hats, Cynthia Miller, Stacey and Mike Mollinet, Jieun Moon, David Moore, Peter Mooseman, Heather Moss, Donna and Joe Nay, New Order, Nine West, Melody and Virgil Oertle, OMD, Blair Ostler, Mindy and Greg Pearson, Karen Penman, Pet Shop Boys, Angela Petty, Vicki Pope, Kyle Powell, Pseudo Echo, Psychedelic Furs, Cory Rallison, REM, Jennifer Rawlings, Real Life, Ronald Reagan, Calee Reed, Samantha Richardson, Mercy River, Paul Santini, Dennis Schleicher, Craig Schofield, Melissa Sedwick, Severian, Bob Shorten, Simple Minds, Soulcatcher, Sparks, Mike Summers/Winters, Tiffany and Lance Sweeten, Emily and Steve Swensen, Vladimir Taltos, Ann Taylor, Lynda and Scott Taylor, Straight Heather and Shayne Taylor, Susan and Kevin Thelin, Spencer Thompson, Ashley Tingey, Denise and Doug Tolley, Jeanene Tyler, Ultravox, Nepanthe and Varthlokkur, Samuel Washburn, Wendy and John Van Wyngaarden, Melvin Walker, Jon Warner, Nancy Wayment, Kim Wilde, Angie and Steve Winchester, Gene Wolfe, Yazoo

Valeria, Shannon, Cathryn, Meaghan, Raechel, Heulyn, Daniel, Allison

Symphony, Melody, Rhapsody

Harmony

Endnotes

1. Nelson, Russell M, "Overcome the World and Find Rest", General Conference, Salt Lake City, October 2022

2. North Star International, "2022 North Star Presidents Address", YouTube, <https://youtu.be/o6sqEypNbPg>, 1'02"

3. North Star International, a church affirming organization for LGBT members of the Church of Jesus Christ.

4. Bird, Charlie, "Without The Mask", Deseret Book, 2020

5. Christofferson, Tom, "That We May Be One", Deseret Book, 2017

6. Mackintosh, Becky, "Love Boldly", Cedar Fort, 2019

7. Schilaty, Ben, "A Walk In My Shoes", Deseret Book, 2021

8. Packer, Boyd K, "The Candle of the Lord", Liahona, December 1988

9. World Professional Association for Transgender Health (WPATH)

10. Mackintosh, Becky, "Navigating Family Differences with Love and Trust", LDS Church Blog, 22 March 2017

11. Bean, Roy, "Rescuing the Lost: Counsel for Parents and Leaders", Ensign, January 2017

12. D&C 100:6 or Matthew 10:19-20

13. Hinckley, Gordon B, "Our Mission of Saving", General Conference, Salt Lake City, October 1991

14. Hinckley, Gordon B, "Converts and Young Men", General Conference, Salt Lake City, May 1997

15. Parkin, Bonnie D, "Personal Ministry: Sacred and Precious", BYU Speeches, Provo, 13 February 2007

16. Ryan C, Russell ST, Huebner D, Diaz R, Sanchez J. "Family acceptance in adolescence and the health of LGBT young adults", Journal of Child and Adolescent Psychiatric Nursing 2010 Nov;23(4):205-13. doi: 10.1111/j.1744-6171.2010.00246.x. PMID: 21073595.

17. Oaks, Dallin H, "Two Great Commandments", General Conference, Salt Lake City, October 2019

18. Inklings: A Hint of Something More, <https://www.emilybellefreeman.com/getting-started>

19. Gong, Gerrit W, "Room in the Inn", General Conference, Salt Lake City, April 2021

[20] Oaks, Dallin H, "Two Great Commandments", General Conference, Salt Lake City, October 2019

[21] Intellectual Reserve, "Teachings of Presidents of the Church: Joseph Smith", 2007, pg 318

[22] Morgan, Trevor, "Elder Ballard's 'questions and answers'", BYU Devotional, 13 November 2017

[23] Church News Staff, "President Oaks' full remarks from the LDS Church's 'Be One' celebration", LDS Church News, 1 June 2018

[24] Holland, Matthew, "Wrong Roads and Revelation", New Era, July 2005

[25] Weaver , Sarah Jane, "Policy Changes Announced for Members in Gay Marriages, Children of LGBT Parents", LDS Church News, 4 April 2019

[26] Morgan, Trevor, "Elder Ballard's 'questions and answers'", BYU Devotional, 13 November 2017

[27] Oaks, Dallin H, "Two Great Commandments", General Conference, Salt Lake City, October 2019

[28] Uchtdorf, Dieter F, "The Merciful Obtain Mercy", General Conference, Salt Lake City, April 2012

[29] Uchtdorf, Dieter F, "Receiving a Testimony of Light and Truth", General Conference, Salt Lake City, October 2014

[30] Official Statement, "Church Applauds Community Efforts to Fight Suicide, Bullying and Homelessness", LDS Church Newsroom, 18 July 2018

[31] Bingham, Jean B, "Ministering as the Savior Does", General Conference, Salt Lake City, April 2018

[32] Holland, Jeffrey R, "Elder Jeffrey R. Holland Urges BYU to Embrace Its Uniqueness, Stay True to the Savior", LDS Church Newsroom, 23 August 2021

[33] Holland, Jeffrey R, "Angels and Astonishment", S&I Annual Training Broadcast for 2019, 12 June 2019

[34] Intellectual Reserve, "Healing", Church History Topics

[35] Durham, Reed C, "Revelation: The Plainest Book Ever Written", New Era, May 1973

[36] Parry, Donald, "Angels", 2013, pg ix-x

[37] Holland, Jeffrey R, "For a Wise Purpose", General Conference, Salt Lake City, January 1996

[38] Franklin, Aaron D, "The Spiritual Physics of Light", BYU Religions Studies Center, 2021

[39] McKay, Kyle S, "The Immediate Goodness of God", General Conference, Salt Lake City, April 2019

[40] Simmons, Dennis E, "But If Not …", General Conference, Salt Lake City, April 2004

[41] Dew, Sheri, "Worth the Wrestle", 2017, pg 88-89

[42] Holland, Jeffrey R, "The Peaceable Things of the Kingdom", General Conference, Salt Lake City, October 1996

[43] North Star International, "I am a Latter-day Saint, I am LGBTQ, and This is What I Know", YouTube, 16 March 2019, <https://youtu.be/HUyUYZ1LkHw>

[44] Nelson, Russell M, "Overcome the World and Find Rest", General Conference, Salt Lake City, October 2022

[45] Napier-Pearce, Jennifer, "Trib Talk: LDS leaders Oaks, Christofferson will appear on Trib Talk to discuss religious freedom…", YouTube, 29 January 2015, <https://www.youtube.com/live/UIJ6gL_xc->, 14'10"

[46] Callaway, Ewen, "Girl with Y chromosome sheds light on maleness", New Scientist, Magazine issue 2704, 18 April 2009

[47] Theisen, J.G., Sundaram, V., Filchak, M.S. et al. "The Use of Whole Exome Sequencing in a Cohort of Transgender Individuals to Identify Rare Genetic Variants", Sci Rep 9, 20099 (2019)

[48] Feusner JD, Lidström A, Moody TD, Dhejne C, Bookheimer SY, Savic I, "Intrinsic network connectivity and own body perception in gender dysphoria", Brain Imaging and Behavior 2017 Aug;11(4):964-976. doi: 10.1007/s11682-016-9578-6. PMID: 27444730; PMCID: PMC5354991.

[49] American Psychiatric Association. (2013). Gender Dysphoria. In Diagnostic and Statistical Manual of Mental Disorders (Fifth Edition ed.). Washington, DC: American Psychiatric Publishing Inc.

[50] Steensma TD, Biemond R, de Boer F, Cohen-Kettenis PT, "Desisting and persisting gender dysphoria after childhood: a qualitative follow-up study", Clin Child Psychol Psychiatry. 2011 Oct;16(4):499-516. doi: 10.1177/1359104510378303. Epub 2011 Jan 7. PMID: 21216800.

[51] Lee, Harold B, "The Teachings of Harold B. Lee", 1996, pg 232
Lee, Harold B, "Fifth Annual Genealogical Seminar Address (Speech)", Fifth Annual Priesthood Genealogical Research Seminar, BYU: Brigham Young University Press, 7 August 1970

[52] Kimball, Spencer W, "Be Ye Therefore Perfect", BYU Speeches, 17 September 1974

[53] Kimball, Spencer W, "God Will Not Be Mocked", General Conference, Salt Lake City, October 1974

[54] Packer, Boyd K, "To Young Men Only", General Conference, Salt Lake City, October 1976

[55] Intellectual Reserve, "Church Handbook of Instruction, Section: Transsexual Operations", 1983, pg. 52-53

[56] Intellectual Reserve, "Handbook 1: Stake Presidents and Bishops", May 2019, pg 68,85

[57] Intellectual Reserve, "General Handbook: Section 38.6.23 Transgender Individuals", February 2020

[58] Intellectual Reserve, "The Family: A Proclamation to the World", 23 September 1995

About the Author

KATHERINE IS AN APPLE fan girl and has NEVER used Windows or Android. (She once had lunch next to Steve Jobs!) New Wave/Alternative music is literally the soundtrack to her life (Can you hear it? Does she need to turn it up louder?) She loves fantasy/science fiction/fandom, but will never read or watch Harry Potter (Don't ask). In her copious spare time she's writing a book explaining the *Book of Revelation*. (She says they've all gotten it wrong. LOL) And she's been called a somewhat decent, tasty cook. (No one has died yet.)

Made in the USA
Middletown, DE
16 October 2023

40878300R00150